Tran

TOPICS IN TRANSLATION
Series Editors: Susan Bassnett, *University of Warwick, UK*
Edwin Gentzler, *University of Massachusetts, Amherst, USA*
Editor for Translation in the Commercial Environment:
Geoffrey Samuelsson-Brown, University of Surrey, UK

Other Books in the Series

Translation, Power, Subversion
  Román Alvarez and M. Carmen-Africa Vidal (eds)
Linguistic Auditing
  Nigel Reeves and Colin Wright
Culture Bumps: An Empirical Approach to the Translation of Allusions
  Ritva Leppihalme
Constructing Cultures: Essays on Literary Translation
  Susan Bassnett and André Lefevere
The Pragmatics of Translation
  Leo Hickey (ed.)
Practical Guide for Translators (3rd edition)
  Geoffrey Samuelsson-Brown
Written in the Language of the Scottish Nation
  John Corbett
'Behind Inverted Commas' Translation and Anglo-German Cultural Relations in the
Nineteenth Century
  Susanne Stark
The Rewriting of Njßls Saga: Translation, Ideology, and Icelandic Sagas
  Jón Karl Helgason
Time Sharing on Stage: Drama Translation in Theatre and Society
  Sirkku Aaltonen
Translation and Nation: A Cultural Politics of Englishness
  Roger Ellis and Liz Oakley-Brown (eds)
The Interpreter's Resource
  Mary Phelan
Annotated Texts for Translation: English–German
  Christina Schäffner with Uwe Wiesemann
Contemporary Translation Theories (2nd edition)
  Edwin Gentzler
Literary Translation: A Practical Guide
  Clifford E. Landers
Translation-mediated Communication in a Digital World
  Minako O'Hagan and David Ashworth
Frae Ither Tongues: Essays on Modern Translations into Scotts
  Bill Findlay (ed.)
Practical Guide for Translators (4th edition)
  Geoffrey Samuelsson-Brown
Cultural Encounters in Translation from Arabic
  Said Faiq (ed.)

For more details of these or any other of our publications, please contact:
Multilingual Matters, Frankfurt Lodge, Clevedon Hall,
Victoria Road, Clevedon, BS21 7HH, England
http://www.multilingual-matters.com

TOPICS IN TRANSLATION 27
Series Editors: Susan Bassnett, *University of Warwick* and
Edwin Gentzler, *University of Massachusetts, Amherst*

Translation, Linguistics, Culture
A French–English Handbook

Nigel Armstrong

MULTILINGUAL MATTERS LTD
Clevedon • Buffalo • Toronto

Library of Congress Cataloging in Publication Data
Armstrong, Nigel.
Translation, Linguistics, Culture: A French–English Handbook/Nigel Armstrong.
Topics in Translation: 27
Includes bibliographical references and index.
1. Translating and interpreting. 2. Language and culture. I. Title. II. Series.
P306.2.A67 2005
418'.02–dc22   2004022672

British Library Cataloguing in Publication Data
A catalogue entry for this book is available from the British Library.

ISBN 1-85359-806-2 (hbk)
ISBN 1-85359-805-4 (pbk)

Multilingual Matters Ltd
UK: Frankfurt Lodge, Clevedon Hall, Victoria Road, Clevedon BS21 7HH.
USA: UTP, 2250 Military Road, Tonawanda, NY 14150, USA.
Canada: UTP, 5201 Dufferin Street, North York, Ontario M3H 5T8, Canada.

Typeset by Saxon Graphics Ltd.
Printed and bound in Great Britain by the Cromwell Press Ltd.

Contents

Acknowledgements. viii
Abbreviations ix

1 The Linguistic Bases of Translation 1
   Purpose of this Book 1
   Saussure's Theory of Language 6
   The Speech Community 12
   The Sapir-Whorf Hypothesis: Linguistic Determinism 14
   Linguistic Relativity. 16
   Codability 17
   Structure of the Book, and Summary 18

2 Approaching a Text 22
   Introduction. 22
   The Translator's Role as 'Secret Agent'. 22
   Text Types 26
   Culture Infused in Language 30
   Culture Detachable from Language 36
   Intermediate Summary 37
   Acceptability and Competence: Strategic Translation Decisions. . 41
   Equivalence. 44
   Translation Loss and Compensation. 46
   Some Genuine Examples of Loss and Compensation 46

3 Translation Issues at the Word Level 49
   The Word and the Morpheme 49
   Word Categories. 52
   Inflectional Morphology: Verb Inflection 55
   Translation Issues at the Morphological Level: Non-Standard
   Forms 59
   Translation Issues at the Morphological Level: Derivation. 61
   Lexical and Grammatical Words 64
   Translation Issues Relating to Word Cohesion 65

Complex Words 68
Denotation and Connotation 70
Style and Register. 73
Nominalisation 77
False Friends 78

4   Words in Combination 82
The Structural Organisation of Meaning: Paradigms and
    Syntagmata 82
Grammatical Paradigms 83
Lexical Paradigms and Polysemy 84
Lexical Paradigms and Synonymy 86
Lexical Paradigms and Hyponymy. 88
The Interaction of Synonymy, Polysemy and Hyponymy. 91
Lexical Paradigms and Antonymy 94
Homonyms 96
Collocation: The Tendency of Words to Co-Occur Regularly 97
Attitudinal Adjectives 100
Word Compounds 103
Idioms. 103
Figurative Expressions 106
Clichés 107

5   Translation Issues at the Syntactic Level 111
Definition of Syntax 111
Syntactic Units. 111
The Sentence 111
The Clause 113
The Phrase 116
Translation of Phrase Function Rather than Structure 120
Apposition. 122
Absolute Constructions 123
Elliptical Constructions 124
Emphasis within the Sentence 126
Prepositions. 131
Idiomatic Constructions 133
Inversion 134
The Passive 135
Structural False Friends. 136
Verbs used Intransitively. 138
Non-Standard Syntax 138
Translation Problems and Procedures in Syntax. 140

6   Translation Types and Procedures 142
      Introduction... 142
      Borrowing 143
      Calques... 146
      Literal Translation 147
      Linguistic Transposition 150
      Modulation 151
      Equivalence, or Pragmatic Translation 152
      Adaptation, or Cultural Transposition 155
      Exegetic Translation.................................... 156
      Gist Translation.. 157
      Non-Translation, or Compression 159
      Some Examples of Transposition and Modulation: Astington's
      Categories 160
      General Comments on Astington's Categories 179
      Ordering of Elements Within the Sentence 180
      Types of Procedure: Cultural or Linguistic? 182

7   Some Miscellaneous Issues 183
      Translating Humour 183
      The Text Level.. 185
      Improving the Source Text 187
      Metaphor 188
      Metonymy 190
      Coherence and Cohesion................................. 191
      Anaphora, Cataphora 193
      Translating Coherence and Cohesion 194
      Multiple Equivalence.................................... 197
      Punctuation... 203
      The Translation Commentary............................. 205
      Example of a Translation Commentary 207
      Concluding Remarks 211

References... 214

Acknowledgements

I am very happy to express my thanks to the following for their help in the preparation of this book: Rosalind Brown-Grant, Aidan Coveney, Yvette Ellis, Russell Goulbourne, Marie-Anne Hintze, Marcel Landric, David Looseley, David Roe, Nigel Saint and Christopher Todd. I am grateful equally to the publisher's readers who commented on an earlier version of the book and improved it greatly by making many invaluable recommendations.

The author and publishers are grateful to the following for their permission to reproduce copyright material: *Le Monde* and *Le Nouvel Observateur*; Cambridge University Press for permission to reproduce material from *Equivalences*, by Eric Astington, 1983; and Presses Universitaires de France for permission to reproduce on the cover an adapted version of a diagram from *La Sémantique fonctionnelle* by Claude Germain, 1981.

Every effort has been made to trace the holders of the copyright of the cartoon on page 157; and on page 183 ('Chimulus'). Any rights not acknowledged here will be acknowledged in subsequent printings if sufficient notice is given to the publisher.

Abbreviations

In this book we refer to some commonly used textbooks and works of references using the following abbreviations and acronyms. Some need no comment; others are commented upon briefly. Full bibliographical references are given at the back of the book.

Astington   Astington, E. *Equivalences: Translation Difficulties and Devices, French–English, English–French*. This is a linguistics-based thematic discussion of translation procedures, now out of print. We comment on it at length in Chapter 6.

Baker   Baker, M. *In Other Words. A Coursebook on Translation*. This is organised a similar way to the present book, looking at translation problems on the linguistic levels in ascending order of magnitude.

Byrne and Churchill   Byrne, L. and Churchill, E. *A Comprehensive French Grammar* (revised and rewritten by G. Price). 'Byrne and Churchill' has been until recently the standard undergraduate English reference grammar of French. It is very useful for checking grammatical terms.

COD, OED   *Concise Oxford Dictionary, Oxford English Dictionary*

Collins-Robert   We refer to the 1998 fifth edition of the one-volume bilingual dictionary.

Fowler   Fowler, H. W. *A Dictionary of Modern English Usage*. The standard short reference book on points of correct usage.

Hervey and Higgins   Hervey, S. and Higgins, I. *Thinking Translation*. Contains many interesting examples, mostly of literary translation.

Oxford-Hachette   We refer to the 2001 third edition of the one-volume bilingual dictionary.

Petit Robert   We refer to the 1986 edition.

Thody and Evans   Thody, P. and Evans, H. *Faux Amis and Key Words*. Very readable; many examples, often accompanied by a discussion of the cultural context behind the particular problem. Good book list in the back.

Vinay and Darbelnet   Vinay, J.-P. and Darbelnet, J. *Stylistique Comparée du français et de l'anglais*, English version *Comparative Stylistics of French and English*. The 'classic' text, the book all the others refer to. Useful as a reference book, as it contains a very large number of examples.

Chapter 1

The Linguistic Bases of Translation

Purpose of this Book

This book is intended both for students of French who need to do translation as a part of their degree course, whether undergraduate or postgraduate, and for students of translation who are interested in the problems posed by the rendering of French into English. The purpose of the book is to make the reader aware of some of the procedures that translators use. The rationale of the book is that an increased awareness of these operations will help to improve translation skills; clearly, this is a practical aim.

At the same time, this book aims to discuss theories of language as they impinge upon translation, and it seems worth stating at the outset why such theories are necessary. Is it not sufficient, one might wonder, to state quite simply that, leaving aside intangibles such as talent, a good translator needs minimally to have very good knowledge of the two languages of interest? In the present case, this will include educated native-speaker competence in English, and knowledge of French that derives in most cases from a study of French literature and other media, and a year spent in a francophone country. This is a likely case, as professional translation is done customarily into the translator's mother tongue, and often by graduates of French. Since language is in large part a cultural practice, very good knowledge of the two languages in question implies also a high degree of general knowledge, or acquaintance with the two cultures; including knowledge of how to find this knowledge. There is a further element of subtlety here, as good general knowledge will include a recognition of where one's general knowledge ends, and hence when a reference tool is required.

These remarks concerning general knowledge apply crucially also to linguistic knowledge, since linguistic problems, being 'structural' and hence built into a text, may be less visible, and capable therefore of inducing a lack of awareness in the translator that a problem is being posed. What do we mean when we say a linguistic problem is structural? Language is hard to think about, partly because, in order to do so, we are

1

using the very system we are thinking about. We examine in further detail below what we mean by saying that a language has a structure, but when we look at a stretch of language, our response is so intuitive – language is 'hard-wired', we are born with a genetic language endowment that seems simply to grow, as our limbs do – that we can find it hard to see the formal structure of that piece of language. This is reflected in a widespread impatience with linguistic enquiry: 'language is for talking about something, not something to be talked about'. From this perspective language is primarily a tool for communication rather than an object of study in its own right. This attitude is a grave shortcoming in any serious student of language, or of any subject closely connected with it, like translation. It has been suggested that the goal of linguistics is 'to present in a precise, explicit and rigorous form facts about language which those who speak it as a native-speaker know intuitively' (Lodge *et al.*, 1997: 2). This goes back to what was said in the first paragraph above about our intention to raise consciousness. Awareness of some of the operations that translators use means explicit knowledge about linguistics, among other things.

This last qualification is important: we do not wish to imply that knowledge of linguistics can improve every aspect of the translator's competence. Leaving aside the obvious fact that general and specialised knowledge are of great importance too, one way of expressing this reservation is to say that translation is as much an art as a science, and that while linguistics, to the extent that it is a science, can provide a rigorous and explicit way of looking at certain translation problems, there are in practice problems beyond the scope of the discipline. This is not necessarily to say that no translation problem is unconnected in principle with linguistics; rather, we would have to be capable of including in a theory of linguistics much more than we can at present, to the extent in fact of having a 'theory of everything'. The resources of linguistics are limited, so that we are not in a position to test in a rigorous way statements about certain differences between French and English. For example, it is often stated that French is a more 'nominal' language than English; that is, French has a tendency to use nouns where English uses other parts of speech. In principle, one could test this impression; in practice, the collection and analysis of enough corpora in the two languages would be a formidable task indeed. So as long as the resources available for systematising every translation problem are lacking, we are obliged to say things like 'English seems to prefer this way of expressing it'. This is a problem of practice, not of principle. At the same time it is a relatively simple problem. Others, such as the analysis of stylistic differences between the two languages, shade into aesthetics and hence are beyond the scope of rigorous theory.

What is required therefore, to the extent that it is possible, is a systematisation of the translator's art; a body of knowledge about translation procedures that might result from a debriefing session aiming to ask an expert to explain the issues that need to be borne in mind when rendering a text into English from French. As the title of this book states, the focus here is upon the cultural and linguistic issues that arise. This may seem obvious; how can a book about translation ignore such issues? The question should seem uncontroversial. Clearly, language is central both to thought and to cultural identity, and the serious student of French, and of French translation, will seek a deeper understanding of how the language works. The double sense of the term 'linguist' is pertinent here: a student of French is clearly a linguist in the polyglot sense of knowing more than one language. At the same time, students of French at any advanced level need also to be linguists in the linguistician sense – the sense of being intensely interested in, and aware of, the structure of the language, and of how it works as a means of cultural expression. The systematic or *linguistic* approach to the study of language offers therefore a means of understanding, beyond the superficial level, how French people think about themselves and their culture; and what distinguishes French from other languages. As was suggested above, non-linguists are in general uninterested in the form of language, being content so long as the content is received loud and clear. Let us emphasise one last time that the microscopic approach to language adopted by the linguistician is necessary for adequate translation.

We can see from this brief discussion of what is required in a good translator, that a simple definition like 'very good knowledge of the two languages of interest' brings us very quickly to the question of what we mean by knowledge, what kind of knowledge, as well as to the question of what we can call 'meta-knowledge', or knowledge about knowledge. While a fully bilingual translator having a very good knowledge of the two cultures may arrive at translation solutions without formal instruction, less privileged individuals seem to require a theoretical training that depends on making explicit two crucial (and related) aspects of the two languages. These are the purely linguistic structures of the languages of interest, and the cultural aspects: by these latter is meant the twofold fact that languages both express a set of cultural practices that can differ quite considerably, and at the same time are conditioned by those practices, often in subtle ways that go beyond lexical items whose culture-specificity is fairly easily apparent.

This book will look therefore at aspects of French both as a linguistic system and as an expression of cultural behaviour. We will proceed largely by looking at examples, mostly from French, although we will consider English examples occasionally where this seems suitable to the issue in question. We may appear to be labouring the point about linguistics, but someone who pursues an advanced-level interest in French unaccompanied by an interest in the linguistics of French is like a student of music who reads no musical theory. An analogy that is sometimes drawn is between language and linguistics on the one hand, and music and musicology on the other. Advanced competence as a linguist (as polyglot) or a musician seems difficult without knowledge of the associated theory. As an example, consider the following passage from *Le Monde* (16 October 2000) about the French adoption of Human Rights legislation as it concerns the right of appeal in the higher courts:

(1)   Au couperet des verdicts succèdera, pour celui que la justice reconnaît criminel, un temps inédit : la possibilité, si le jugement ou la peine ne lui conviennent pas, de faire appel et d'être rejugé.

As Newmark (1988: 39) suggests: 'any translation is an exercise in applied linguistics'. The phrase 'applied linguistics' has several senses, the commonest being its use in language-learning theory and practice, but we can paraphrase it in this context as 'the application of knowledge of linguistics to aid translation'. Among the fundamental concepts of linguistics is that of the 'level of linguistic analysis', or simply 'linguistic level'. Three are normally distinguished: phonology (the sound level); grammar, comprising morphology (word formation) and syntax (sentence formation); and lexis (vocabulary). This threefold division makes sense a lot of the time, as we can often analyse the sounds of a language without reference to its grammar, and so forth. In other words, these three levels can be thought of as independent of one another and useful for clear analysis. If we examine the sentence quoted above, we quickly see that the levels of grammar and lexis provide useful frameworks for thinking about the problems the passage poses for a translator. The sound level can be relevant when dialogue is being translated, but is a fairly marginal issue in written translation. In the following chapter we will however examine this level from the viewpoint of how certain sounds communicate culture-specific information.

If we attempt a word-for-word translation of the first part of passage (1), problems of grammar and lexis surface very quickly:

(2)   'To the guillotine-blade [chopper, cleaver, etc.] of [the] verdicts will succeed, for he whom justice recognises [as] criminal ...'

It seems useful to be able to use a set of linguistic terms to articulate the translation problems here. Why does the very first word *au* potentially give trouble? Perhaps because it is a frequent word, and its less usual function is capable of being overlooked in the present context. At first sight the translator may analyse *au couperet* as 'at the guillotine-blade', without seeing that *au* depends on the following verb. This problem is present in turn because the sentence structure is inside out, or 'inverted' in the terminology, which goes against the English tendency. A smooth English version will put in very first position the clause which in the French original is placed second, *pour celui que la justice reconnaît criminel*, followed by the subject of the sentence, *un temps inédit*, with as a result something like:

(3) For those found guilty, an unprecedented era will follow these [brutal and] irreversible decisions: the possibility of appeal and retrial if they do not accept the judgment or sentence.

A further linguistic operation worth pointing out is that performed on *couperet*. Literally 'chopper', 'cleaver', 'guillotine-blade', these terms seem unsuitable in English for several reasons. Evocation of the guillotine especially produces 'static' or interference, in the form of unwanted resonance or 'connotational meaning' to do with UK parliamentary procedure or the French Revolution. The other terms are similarly rich in needless connotation: that is, the peripheral meaning that overlays the central 'denotation' or reference the word makes to a concept from the stock shared by the linguistic community. We discuss connotation and denotation in more detail in a later chapter. The operation performed here is one of *abstraction*: identification is made of the non-concrete qualities referred to by the blade metaphor, and these replace the concrete French word.

   Other aspects of this brief stretch of language are equally worthy of comment: for example, the sense of *inédit*, which here, in collocation with *temps*, needs to be translated as 'new' or 'unprecedented'. But the general point of this discussion is to emphasise the advantages conferred by an explicitly linguistics-based approach to translation. We are concerned here with a consciousness-raising process, to do with the minutiae of language at every level. So for instance, in the text discussed above the translator needs to be aware of a piece of terminology like 'prepositional phrase', the term that describes *au couperet*, as well as of the level upon which this linguistic item is situated, and the consequent fact that certain verbs construe with, or have to be accompanied by, certain prepositions. Other concepts required to deal adequately with this stretch of language are inversion (which in turn implies the notion of the subject + verb sentence structure); metaphor; collocation; and connotation. As Newmark (1988: 8) states: '[a translator] is consciously or intuitively following a theory of translation, just as any teacher of grammar teaches a theory of linguistics'.

We can expand further on this by saying that a theory of translation is most obviously a linguistic theory. We will discuss the fundamentals of the theory in this and the next chapter, before considering individually the linguistic levels referred to above. A further point is that the degree of consciousness or intuitiveness employed by the translator will probably be connected with the stage of competence reached. It is common knowledge that beginners in any highly skilled procedure proceed slowly and hesitantly at first, because they are still at the stage of consciously applying the body of knowledge they have acquired, before that knowledge has been fully internalised at an intuitive level. What is slightly paradoxical is that translators often appear not to receive a body of knowledge as such, at least compared to practitioners of professions requiring a similar level of skill. As stated above, the minimum knowledge required by a competent translator is very good knowledge of two languages and their associated cultures. We have argued above that this knowledge implies a further layer to make it explicit, namely linguistic theory.

Finally in this introductory section, we need to consider the point that the use of the term linguistic *theory* may imply something contentious; after all, we only theorise on matters about which we are not certain. But in this book, we present linguistic theory very largely as description, so far as that is possible in relation to a subject like language, which is not amenable to direct observation. By this is meant that we can only look at individual examples of language, each of which can differ considerably from speaker to speaker, so much so that it is possible to ask whether 'the English language' exists independently of the sum of the Englishes spoken by its speakers. If it does, it is clearly rather an abstract entity. Nevertheless we present here foundational theories of language that have stood the test of time and are generally accepted in the community of linguists.

Saussure's Theory of Language

If we accept that an adequate understanding of the underlying issues surrounding translation requires an acquaintance with linguistics, any discussion of the fundamentals of the present-day discipline will be widely agreed to have to start with Ferdinand de Saussure (1857–1913). Saussure, a Swiss linguist, was responsible for clarifying many previously muddy ideas about the nature of language. Culler (1976: 7) refers to him as 'the father of modern linguistics, the man who re-organized the systematic study of language and languages in such a way as to make possible the achievements of twentieth-century linguistics'. Among Saussure's crucial insights is the notion of language as *structure*. Indeed, Saussure's theory of language is often referred to as 'structural linguistics'. When we speak of the structure of anything, we refer to the relation of its parts to each other, and to the whole; which elements are more closely associated with each other than others; how they are disposed in a hierarchy; and so on. One of Saussure's most striking statements is that language *is* structure, and that form is unimportant, or at least secondary. What follows from this is that language achieves meaning through a system of oppositions.

To illustrate this, one of the famous analogies that Saussure used in order to explain the structural view of language was with the pieces used in chess. Although chess pieces have conventional shapes, we recognise each piece, both in itself but also by virtue of its differences from the others, and a chess set could be (and no doubt has been) assembled from bottle-tops, pebbles, etc. for lack of a conventional set. In this latter case, what is important is (1) that the players should recognise and agree on the value of the unconventional pieces; and (2) that these pieces should be differentiated one from the other. This is what is meant by the achievement of meaning through a system of oppositions. As Saussure expresses the matter: 'leur plus exacte caractéristique [des termes] est d'être ce que les autres ne sont pas' (1973: 162); or even more starkly (and famously): 'dans la langue il n'y a que des différences' (1973: 166). Thus, it so happens that we produce language by issuing pulses of air from our lungs, and by modifying these pulses through the movements of our vocal organs. This process results in a series of pops, clicks, hisses and notes, or 'consonants' and 'vowels' to use the commonly accepted terms, and we combine these in groups we know our hearer will convert back into meaning. The secondary language system deriving from this relies (typically) on black shapes imposed on a white ground of some sort; that is, writing. We take these systems for granted so much that we cease to see them as conventional, but other systems relying on the rapping of our knuckles on a hard surface, air entering the lungs rather than issuing from them, the production of puffs of smoke, and so forth, are quite conceivable, and indeed some have been devised.

The important point here then is that it is not the form of language that achieves meaning, but its structure, or the relationships between the items that compose a language. Put at its most crudely, we know what 'cat' means, not because of some mystical virtue inherent in the phonetic sequence /kat/, but because, or partly because, /kat/ contrasts with

/hat/, /bat/, /fat/, /rat/ and so on. On the lexical level, important contrasts are between 'cat' and 'dog', etc. In the following discussion we indicate the concept using inverted commas, as 'cat', while concrete examples are italicised, as *cat*.

The next step that follows clearly from this is that the linguistic forms that make up the structure of a language are *arbitrary*; that is, they bear no necessary relation to the concepts to which they refer (their referents). So-called onomatopoeic words, those that mimic their referents in the world, are marginal phenomena, and contain in any case a considerable conventional or arbitrary element. As Pinker (1994: 152) points out: 'in English, pigs go "oink"; in Japanese, they go "boo-boo"'. We notice that linguistic forms or 'signs' are arbitrary the moment we begin to learn a second language, and once we realise that English has *dog* while French has *chien*, German *Hund* and so forth, this fact seems perfectly obvious. However, the arbitrary nature of the sign, or 'l'arbitraire du signe' in Saussure's celebrated phrase (1973: 100), goes even beyond this, and has consequences for translation that are momentous and far-reaching. We discuss some of these after having laid out the rest of the structural view of language. We should emphasise at this point that the term 'arbitrary' lays stress on the absence of any necessary or motivated link between sign and referent. More accurate terms are perhaps 'conventional' or 'unmotivated', since there is universal agreement in any linguistic community on the sign–referent links that have historically been set up. These links are not arbitrary in the sense that speakers are free to set up their own.

The following step in the argument is that it is not only the form of the sign that is unmotivated in relation to its referent; beyond this, the sign–referent relationship itself is not a necessary one, because the sign evokes a *concept* of the referent, not the referent itself (note that 'concept' was used from the outset above, not 'thing', 'object', 'entity', etc.). It would be going too far to say the sign–referent relationship is wholly arbitrary. It seems rational to assume that there is a world out there that is independent of us; and furthermore that languages describe this world in ways that are essentially similar across cultures, and that refer to real differences between classes of entities. Nevertheless, the important point here is that we perceive the world *through our mind*, not through our senses (or through our mind via our senses). We see this most clearly in ambiguous optical illusions of the well-known type in Figure 1.1, where it is possible, through a purely mental operation, to see the cube in two opposing depth perspectives:

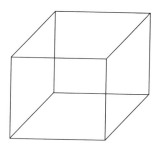

Figure 1.1 The ambiguous Necker cube

To what extent can we draw a parallel between a phenomenon of this kind that is universal, related to the cognitive or information-processing properties of the mind, and hence not cultural, and the relation between language and the world? Clearly, the influence of our mind upon our perceptions as shown in language will generally be subtler than the effect illustrated in Figure 1.1. Moreover, the influence exerted by or reflected in language upon our perception of the world is a cultural, society-wide phenomenon, even though it has psychological origins: in the jargon, it is 'psychosocial'. We call the problem raised by the Necker cube a cognitive one, since ambiguity is present in the geometrical shape shown in Figure 1.1 as a result of its shape, which does not favour either of the two hypotheses our mind makes about its 3D projection. If we conduct a discussion of the problem in terms of 'hypotheses', the word used previously, we find interesting consequences when we attempt to demonstrate a parallel between the Necker cube effect and the relation between language and the world. This term implies that our mind uses visual (and auditory, etc.) input in order to make guesses about how the world is organised. We have all had the experience of looking at an object (not a constructed one, as in Figure 1.1) or hearing a sound, and being unable at first to interpret its meaning. Does everyday language show that cultures form hypotheses about the world in order to clear up ambiguity, aside from obvious areas of enterprise such as science, or relatively trivial cases such as ambiguous geometrical figures? To examine this question, a diagram will again be useful.

The relation between the linguistic sign and its referent is expressed in Figure 1.2. This diagram is designed to illustrate the indirect or perhaps, to reprise again the term we started by using, 'hypothetical' nature of this relationship. The left-hand side of the diagram shows that the sign (the word for the purposes of this discussion) has a double aspect: its form,

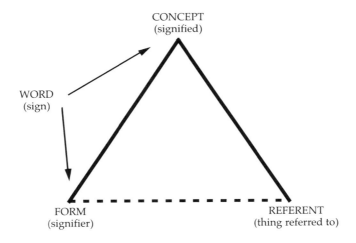

Figure 1.2 The semiotic triangle (cf. Lyons, 1968: 404)

whether phonic or graphic (the 'signifier') and the concept, or 'signified' (*signifiant* and *signifié* in Saussure's terminology). The sign can be compared to a coin, made up of the signifier on one side and the signified on the other. The coin image is meant to suggest that the two aspects of the sign are inseparable, and indeed this makes sense intuitively. We cannot say or hear, read or write the word (signifier) *cat* without evoking the concept (signified) 'cat'. We discuss below whether this is also true of more complex signs, and its consequences for the translation process.

The bottom, broken line in Figure 1.2 shows the indirect or arbitrary relationship, already discussed, between the signifier and its referent. Recall that the relationship is arbitrary because the phonic or graphic sequence *cat* has no necessary connection with the furry quadruped. The apex of the triangle shows the new element in this discussion: the concept or signified that the sign refers to. What is important to notice here is that there is a direct link between one aspect only of the sign: between the signified aspect of the sign and its referent. The diagram is designed to show that languages do not put names on things, but on concepts. Saussure explained this view of language in the following way (1973: 98): "le signe linguistique unit non une chose, mais un concept et une image acoustique". (Note that Saussure accords primacy to the spoken language, as is customary in linguistics. This is because speech is primary, writing derives from speech, and many languages have no writing system.) Saussure also expresses this idea in another way, by saying that language is not a 'nomenclature', that is, a list of words attached to things: 'si les mots étaient chargés de représenter des concepts donnés d'avance, ils auraient chacun, d'une langue à une autre, des correspondants exacts pour le sens; or, il n'en est pas ainsi' (1973: 161).

Saussure's view is therefore that each language is composed of a system of signs, each of which 'unit non une chose, mais un concept et une image acoustique'. Furthermore, these concepts are not 'donnés d'avance'; that is, they do not exist independently of the speech communities that form them. If they did, language learning and translation would be simple tasks, consisting in finding one-to-one correspondences between the signs of the languages in question, at least where vocabulary is concerned. Here we come back to the notion of the hypothesis discussed earlier. We saw that our mind can entertain two hypotheses about the Necker cube, thereby forming two visual perceptions of its position on space. To go back to our example of the cat, it may seem rather odd to say that speech communities have a hypothesis of what a cat is. Moreover, European cultures, and therefore languages, coincide in their view of what characteristics distinguish cats from (say) dogs. Nevertheless it is not difficult to imagine a culture that is not interested in the cat–dog distinction, and this different conceptual organisation would be reflected in the system of linguistic signs employed by that culture's language. Using the terminology in Figure 1.2, we suggest that concepts differ across cultures, and that certain cultures may, for whatever reason, neglect to isolate the 'cat' concept. This way of expressing the matter seems less idiosyncratic than suggesting that a culture 'has no cat hypothesis'.

For the purposes of our discussion, it does not really matter that many if not most cultures have got the cat–dog distinction 'right', in the sense of corresponding to the best efforts of biologists to classify the living world in a systematic way reflecting real divisions in the world – here the criterion is of course overlap of genetic material, since cats and dogs are incapable of mating and belong therefore to different species. Of interest here at a more general level of explanation is the psychological notion of the 'prototype', which suggests that we organise the world into fairly abstract categories such as 'bird', subsequently making decisions as to which are good, central examples of the prototypical bird and which marginal. The abstract prototype is characterised by features – in the bird's case beak, wings, egg laying, nesting, flight – and individual examples are perceived as fitting more or less well with the abstraction. We can assume that the abstract prototype will be culturally conditioned, so that a blackbird or robin may be 'good' examples of birds in western Europe, while ostriches and penguins match the prototype less well.

The notion of the prototype as a mental tool or procedure, used by speakers and cultures in their attempts to classify the world, seems to explain certain cross-cultural differences. Our imagined example of a society that draws no distinction between cats and dogs is perhaps plausible if we assume a superficial cat–dog continuum based on appearance, with in the middle a blurry distinction between large cats and small dogs. We have in any case other, less fanciful examples that are not far to seek: Thody (1997: 103) in a discussion of dietary taboos, points out that creatures which are perceived as falling between categories, such as bats (mammal or bird?) or owls (birds, but they fly only at night) are shunned as food in many cultures. These examples may seem exotic from a Eurocentric point of view, but Thody (1997: 105) explains the taboo in Western cultures forbidding us to eat cats and dogs by suggesting that we regard them as partly human, since they are kept for company. Eating a cat would therefore be akin to cannibalism. Slobin (1979: 177) gives an example from Chinese, which has an overall category or superordinate term that corresponds to English '(dried) fruit and nuts'. This seems explicable using the prototype notion, since fruit and nuts seem to belong more or less in the same semantic 'envelope' of 'edible [dried] plant seeds'. All of these examples show that cultures can have distinctions between categories that differ in fairly subtle ways, provided that the entities subject to categorisation are not grossly dissimilar. But we should be surprised to learn of a culture that had no elephant–mouse distinction, if both of these creatures were elements in their situation. In this discussion we leave aside the famous but rather obvious examples such as snow and ice vocabulary, supposedly rich in Inuit languages but almost non-existent in (say) Aztec. We assume it is sufficiently plain that cultures having little occasion to refer to a concept or set of concepts will have a correspondingly scanty lexicon in that area.

The Speech Community

The notion of the prototype explains the fact that differences in conceptual organisation will tend to be relatively subtle, at least across cultures that are not grossly dissimilar. One well-known example of an organisation that differs between French and English is expressed in the *fleuve ~ rivière* lexical pair. Both of these terms can translate as English 'river', while dictionaries differ in their interpretation of the distinction between these terms. The Collins-Robert gives *fleuve* as 'river' (lit.) and this 'literary' label is reflected in the fact that *fleuve* collocates with *roman* in the phrase *roman fleuve*, a multi-volume 'saga novel' like *A la recherche du temps perdu*. The monolingual *Petit Robert* gives a specialised meaning of *fleuve* as a *grande rivière [qui] aboutit à la mer*. In this sense of the word, the Seine is a *fleuve* while a river like the Yonne, which flows into the Seine, is a *rivière*. The 'major river' ~ 'tributary' distinction that depends on one of the senses of *fleuve* is used in Lodge *et al.* (1997: 52) to illustrate how the lexical structure of languages can differ. It seems then that speakers of French have a 'hypothesis of rivers' that differs from the English one; or if we feel that this term is being stretched too far, we can say that the French language makes explicit a view of river systems that is latent is English, since the latter language does not encode this distinction so compactly. However, given that the *Petit Robert* gives the 'major river' sense of *fleuve* as only a specialised sense of the word, it is possible to wonder how important this 'major river' sense is for a majority of French speakers.

One very important point that emerges from the foregoing discussion is that much of language is cultural, as suggested previously. Hudson (1996: 73), pointing out the difference between stretches of language that might be called non-cultural and cultural, gives the example of 'I had sausages for lunch today' as non-cultural, in the sense that it is 'known to be true from one's own experience', while 'Columbus discovered America' 'clearly belongs to culture, as something one has learned from other people'. Of course, even the statement 'I had sausages for lunch today' contains elements of cultural knowledge in the sense defined by Hudson, since sausages differ across cultures; even so, the statement concerning sausages is directly verifiable in a way that Columbus's discovery of America is not. The significance of this for our present discussion is that cultural knowledge is distributed unequally, within as well as across 'speech communities'. This latter term is rather hard to define with precision: Crystal (1991: 323) refers to it as 'any regionally or socially definable human group identified by a shared linguistic system'. The problem here is that the speech community is defined socially, and that social groups are not homogeneous. So the most problematic terms in this definition are 'shared' and 'linguistic system': how much of 'English' is shared by (say) all UK English speakers? What is meant by the 'linguistic system' – the core grammar, or the culture-dependent elements of the type we have discussed above? Both the linguistic system and the more peripheral elements can vary to a surprising degree across speech communities, and it probably makes sense to say that the wider the degree of variation in social terms – whether geographical or social – the greater the potential for linguistic difference. Milroy (1992: 33) has the following example of a serious misunderstanding on the part of speakers of standard and Hibernian English:

(4)   **A:** How long are yous here?
       B: Oh, we're staying till next week.
       (silence of about two seconds)
       C: We've been here since Tuesday.
       A: Ah well, yous are here a while then.

Speaker A, a Hiberno-English speaker, has a non-standard temporal system which uses the present tense where standard English has the present perfect: 'How long have you been here?'. Speaker B misinterprets A's first utterance as meaning: 'How long are you / will you be here (for)?', and confusion prevails until C repairs the situation. Milroy (1992: 34) states that 'there is no doubt that [communicative] breakdowns arising from the different [grammatical] structures of divergent dialects are quite common'. Certainly example (4) shows the quite striking extent to which 'English' can vary across speech communities, and what relatively deep structural levels this variation can pervade; it is not just a question of vocabulary differing across communities.

These considerations are relevant to our *fleuve ~ rivière* discussion in that the translator who encounters the word *fleuve* needs to be aware of the sense attributed to it as a result of the surrounding context. In other words, we need to put Saussure's structural view of language, or at least the part stating that different languages cut up the world along different lines, into its social context by having clearly in mind the 'speech community' at either end of the translation process. This is a question we will come back to repeatedly.

In the following section we look at a linguistic theory that develops ideas that are latent in Saussure's structural view of language, presenting them in a form that relates them to the translation issues we are considering.

The Sapir–Whorf Hypothesis: Linguistic Determinism

The American linguists Edward Sapir (1884–1939) and his pupil Benjamin Lee Whorf (1897–1941) are the most recent names to be associated with the notion that language and thought are interdependent. The strong form of this view, 'linguistic determinism', suggests that speakers' thoughts and perceptions are determined or conditioned by the categories that their language makes available to them. We can note historically that this is a recent expression of a view going back to earlier romantic thinkers, with their emphasis on cultures so diverse as to be incompatible, and was influenced by the linguistic activity in the United States in the earlier part of this century. This activity focused to some extent on the description of native-American languages, and their considerable structural differences from (to the linguist) more familiar languages were noticed. Sapir (in Mandelbaum, 1958: 162) expresses this view as follows:

> Human beings do not live in the objective world alone, nor alone in the world of social activity as ordinarily understood, but are very much at the mercy of the particular language which has become the medium of expression for their society. It is quite an illusion to imagine that one adjusts to reality essentially without the use of language and that language is merely an incidental means of solving specific problems of communication or reflection. The fact of the matter is that the 'real world' is to a large extent unconsciously built up on the language habits of the group [...]

Sapir's contention is that if two languages differ considerably in their structure, then this implies two world-views that also differ considerably. This seems untrue, however, at least so far as philosophically interesting categories like colour, number, time, shape, are in question. It would indeed be remarkable if a given language that did not express or 'encode' a certain category – more than three colours; more than three numbers; certain geometrical forms – prevented its speakers from perceiving or thinking about the categories not encoded in their language. A large amount of empirical research had been devoted to investigating this problem, and it seems that the most we can say is that a language can have a certain effect on the memory and learning processes of its speakers. For example, monolingual speakers of a language that does not encode the difference between orange and yellow may have difficulty in re-identifying objects of the colour not encoded in their language. Against this, speakers of languages possessing only three colour terms find it easy to learn names for 'good', central examples of other colours: i.e. colours cited as good examples by speakers with more than three colour terms. Children who speak a language that emphasises the shape of an object over its colour will group objects together on the basis of shape rather than colour. On the other hand, speakers of a language who have no familiarity with regular geometrical shapes like squares or triangles prefer 'good' examples of these, when invited to compare them with imperfect examples.

What these examples seem to show is that certain categories and faculties exist in the world and in the mind independent of language, and if language does influence memory, perception and other faculties, it does so in a non-radical way. Sapir's version of linguistic determinism seems to assume that thought is impossible without language; we can rebut this by pointing to the quite familiar experience of having a thought that we find difficult to put into words. Yet again, linguistic determinism implies an odd conception of bilingualism: namely, that bilinguals would need to operate with two quite different world-views, switching from one to another as they switched language. A more plausible explanation is that bilinguals mediate their single world-view through each language as required. We need therefore to modify Sapir–Whorf in a less radical direction.

Linguistic Relativity

The weaker form of the Sapir–Whorf hypothesis expresses in more explicit form Saussure's statement that 'language is not a nomenclature'. This version of Sapir–Whorf is referred to as 'linguistic relativity', and states that the linguistic structures of different languages, which can be very diverse, encourage or oblige their speakers to pay greater attention to certain aspects of the world at the expense of others. At the same time, these structures of course reflect the world-view of the culture concerned. There are several issues involved here. Examples supporting the weak form come easily to hand. Slobin (1979: 179) makes the distinction between items that reflect linguistic relativity on the levels of grammar and lexis, and suggests that grammar is the more interesting linguistic level in this regard, because certain grammatical sequences are obligatory in a way that lexical items may not be.

The most notable area of grammar in French that endorses Sapir–Whorf, and is capable of proving problematic to the translator, is probably the pronoun system. Everyone who learns French soon becomes aware of the so-called 'T/V system' built into French, in common with many other languages. We are concerned principally here with Sapir–Whorf as it affects the translator, and clearly a French sequence like: *on se tutoie, d'accord?* can have no literal translation in English. We shall discuss problems of this kind more fully in a later chapter, when we look at different types of translation. We can note here, however, that a language like French, in which the T/V system is a structural part – one is obliged to choose between *tu* and *vous* when addressing someone, as it rather hard to avoid using a 2nd-person pronoun when talking to another person – shows in quite a vivid way the influence language can have upon perception. As Slobin suggests (1979: 181–2), when speaking a language that has no T/V system 'you do not have to go through the sort of agonizing decision you would have to make in many cases if we were all compelled to speak French, for example, and thus were CONSTANTLY REQUIRED to decide which pronoun, or which verb form to use – in almost every remark' (emphasis in original). Describing a decision like this as 'agonising' is perhaps a little exaggerated, but certainly the unavoidable obligation to choose a pronoun plus verb form as a function of the relationship one has with one's interlocutor, which in turn depends on a perception of that person's social status, as well as other factors such as the degree of intimacy or solidarity subsisting between the speakers, seems a good example of the weak form of Sapir–Whorf. Equivalents in English of the T/V system seem less salient, and are also subject to choice: for example, one may hesitate between the use of title plus last name and first name when addressing someone one does not know very well, but equally one can simply avoid the option altogether, and say something like: 'Er … excuse me'.

We can note further in passing that the T/V system in French and other languages is a good example of how language change lags behind social change. The dual pronoun system is a remnant of a more deferential epoch, when someone highly placed in the social order, such as the Lord of the Manor, would address his social inferiors as *tu*, and expect *vous* in return. This is linked with the association between power and impersonality, or duality – the 'royal we', and the English upper-class habit of referring to oneself as 'one', are further examples. Such non-reciprocal *tu–vous* usage, along with the rigid hierarchical social organisation it reflected, has now largely vanished, but clearly, a feature such as the pronoun system is such a central part of a language that it cannot itself be eradicated, in the way that an obsolete term referring to an outmoded cultural practice can. Quite obviously, the speakers of a language cannot immediately abandon such a central part of it as the pronoun system, in response to changing social conditions. What happens rather is that while the system does not change, the use of it made by speakers does: from articulating deference versus dominance, the T/V system shifts to the expression principally of intimacy versus distance.

We turn now to the relationship between culture and language in the other direction: that is, the influence of culture upon language, rather than language upon culture. This is seen in various ways, but the key notion that is very often of relevance here is 'codability'.

Codability

We have already touched on the concept of codability when considering the prototype as a kind of procedure used by speech communities in their efforts to classify the world. We noted that languages draw lines between categories in different ways, reflecting the fact that a word refers to a concept, not a thing. The next step, perfectly obvious once it is formulated, is that languages having occasion to refer to concepts that are important in their culture will encode them in a terse form, and this is what is meant by 'codability', not the most transparent term that could have been devised. The idea behind the term is 'compactness of encoding'. We can assume that any concept can be expressed in any language (and therefore that any concept can be translated), but a concept that is familiar and important in a given culture will find compact expression in the language – obviously, since linguistic items that are important in a culture, and hence frequent in its language, are generally encoded in less linguistic material, so as to save time and effort. Examples are very numerous: the French term *système D* refers, in three syllables, to a Gallic conception of the relationship between individual and state that 'resourcefulness', a typical English translation, by no means fully captures.

The English term 'LBW', or even 'LB', is similarly culture-specific, and depends for its understanding on a fairly thorough knowledge of the rules of cricket. This term illustrates the point that compactly coded terms can be the property of whole cultures or sub-cultures. What *système D* and 'LBW' have in common, however, is their concise reference in the two languages to substantial areas of cultural practice. Our purpose here has been to describe the notion of codability and emphasise its centrality in any theory of translation. We can note further that the phenomenon of codability is not static, but is a *productive* process. The notion of productivity in linguistics is used to describe the process whereby a linguistic feature is capable of being applied repeatedly to produce new items – words or phrases are of interest to us here. So, the English suffix *–s* is overwhelmingly used to produce new noun plurals, unlike vowel alternations such as 'mouse' ~ 'mice', for example, which were productive at an earlier stage of the language but are no longer. Productivity in compactness of encoding can raise problems for the translator, most notably because new compact forms take a while to find their way into reference resources – although Internet-based resources are becoming increasingly flexible in this regard. A recent example is the French noun *Tanguyisme*, deriving from the (2001) film 'Tanguy' and referring to the trend for 20-somethings to stay on at home rather than set up on their own. The productive process here is the addition to a noun of the *–isme* suffix to produce a new, abstract noun.

In a later chapter we will consider various solutions available to the problems posed by the phenomenon of codability.

Structure of the Book, and Summary

This book is structured partly in ascending order of magnitude of the problems facing the translator. In the present chapter we have been looking at the essential structure of language (Saussure) and the relationship between language and culture (Sapir–Whorf), using examples provided by individual words and phrases for the most part. In Chapter 3 we consider the word in more detail, looking at French and English word structure as they affect translation issues. In Chapter 4 we look at the relationships that make up the lexical structure of French: the principal relationships of interest are hyponymy and synonymy. We will see that some translation problems beyond the word level can also be discussed with profit in the light of the theories of Saussure and Sapir–Whorf. In Chapter 4 we consider also some concepts in lexical semantics that are useful in translation. When we reach Chapter 5 we will see that Saussure and Sapir–Whorf are less useful when we consider the translation problems caused by syntactic differences across the two languages. Chapter 6 summarises the suggestions we have made in the book by considering the various types of translation that can be performed. In Chapter 7 we discuss some miscellaneous issues that do not fit in neatly elsewhere.

In the next chapter we lay the other foundation stone of the book by considering the translator's role in relation to the type of text that is being translated, and hence the type of reader assumed. This is a central issue, and many translation failures are caused by insufficient attention to it.

In the present chapter we have already touched on the three concepts that are of crucial interest to the translator. Recall that early in this chapter we said that linguists study (1) the structure of the language, and (2) how it works as a means of cultural expression. These are the first two pillars of our edifice. The third is the relationship between writer, text and reader, as mentioned in the previous paragraph.

When we said that linguists study the structure of the language, and how it works as a means of cultural expression, we were over-generalising. Linguists can and do study the structure of language without paying much heed to its role in cultural expression, and the most famous sentence in linguistics has little to do with the culture behind it:

(5)   colorless green ideas sleep furiously

This sentence, devised by Noam Chomsky (b. 1928), the leading figure in linguistics since Saussure, is designed to illustrate the relationship between syntax and semantics. We can see that the sentence has an acceptable syntax, even though it makes no sense as ideas cannot be green; if they were they could not be colourless, and so on. From our recognition that the sentence makes no sense but is syntactically well-formed, we can go on to devise a theory of the human language faculty that tries to explain how we are satisfied by the syntax of example (5) while still recognising its nonsensicality. For instance, we could hypothesise that words in the mental lexicon are 'tagged' in some way, so as to ensure they do not co-occur in ways that produce nonsense.

The type of linguistics done by Chomsky and his followers is 'pure' in the sense of having little social input. Linguistics of this kind is sometimes called 'armchair linguistics', as it is possible to do it by constructing examples in the comfort of one's office. There is little social input, as sentence (5) illustrates, since the influence of social or cultural factors is not of interest. It would not therefore be difficult to translate sentence (5) into a language having a similar structure. However, theoretical linguistics is of help to the translator, if only because it provides the tools necessary for the rigorous analysis of language, as we hope to have demonstrated in this chapter.

As well as the purely theoretical help that linguistics can provide, we have already discussed several examples of the relationship between the structure of language and how it works as a means of cultural expression. Examples like *système D* and 'LBW' are the tip of a very large iceberg; the scope of 'culture' is as large as it is multi-dimensional. We suggested above that a term like 'LBW' is the property of a sub-culture. Social groups or sub-cultures split along many dimensions, with different linguistic consequences in each case. Very compactly encoded lexical items such as those just quoted are the most obvious consequences, but all three linguistic levels are in question here, with variation taking place across our two languages of interest in the way pronunciation, grammar and lexis reflect cultural variation. We shall discuss one last example before we approach the relationship between text, writer and reader. The following example is designed to show that the linguistic and cultural aspects of translation issues can be indissociable. Grammatical variation is a salient feature of French, in the sense of being shared by all speakers, to an extent that seems less noticeable in English. So for instance, in informal French a speaker has the option between *quelle* and *quoi* as question words in sequences of the following type. The symbol '~' here means 'varies with':

(6)   tu es de quelle origine? ~ tu es d'origine quoi?

We discussed above the example of the T/V system mostly from the point of view of the influence of language on perception, pointing out only in passing that sequences like *on se tutoie, d'accord?* cannot be translated literally. To expand this point, we can say that this is clearly because standard English no longer has the 'thou/you' alternation. So, although the alternation still persists in a few out-of-the-way places, an attempt by a translator to render this French sequence by 'let's use "thou" to each other, shall we?', even if understood at all by a reader, will carry totally unsuitable associations – if anything, the social message will be archaic or rural. So although the French T/V system carries strong social coding, the socio-cultural dimensions along which we analyse the coding – solidarity versus power, intimacy versus distance – are at variance with any social coding the vestigial English T/V system continues to convey.

The example of alternation between 'Q-interrogatives' (so called because the question-word begins with a Q) illustrates the same point, but again along different socio-cultural axes, this time to do with how language varies according to its use by speakers of different age-groups, social classes, and in situations differentiated by their formality. The non-standard alternant of the pair shown in (6), *tu es d'origine quoi?*, is also untranslatable in any literal way, because the interrogative system of English has little social variation in it. An attempt to render into English the very informal nature of *tu es d'origine quoi?* would probably have to use resources from a linguistic level other than syntax.

In summary, we have sketched a view of translation in this chapter with the aim of showing three things:

(1) A linguistic approach needs to look at the structure of the language itself, perhaps without any need to consider the way in which culture bears upon the language. The various structural linguistic considerations discussed in relation to the passage on Human Rights legislation was designed to show this.

(2) When we view language as a vehicle of cultural expression, we soon see that culture-specific concepts enjoy special linguistic privileges, as they are compactly encoded. We will return to this issue repeatedly in what follows.

(3) Our last point is perhaps another version of point (3). Cultural expression can be encoded in a language in such a structural way – in the grammar and sound system – that no equivalent is available on the same linguistic level in the other language. We might call this a structural encoding of social meaning, as against the often more superficial encoding that finds expression in vocabulary.

We turn now to the study of text types.

Chapter 2

Approaching a Text

Introduction

In this chapter we consider some of the sociolinguistic factors that need to be borne in mind as a text is being translated. These factors are social, since they have to do with the characteristics of the intended readership and the process of translation as an act of communication, which in turn has to do with the intention of the author of the 'source text' (ST) – the text out of which translation is taking place. At the same time the factors influencing translation are inevitably linguistic, since they find expression in language. We look first of all at the question of the extent to which the translator should aim to be unobtrusive. Assuming that on the whole the translator's art needs to be concealed, we examine subsequently some of the factors that help or hinder the effort to do so. From now on, as well as ST, we use the terms 'source language' (SL), as well as 'target text' (TT) – the translation – and 'target language' (TL), the language of the target text. Other new terms are 'decode', which means simply to determine the meaning of an ST term, and 'encode', to render that meaning into the TL.

The Translator's Role as 'Secret Agent'

By and large, we will not be concerned very much here with the question of the extent to which the translator should be 'invisible'; we shall simply assume that in the vast majority of cases this should be so. There has been a certain amount of discussion of this question in the scholarly literature on translation; for instance, Venuti, in his book entitled The *Translator's Invisibility*, criticises 'United Kingdom and United States cultures that are aggressively monolingual, unreceptive to the foreign, accustomed to fluent translations that invisibly inscribe foreign texts with English-language values and provide readers with the narcissistic experience of recognizing their own culture in a cultural other' (1995: 6). This view interprets the translator's status as comparable to that of the author of the ST, rather than as an intermediary whose work, if it is well done, should be undetectable. We may deplore the largely monolingual cultural hegemony enjoyed by the UK and US that requires a translation bearing little or no trace of the ST; at the same recognising this dominance and the need to work within its constraints, at least at the commercial level. This view is reflected in guidelines issued by professional bodies; for example, the Institute of Linguists, a UK organisation that sets translation examinations to professional standard, expresses one marking criterion in the following terms: '[an excellent translation] reads like a piece originally written in the target language; sentence structure, linkages and discourse are all entirely appropriate to the target language.' A literary translation may of course aim to convey some of the foreign characteristics of the ST, and this is recognised in the translation literature as 'foreignising translation'.

It certainly appears that the translator who uses 'foreignising strategies' that infuse elements of the SL into the TL in a clearly visible way, will usually be doing so for some special stylistic effect. For instance, Ernest Hemingway's novel *The Sun Also Rises* (1954: 240) (*Fiesta* in the UK) has the following passage, where the narrator and his interlocutor are clearly portrayed as speaking in Spanish (the setting is Madrid, where the narrator is talking to a hotel employee):

(1)   Did I want to stay myself in person in the Hotel Montana?

Of that as yet I was undecided, but it would give me pleasure if my bags were brought up from the ground floor in order that they might not be stolen. Nothing was ever stolen in the Hotel Montana. In other fondas, yes. Not here. No. The personages of this establishment were rigidly selected. I was happy to hear it. Nevertheless I would welcome the upbringal of my bags.

Here the dialogue is conveyed indirectly, and we may assume that Hemingway is seeking to provide amusement by writing English of a kind that gives the impression of being translated more or less directly from the Spanish. This is done principally through the use of word order and vocabulary that is unidiomatic, as well as of words that simply are not found in English, such as 'selected' and 'upbringal', but whose sense is nevertheless clear. We are not of course concerned directly in this example with translation, which proceeds normally through the intervention of a mediator between the reader and the original author. Nevertheless Hemingway's example illustrates that a foreignising translation is the exceptional case, reflecting a special intent (or ineptitude on the translator's part). We can contrast Venuti's view with that of the writer Norman Shapiro (cited in Venuti, 1995: 1), who expresses very vividly the dominant requirement imposed upon the translator:

I see translation as an attempt to produce a text so transparent that it does not seem to be translated. A good translation is like a piece of glass. You only notice that it's there when there are little imperfections – scratches, bubbles. Ideally there shouldn't be any. It should never call attention to itself.

'Calling attention to itself' is precisely what Hemingway's translation-composition is doing. In a similar vein, it is worth considering the following poem by Kingsley Amis, which is a translation-cum-pastiche of Baudelaire's well-known poem 'L'Alabatros'. The ST and TT are given in parallel below:

(2)

L'Albatros	The Helbatrawss
Souvent, pour s'amuser, les hommes d'équipage	Qvite horfen, for a lark, coves on a ship
Prennent des albatros, vastes oiseaux des mers,	Ketches a uge sea-bird, a helbatrawss,
Qui suivent, indolents compagnons de voyage,	A hidle sod as mucks in on the trip
Le navire glissant sur les gouffres amers.	By follerin the wessel on its course.
A peine les ont-ils déposés sur les planches,	Theyve ardly got im on the deck afore,
Que ces rois de l'azur, maladroits et honteux	Cackanded, proper chokker – never mind
Laissent piteusement leurs grandes ailes blanches	Es a igh-flier – cor, e makes em roar
Comme des avirons traîner à côté d'eux.	Voddlin abaht, is vings trailin beind.
Ce voyageur ailé, comme il est gauche et veule!	Up top, yus, e was smashin, but es grim
Lui, naguère si beau, qu'il est comique et laid!	Like this; e aint alf hugly nah es dahned:
L'un agace son bec avec un brûle-gueule,	Vun perisher blows Voodbine-smoke at im,
L'autre mime, en boitant, l'infirme qui volait!	Anuvver tikes im orff by oppin rahnd!
Le Poète est semblable au prince des nuées	A long-aired blokes the sime: ead in the clahds,
Qui hante la tempête et se rit de l'archer;	E larfs at harrers, soups is cupper tea;
Exilé sur le sol au milieu des huées,	But dahn to earf in these ere bleedin crahds,
Ses ailes de géant l'empêchent de marcher.	Them uge great vings balls up is plates, yer see.

Amis's poem is a more suitable example for our present purposes, as it is a translation in a more straightforward sense than the fragment of 'self-translation' from Hemingway quoted previously. What is striking in Amis's translation of the Baudelaire poem is the use of non-standard items from each of the three linguistic levels of analysis, pronunciation, grammar and vocabulary. Line three contains at least one example from each linguistic level; thus 'a hidle sod as …' could be rendered in standard English by 'an idle fellow who …'.

In contrast to the Hemingway example, it so happens that we know the motivation behind Amis's attempt to reproduce an unusual or highly marked variety of English. Amis chose to translate the French of Charles Baudelaire (1821–67) into a stylised archaic Cockney, such as can be found in works of 19th-century literature like Dickens's *The Pickwick Papers* and other novels, and some Victorian light verse. He did this to poke fun at a dialect revival that was taking place around the time he composed the translation (1954), and the poem was included in a tongue-in-cheek article that he published (under the pen-name 'Anselm Chilworth') in *The Spectator*, entitled 'The Cockney Renaissance'. 'The Helbatrawss' was presented as the work of 'Helfred Uggins', and was accompanied by 'glosses' into standard English such as *'soups is cupper tea*: he is most at home in foul weather'. The dialect revival that was taking place concerned 'Lallans' (Lowland Scots English). The source of the humour in Amis's piece is therefore the suggestion that Cockney is a dialect with a similar status to rural varieties like Lallans and hence a suitable vehicle for literary expression.

The most notable feature of the Cockney used is no doubt the crossover in the use of /w/ and /v/, as in 'quite' pronounced *qvite* and 'vessel' pronounced *wessel*. Other striking features are the use of /h/: absent in contexts where it is present in standard English, as in 'long-aired', but present where it is ruled out in the standard variety, as in 'harrers' for 'arrows'. This is again an old-fashioned Cockney stereotype. Other features are perhaps more familiar, by reason of still being found in Cockney and of spreading into contemporary 'Estuary English' and beyond: replacement of 'th' (/θ/ in phonetic script) by /f/, as in 'earf' for 'earth'; and of the standard /aw/ vowel in 'clouds' and 'crowds' by a long /a/ sound ('clahds', 'crahds').

As in Hemingway's example, sheer playfulness seems to be an important motivation behind Amis's Baudelaire translation – which is however quite an accurate one, leaving aside the dialect features. However, the point at issue is that, as stated previously, we can contrast 'marked' translations such as those of Hemingway and Amis with those (the majority) which aim simply to render the ST into a TT that is 'so transparent that it does not seem to be translated'. There is nevertheless a level of complexity beyond this fairly straightforward view, for the features in an ST that result in its calling attention to itself need to be matched in the TT so far as possible. We consider this issue in the following section, when we look at another literary text.

Apart from the author's intention, an important characteristic of the texts discussed above is their subjectivity or expressive character. By this we mean that the authors are expressing either a point of view that is personal to the author and open to debate (is a poet like an albatross or not?) or simply playing about with words, as in the Hemingway extract. Other texts, most notably those that are informative and universal in their reference, contrast sharply with texts whose bias is subjective and expressive. As Newmark (1988: 13) points out regarding poetry, the amount of attention the translator needs to pay to the readership may be very small. Newmark suggests that this is because the composition of poetry is often prompted by the impulse to self-expression, without necessarily having regard to any potential reader at all, or more than a small circle of readers whose identity may be known. The author's intention is therefore again an important factor here: a poet may not necessarily be much or even at all concerned with getting a 'message' across, but rather with constructing a pleasing sound-sequence whose meaning is secondary. Obviously, this grants the translator a good deal of latitude.

This leads us on to a consideration of the notion of the 'text type'.

Text Types

In the previous section we discussed the translator's intention, suggesting that by and large it was concerned with the production of a TT that should leave as few traces as possible of the ST. Following on from the discussion in the previous section, let us consider the two passages below. We are considering from this perspective the original author's intention, rather than the translator's. These passages are examples of different text types.

(3) Functions play an important role in science. Frequently, one observes that one quantity is a function of another and then tries to find a formula to express this function. For example, before about 1590 there was no quantitative idea of temperature. Of course, people under-stood relative notions like warmer and cooler, and some absolute notions like boiling hot, freezing cold, or body temperature, but there was no numerical measure of temperature. It took the genius of Galileo to realise that the expansion of fluids as they warmed was the key to the measurement of temperature. He was the first to think of temperature as a function of fluid volume.

(4) There hastened forward another plump man with a moustache and a notable jacket, one resembling an abbreviated dressing-gown. He too cut the air a good deal, proclaiming himself generally to be the proprietor, and of an Italian restaurant too. His greeting to Rhiannon fell short of kissing her hand but not by much. If he was not Italian himself by blood, which in this part of South Wales and in the catering trade he might quite well have been, he was the next best thing, perhaps even one better: a Welshman putting it on all-out.

Peter got something different from him, the graver reception appropriate to a senator or international operatic tenor.

When thinking about text types as objects of translation, we can consider their distribution, or where they are typically found: in textbooks, novels, newspapers, in an instruction manual, on a stand in a tourist office, and so on. A related approach is to consider, as we suggested above in relation to the author's intention, the purpose of a given ST; what is the author trying to achieve? Texts (3) and (4) above represent examples that would be situated rather far apart from each other on any scale designed to indicate the author's intention; (3) is clearly a good example of an informative text, taken from an introductory mathematics textbook (McCarthy, 1986: x), while (4), again by Kingsley Amis, seems similar to 'The Helbatrawss' in its intention to entertain. It is an extract from his novel *The Old Devils* (1986: 182).

In what follows we shall initially take the more difficult route (for the native English speaker) and attempt to render these texts into English, so as to highlight more vividly some of their features considered as elements that indicate a certain text type. In this way, one can see that different text types are characterised by certain linguistic features, which in turn are an expression of the author's intention. The author's intention is, in turn, related to the perception s/he has of who the text is aimed at. Yet again, the author's intention is capable of being related to the socio-cultural conditions surrounding the text. From this point of view, it is obvious that text (3) is relatively easy to translate while text (4) is more difficult.

The first sentence of text (3) goes into French with little difficulty: *Les fonctions jouent un rôle important dans les sciences*. This ease of translation is due partly to the fact that the topic under discussion, as well as the register in which it is being discussed, draw upon vocabulary that is common to both SL and TL. We will develop this point below, but concentrating for the moment on the author's purpose, we can say, fairly obviously, that this purpose is to convey information in as clear a way as possible. A crucial factor here is shared knowledge; the author has an advanced level of competence in mathematics, but is concerned to explain an area of the subject to a readership that has more limited knowledge. A large number of the linguistic features in the text stem from this; for example, the first sentence has a very simple subject-predicate structure which we can presume is connected to the author's concern for ease of readability, and which in turn makes for ease of translation. We can therefore modify our definition of the author's intention by saying that the function of the text is expository or explanatory rather than more broadly informative: from a position of expertise, the author is explaining a complex subject as clearly as possible, for the benefit of a readership less fully acquainted with subject.

With this in mind, we can notice further that the author has chosen to use an image that is convenient for the translator's purpose, as it is shared by French and English: that of 'playing a role'. As both languages commonly use this image, a literal translation is possible. This is a happy accident here, but a more general point is that imagery is central to the use of language – as shown by the fact that we have just used an image to express this notion, the pictorial or spatial notion of centrality. Language that puts a premium on the communication of information to a non-expert readership uses a fair amount of imagery, although it is not quite clear why – it seems that both writers and readers prefer the concrete to the abstract in many types of text where the amount of knowledge shared by writer and reader is limited in some important way. A contrasting case is technical or academic prose, where the advanced degree of speciali-sation shared by writer and reader is reflected in the highly abstract, i.e. non-concrete, non-pictorial, etc. nature of the writing. It is lack of imagery, as much as a high degree of specialisation reflected in the use of technical terms, which often makes for prose that is hard to read. The use of imagery can both help and hinder the translator; clearly, where there is identical use of an image in SL and TL, this makes possible a literal trans-lation. Where there is non-equivalence, an alternative image or expression must be sought, as in the case of the 'key' image used in the ST (line 9), where *moyen* is perhaps most suitably substituted as an idiomatic rendering of 'key', since *la clé du calcul de la température*, while possible, reads rather clumsily.

If we reproduce (3) in modified form, along with a speedy translation that does not pretend to any great elegance, underlining words that are similar in ST and TT, we see a pattern that is quite striking:

(5) Functions play an important role in science. Frequently, one observes that one quantity is a function of another and then tries to find a formula to express this function. For example, before about 1590 there was no quantitative idea of temperature. Of course, people understood relative notions like warmer and cooler, and some absolute notions like boiling hot, freezing cold, or body temperature, but there was no numerical measure of temperature. It took the genius of Galileo to realise that the expansion of fluids as they warmed was the key to the measurement of temperature. He was the first to think of temperature as a function of fluid volume.

(6) Les fonctions jouent un rôle important dans les sciences. Fréquemment, on peut observer qu'une quantité est fonction d'une

autre, et on tente alors de trouver une <u>formule</u> pour <u>exprimer</u> cette <u>fonction</u>. Par <u>exemple</u>, avant 1590 environ on n'avait pas d'<u>idée</u> <u>quantitative</u> de la <u>température</u>. Bien entendu, on comprenait des <u>notions</u> <u>relatives</u> comme «plus chaud» ou «plus frais», et certaines <u>notions</u> <u>absolues</u> comme <u>bouillant</u>, gelant ou la <u>température</u> corporelle, mais il n'y avait pas de <u>mesure</u> <u>numérique</u> de la <u>température</u>. Il fallut le <u>génie</u> de Galilée pour découvrir que <u>l'expansion</u> des <u>fluides</u> qui se chauffent était le moyen de <u>mesurer</u> la <u>température</u>. C'était le premier à concevoir la <u>température</u> en tant que <u>fonction</u> du <u>volume</u> des <u>fluides</u>.

A further important feature of a text type is its subject matter. Paradoxically, it is in large measure the abstract nature of the ST that makes it fairly easy to translate. Of the 109 words in text (3), 32, almost one in three, are abstract words that have an easily recognised counterpart in the TL, some repeated more than once:

> functions, important, role, science, frequently, observes, quantity, formula, express, example, quantitative, idea, temperature, relative, notions, absolute, numerical, measure, genius, expansion, fluids, measurement, volume.

For the most part these words go straight into French with the minimal amount of adaptation that is necessary. Clearly, one reason for this is that French and English, being quite closely related languages that furthermore have a millennium or so of shared history, have a scientific word-stock that is very largely common to both, since by and large their abstract vocabulary is drawn from Latin and Greek. At the same time the translator can render words like 'temperature' and 'function' into French in a straightforward way, because in this text their meaning is independent of any cultural considerations – 'temperature' is here a universal concept, as is 'function' where its sense refers to mathematics. In this text, therefore, we can translate these words without worrying about their sense in relation to the surrounding text, or their collocational value. We discuss collocation in a later chapter, but briefly, collocation refers to the way groups of words are commonly found together: we talk about 'rancid cheese', but not, except for special effect, 'rancid aluminium'. Thus the words 'rancid' and 'cheese' show a tendency to collocate (co- locate: locate together). It is of course possible to employ 'temperature' and 'function' in a figurative sense that might rule out a literal translation.

In a broader perspective, text (3) contains quite a large number of words that are abstract without referring to the scientific enterprise, and many of these words are again common to the Greco-Latin word-stock shared by the two languages. But as so often, we need to be alert to the presence of false friends, and 'realise' is a case in point here.

In summary, the main difficulties associated with translating this text relate to the structural linguistic differences between ST and TT: translating 'is a function' as *est fonction*, 'he was the first' as *c'était le premier*, 'fluids as they warmed' as *des fluides qui se chauffent*, 'the key to' as *le moyen de*, etc. This is the linguistic aspect of translation, discussed at the end of Chapter 1, which is only tenuously connected with cultural differences. A general point, obvious enough but worth making nevertheless, is that in a 'service translation' such as we have just discussed – a translation out of the translator's mother tongue, in the direction which is not customary – the difficulty is to find the grammatical and (ideally) idiomatic construction in the TL that is equivalent to the SL construction, while avoiding the influence of the SL. Short of being fully bilingual, one is therefore operating at a lower level of competence, and often simply avoiding ineptitude when translating in this direction. In the normal direction of translation, into one's mother tongue, we can assume, in the best of cases, a very much fuller availability to the translator of grammatical and idiomatic constructions in the TL that can be used to render SL sequences. At the same time, SL influence needs to be avoided; if we imagine *des fluides qui se chauffent* as an original ST fragment, it is not difficult to imagine unhappy SL influence resulting in 'fluids that heat' or something similar.

Culture Infused in Language

Turning now to the Kingsley Amis text, we can argue that the translation difficulties inherent in it are due very largely to the author's intention, considered once again in relation to the linguistic-cultural context in which the text is situated. Amis stated that he hoped to be remembered as a funny writer, and that a writer who failed to amuse himself as he wrote was unlikely to amuse his readership. One may or may not agree on the success of the humour to be found in text (4), but what is certain is that Amis is making copious use of what we might call 'marked' language, presumably in the interests of achieving humour. The concept in linguistics of a marked linguistic item or construction refers to the listener's or reader's expectations: the theory is that we assume the unmarked case in the absence of information to the contrary. According to the theory, we assume for instance that nouns will be singular, tenses will be in the present, and so forth, unless we are alerted otherwise. We can extend this concept to include words, constructions and collocations that are used where a more common variant is available. Thus the first sentence of the Amis passage begins with a so-called 'expletive' construction, 'There hastened forward a plump man' where a less elaborate construction could have been used: 'A plump man hastened forward'. Such constructions are called expletive because the first word, 'there', does not contribute any meaning but is present merely to fill a gap that the syntactic construction in question happens to require. 'Expletion', from the Latin, means 'filling out', and in its origin has nothing to do with swear words. Expletives in this latter everyday sense are of course often used fill to a gap, adding little or nothing to the sense.

Why did Amis phrase things the first way round? In contrast with his 'marked' translation of *L'Albatros*, we are once again in the realm of conjecture. The humour here depends perhaps on a tension between the everyday subject matter (having a drink in an unpretentious restaurant in South Wales) and the language in which it is narrated. The construction 'There hastened forward' may be intended to evoke subliminally in the reader's mind the sort of language found in the King James Bible, where phrases structured in this way, such as 'There arose then a great multitude', are not uncommon. This particular construction does not test the translator too severely, although s/he must of course be aware of the equivalent construction: the syntax of *Il s'avança avec empressement un homme potelé …'* conveys much the same old-fashioned feel in French.

A further difficult feature of Amis's text relates to collocation, and this is an aspect of translation that causes problems both into and out of the translator's native language. The difficulty here is the use by Amis of marked or unusual collocations like 'abbreviated dressing-gown' and 'notable jacket'. If we were set the task of translating the text into French, the difficulty here would be to match a native-speaker's intuition as to the unusual nature of equivalent collocations. Other difficulties are idiomatic phrases like 'cut the air' – obviously, 'to gesture', but a French equivalent drawn from a similar register could prove hard to find. The same remark applies to 'putting it on all-out'. Culture-specific references such as the allusion to the presence of inhabitants of Italian origin in South Wales are implicit in the English original, but might need expansion in a translation. Difficulties to do with nuances of words – finding a close equivalent for 'plump', for example – should not tax the advanced translator too severely.

It should be clear that the problems attending an English–French translation of the Amis text stem from the threefold issue we referred to briefly at the end of the previous chapter, what we might call the reader-writer-text nexus. Amis is not at all concerned with issuing decontextualised information in as clear a way as possible. On the contrary, any 'information' in text (4) is highly context-dependent, the context here being something like 'the English literary tradition'. If we had to define the purpose of text (4), we might suggest, as previously, that it is to provide entertainment of a sophisticated order. More precisely, the author is (among other things) playing a game using some of the sociolinguistic resources of English. If we pursue further the analogy of a game, we can state that sophisticated games presuppose a set of rules unfamiliar to some if not most potential readers. In these terms, a further contrast between (3) and (4) is that the author of (3) is concerned to make his initial presentation at least as accessible and universal as possible (to interested readers of English, in any event), while this is not an important concern in the case of (4). In any case it is possible to argue that the motive behind literary composition is not 'communication', at least as that term is ordinarily understood. As the novelist and literary critic David Lodge has pointed out (1997: 192): 'the fact that the author is absent when his message is received, unavailable for interrogation, lays the message, or text, open to multiple, indeed infinite interpretation. And this in turn undermines the concept of literary texts as communications.' The general conclusion seems to be that the more literary the text, the more tenuous is the link between writer and reader, with the implications for difficulty of translation we have discussed above.

A further source of difficulty is 'intertextuality', a common theme of literary criticism. We are told by modern critics that all texts refer to previous texts, however tenuously. This is part of the game referred to above. Where intertextuality takes place between texts in the same language, the universality of the language is diminished unless texts have a common source that many languages have drawn upon – the Bible, for instance. But even in the latter case, we may see the kind of indissociable fusing of language and culture we discussed in the previous chapter in relation to French grammar. This is because translations of the Bible can be quite highly culture-specific; the King James Bible is valued as much for its literary worth as for its value in religious teaching. This explains the biblical echoes so often found in literature. The poem quoted below shows a fairly extreme example of a writer playing language games using the sociolinguistic resources of English, including biblical resonances:

(7)   What does little Ernest croon
      in his death at afternoon?
      (kow dow r 2 bul retoinis
      was de woids uf lil Oinis).

This poem is by e. e. cummings (*sic*), an American poet, and is a *jeu d'esprit* directed against Ernest Hemingway. The amount of cultural and linguistic knowledge required to decode the text is surprisingly large for such a short fragment, and is commensurate with the difficulty of translation. Firstly, one needs to be familiar with the title of one of Hemingway's books, *Death in the Afternoon*, a book about bullfighting, which was one of Hemingway's obsessions. The second couplet interweaves literary reference and non-standard language in quite a complex way: The third line evokes a modified fragment from the Burial Service: 'Dust thou art, to dust returnest', while the spelling of 'retoinis', 'woids' and 'Oinis' seem designed to convey a low-class Brooklyn accent. In addition there appears to be sheer playfulness in the use of numbers and single letters to indicate full words – 'r 2' –, though one could argue that this intensifies the subversive thrust of the text. The effect is to mock Hemingway's solemn attitude to bullfighting, perhaps by suggesting that his approach is too reverential (the reference to the Book of Common Prayer) while poking fun at his high aesthetic pretensions by attributing to him a lower-class origin (the Brooklyn vowels).

How much of this can be translated? As suggested above, what is cross-cultural lends itself best to translation – and here there is very little that is cross-cultural, since the Burial Service is an English text, is indeed part of the English literary canon. Similarly, the non-standard language in which it is couched can have no direct equivalent. This is also the case where language and culture are literally inseparable, because built into the very structure of the words ('retoinis', 'woids', 'Oinis'). If we are aware of the Brooklyn stereotype, the English spelling sequence <oi> will trigger it, because the spelling evokes the vowel sequence linked to the social stereotype.

We have concentrated so far on English texts to illustrate the point that language can be so saturated in the culture to which it refers as to rule out any kind of literal translation. Below is a French fragment that broadly endorses the same point, although here the fusion of language and culture is not so uniformly close. It is taken from Queneau's *Zazie dans le Métro* (1959: 47):

(8)   Le type paie et ils s'immergent dans la foule. Zazie se faufile, négligeant les graveurs de plaques de vélo, les souffleurs de verre, les démonstrateurs de nuds de cravate, les Arabes qui proposent des montres, les manouches qui proposent n'importe quoi. Le type est sur ses talons, il est aussi subtil que Zazie. Pour le moment, elle a pas envie de le semer, mais elle se prévient que ce sera pas commode. Y a pas de doute, c'est un spécialiste.

Elle s'arrête pile devant un achalandage de surplus. Du coup, a boujplu. A boujpludutou. Le type freine sec, juste derrière elle. Le commerçant engage la conversation.

One of the notable features of *Zazie dans le Métro* is its importation into the narrative of some non-standard features of spoken French, which are moreover found throughout in the dialogue and narrative of the novel. Queneau was by no means the first to use this device; it can be found in Céline, Zola, Hugo and Balzac. One can apply similar observations here to those made concerning the Amis texts: Queneau seems here to be playing a sophisticated literary game, deploying sociolinguistic resources to provide high-level diversion for the reader who shares them. One way of analysing this is to suggest that the amusement deriving from the quite frequent infusion in the book of non-standard language into narrative depends again on a tension, here between expectation and literary practice. The practice employed by Queneau goes against the convention used in most novels, where narrative and dialogue are sharply demarcated, so that in the passage cited above, colloquial elements like *y a pas de doute* contrast with carefully chosen literary words such as *s'immerger*. As in the e. e. cummings poem discussed above, where conflicting literary elements are interwoven very tightly, the translation difficulties become formidable. This is most vividly apparent in the sequence: *Du coup, a boujplu. A boujpludutou* in the above passage. In a more standard register of French this is: *Du coup, elle (ne) bouge plus. Elle (ne) bouge plus du tout.* Here the words written solid evoke the stream of speech, where there are no gaps between words, while the semi-phonetic spelling seems to have been triggered by the author's decision to represent *elle* as *a*, an old working-class Parisian feature. This playfulness, as well of course as the culture-specificity, again evoke the 'retionis', 'Oinis' etc. of the cummings passage.

We are perhaps employing a little too much subtlety in evoking the use in narrative of non-standard language to explain the difficulty of this passage as regards translation. It is possible to separate out the standard and non-standard linguistic elements in the *Zazie* passage in a way that is less easy with the cummings poem; indeed, it is essential for any translator to be keenly aware of these shifts in register. At any rate, it is enough to suggest that sequences like *Du coup, a boujplu. A boujpludutou* are untranslatable in anything approaching a literal sense, because stretches like these refer to aspects of the culture underlying the language in such a specific way. Thus, any attempt to render a working-class Parisian feature would by definition have to refer to something non-Parisian, and hence a more or less approximate equivalent – Cockney, perhaps. A recent translation (Queneau, 2000: 36) renders the above sequence as:

(9)   What a sight; she doesn't budge. She doesn't budget all.

Here the translator seems to have decided to substitute for the omission of *ne* and the Parisian /a/ vowel respectively, a contraction: 'does not' > 'doesn't'; and a pun: 'budge at all' > 'budget all' (Zazie has just seen some blue jeans for sale on the market stall, and she is very eager to acquire a pair). We discuss in a subsequent section what is meant by equivalence in translation, but clearly the rendering of *A boujpludutou* by 'She doesn't budget all' produces a very broad effect: what is retained is the rather whimsical humour of the original. All else is lost.

Problems that are similar to, but less drastic than the *A boujpludutou* issue are posed by reduced forms like *y a pas de doute* (full form *il n'y a pas de doute*). This is a large and complicated subject, but in the case of *y a pas de doute*, the non-standard or colloquial effect is connected with reduction – the omission of *ne* and of the pronoun *il*. Thus *il n'y a pas de doute* would be transcribed in the International Phonetic Alphabet as [ilnjapaddut], while the reduced sequence is pronounced [japaddut]. The problem here is to determine whether reduced forms have equivalent social significance in French and English. Both languages (like all languages) make use of reduction in less formal speech styles, and as was pointed above, the reduction in *a boujplu* was conveyed by a reduction in the TT: 'she doesn't budge'. Does this produce an 'equivalent' effect? All we can say is that the translator presumably thought so; she was aware that the reduction in the French sequence had a certain non-standard value, and decided to use a resource in English that was similar on the same linguistic level. Where a linguistically similar resource is available across two languages, it seems defensible to transfer it from ST to TT. Where socially coded features are related, not to reduction but to features like alternations on vowel quality, as in the /a/ vowel above, the translator's task is much more difficult. We can note in passing that features of this latter type are numerous in English: recall the variants in the Amis poem discussed above, such as 'crowds' ~ 'crahds' and 'albatross' ~ 'helbatrawss'.

The ease with which we can imagine a solution to the translation of a stretch of non-standard language depends on the availability of a feature in the TT that is more or less comparable. For instance, the famous opening passage of *Zazie* is presented as straight speech, or more precisely as interior monologue. The first two sentences are as follows:

(10)   Doukipudonktan, se demanda Gabriel excédé. Pas possible, ils se nettoient jamais.

Queneau's use of his semi-phonetic system right from the outset seems to proclaim his commitment to the celebration of spoken *français populaire*. *Doukipudonktan* seems to mean *D'où qu'il(s) pue(nt) donc tant?* (Gabriel is standing in an apparently unwashed crowd) and we can imagine a translation that would replace the non-standard syntax of *d'où que* with English non-standard lexis, perhaps something like either: 'Why do they smell so bloody awful?' or 'Where's that bloody awful hum coming from?', depending on the interpretation of *Doukipudonktan*. The same translation of *Zazie* as that referred to above (Queneau, 2000) renders these sentences as:

(11)   Howcanaystinksotho? Ts incredible, they never clean themselves.

We can see that the translator has again resorted to reduction to achieve an approximation to the non-standard effect in the ST: 'they' reduces to 'ay', 'it's to 'ts', and quite ingeniously, 'though' to 'tho', using non-standard spelling to suggest non-standard speech. The rather odd collocation of *nettoyer* with an animate object goes straightforwardly into English using the verb 'clean', which likewise sounds dubious when collocated with people. Clearly, the non-standard syntax of *d'où que* has no equivalent in English on the grammatical level.

Culture Detachable from Language

In the preceding discussion, we have seen that where socio-cultural features are structurally inherent in linguistic units, translation is difficult. This depends however on the linguistic level on which the unit is situated; the passage below, an extract from an article in the weekly magazine *Le Nouvel Observateur*, contains some quite highly culture-specific elements, but these are all in the vocabulary. The article concerns what the author calls *les nouveaux bourgeois*: baby-boomers who have done well in their career, so much so that their income is at *bourgeois* level, but whose post-hippy lifestyle differentiates them from the traditional *bourgeois*.

(12)   Depuis le déclin politique d'Edouard Balladur, dont les manières avaient provoqué un bref revival des valeurs bourgeoises, les Français ne s'identifient plus au personnage austère et courtois, amoureux de la richesse et de l'ordre, qui fut immortalisé par Flaubert et Bazin, par Daumier et Sempé. L'existence statistique du bourgeois ne subsiste qu'à l'état de traces. Entre 1966 et 1996, les sondés déclarant appartenir à la bourgeoisie sont passés, selon la Sofres, de 7% à moins de 3%. Aveux de provinciaux vieux jeu, sans doute. Pour sa part, l'Insee a radié cette catégorie de sa nomenclature. En tant que classe sociale, la véritable bourgeoisie se réduit en effet à la partie non nobiliaire des 40 000 patronymes répertoriés dans le 'Bottin mondain'. C'est un isolat, qui paie des conseillers

fiscaux pour diminuer son lourd impôt sur la fortune. Un collectif dynastique qui se réunit lors des vernissages les plus chics, les dîners de charité et les premières à l'Opéra, pendant que ses enfants éduqués à Sainte-Croix ou Sainte-Marie de Neuilly font connaissance dans les rallyes les plus cotés. (© *Le Nouvel Observateur*)

Words referring to French cultural practices, like *Sofres, Insee* and *Bottin mondain*, as well as to names like Flaubert, Bazin, Daumier and Sempé, would clearly require careful thought by the translator, but their rendering into English is a relatively mechanical matter, depending on the translator's estimation of the target reader's cultural background. So a term like *Bottin mondain*, which has no direct English equivalent, may need expansion in the text or explanation in a footnote, depending on various factors: the translator's estimation of the target reader's cultural background; whether the translator is willing to hold up the flow of the text while a gloss is provided. The issue here though is that these items are detachable from the structure of the text in a way that those discussed in the previous section are not.

Intermediate Summary

We started this chapter by considering the extent to which the translator should intrude in a TT, stating the professional view that a good translation should ideally bear no traces of the original. Moving on to the relation between type of text and type of translation, we then looked at some idiosyncratic translations, and concluded that where a TT is non-standard in the sense either of diverging considerably from the original ('The Helbatrawss') or showing noticeable features of the original (Hemingway's 'self-translation') this was because of the nature of the text or the author's intention, or both. Indeed, these two factors are inseparable, since we have seen that the intention to amuse will result in a certain text type, the intention to inform in another, and so on. These two factors are linked in turn to the reader, and it seems that the writer who has a clear notion of who s/he is writing for will provide a text that will lend itself to straightforward translation. But an important qualification to this is the degree to which a text is culture-specific: while a poet may be writing with a sub-group of like-minded poets in mind as potential readers, the text in question may be situated within a narrowly focused linguistic-cultural context. The clearest instances of straightforward translation might seem to occur where informative intention, clearly defined readership and cross-cultural theme line up together.

We need however to define what we mean here by 'straightforward'; a better term is perhaps 'literal'. We mentioned literal translation in connection with the texts on mathematical functions, and noted that the ST sentence 'functions play an important role in science' was translatable literally as *les fonctions jouent un rôle important dans les sciences*. From this we can conclude that literal means more or less 'word-for-word' translation, leaving aside basic structural features of the SL and TL, in this case definite and indefinite articles. Obviously, a truly word-for-word translation would give: **fonctions jouent un rôle important dans sciences*; which is ungrammatical in French except in a context where brevity is important: e-mail perhaps (in linguistics, an asterisk indicates an ungrammatical sentence).

One might think that the purest examples of texts of this kind are weather forecasts and air-traffic control instructions, where culture-specific information is at a minimum. A more everyday text of this type is shown in (13) below, where we can see that culture-specific differences are virtually absent, the informative intention is very important, and the readership clearly defined

The remarks made concerning the purely grammatical difficulties in text (3) in a previous section (the text on mathematical functions), apply also to the Fablon parallel texts below. But there are important differences: in the texts in (13) we see language reduced pretty much to the minimum while still avoiding the use of telegraphic language, and the translation difficulties that would attend the rendering of either text into the other language illustrate the structural or grammatical differences between the languages, and almost nothing else. The only culture-specific issue in the texts relates to the mismatch between the Imperial and Metric systems of measurement (paragraphs 2 and 4). We suggested previously that text (3) above on functions would present relatively little difficulty to a translator, and said that this was partly because of the subject matter, partly because of the intention of the writer of the ST. This intention seems to have been to present information as clearly as possible. As mentioned previously, we defined the author's intention in text (3) as expository or explanatory rather than more broadly informative: the expert author is explaining a complex subject as clearly as possible, for the benefit of a less expert readership. This was reflected in the use of examples and metaphors.

(13)

Pour les grandes surfaces

Pour recouvrir du plâtre ou du bois égalisé et peint.

1. Prendre des mesures et découper le Fablon selon les instructions, puis mouiller la surface à recouvrir avec une solution étendue de détergent.

2. Décoller sur un mètre le Fablon de son papier support et le mettre en position. La surface mouillée facilite l'opération.

3. Décoller le papier support restant et lisser le Fablon jusqu'à ce qu'il soit bien en place. Eviter la formation de bulles.

4. Une fois l'eau séchée, le Fablon est collée. S'il subsiste des bulles, les percer. Les jointures doivent se recouvrir de 5mm.

Covering large areas

The following is suitable for smooth painted plaster or wood.

1. Measure and cut the Fablon to size, as instructed, and wet the areas to be covered with a weak solution of detergent in water.

2. Peel back one metre (one yard) of backing paper and position the Fablon. The wet surface makes adjustment simple.

3. Peel off remaining backing paper. Smooth the Fablon home. Avoid bubbles.

4. When the water has dried out, the Fablon will be stuck. Prick out any bubbles. Overlap joins by 5mm (¼″).

The informative intention is paramount in the Fablon texts above, yet if we apply the same test to the text in (13) as to text (3), translation in the more difficult direction for a non-native speaker of French, we see a difference. There are no examples, metaphors or other images, and shared knowledge concerning DIY is assumed between reader and writer. As a result, we need to refine our concept of what we meant above by referring to a 'clearly defined readership' when we suggested that translation is straightforward where informative intention, clearly defined readership and cross-cultural theme coincide closely. A further factor is the relationship between writer and reader, and we have already hinted at the importance of this dimension by remarking that technical writing is generally empty of imagery. We can say that the texts under (13) are quasi-technical, and reiterate that the relationship between writer and reader is one of greater equality than that apparent in text (3).

On the one hand, therefore, much shared knowledge is taken for granted in texts under (13), and on the other, the conventions governing how texts of this type are written make for a brief document – it is true that space constraints may be important where instructions are concerned, but a somewhat arbitrary convention seems to insist on the terseness of this type of text. The translator is thus obliged to concentrate on an idiomatic rendering, on the one hand of grammatical sequences, and on the other of quasi-technical terms. Even a translation in the easier direction (for a native-English speaker) brings up terms like *solution étendue* (paragraph 2), while the English translation of *La surface mouillée facilite l'opération*, a general, atemporal statement, seems to have been influenced by the French. A conditional like: 'If the surface is dampened …' seems more idiomatic.

A further way of classifying the texts in (13) is to call them 'authoritative', in Newmark's definition (1988: 282): "An official text, or a text where the status of the author carries authority". Texts of this kind clearly accord the translator little freedom in their rendering.

As a final English example serving to illustrate the complexity of the text–reader–writer relationship, consider text (14) below.

(14)   In my youth there was always a bad smell in our house. Sometimes it was so bad that I asked my mother to send me to school, even though I could not walk correctly. Passers-by neither stopped nor even walked when in the vicinity of our house but raced past the door and never ceased until they were half a mile from the bad smell. There was another house two hundred yards down the road from us and one day when our smell was extremely bad the folks there cleared out, went to America and never returned. It was stated that they told people in that place that Ireland was a fine country but that the air was too strong there. Alas! there was never any air in our house.

If we apply again the translation-into-English test, we see that this stretch of language is straightforward: *Pendant ma jeunesse il y avait toujours une mauvaise odeur dans notre maison*, etc. This extract is from *The Poor Mouth* (1973: 22) by the Irish author Brian O'Nolan, writing here under one of his pseudonyms, Myles na Gopaleen. The fact that the text above is an English translation from the Irish makes this example somewhat more convoluted, but the author's intention here, through the use of a very straightforward register of English, seems to be to present the unsophisticated viewpoint of a stereotypical Irish peasant: the next paragraph of the book reveals that the cause of the unpleasant smell is a pig living in the house. The point at issue here is that this naive passage is embedded within a complex cultural tradition that has to do with how Irish people perceive themselves and their history. The simplicity of the passage is feigned, assumed as part of a complex cultural game. This does not of course make any difference to the ease with which the passage could be translated, but is of theoretical interest nonetheless. The complexity of the writer–reader–text relationship can produce quirky results.

In the next section we pull together the conclusions we have drawn in this chapter so far concerning the strategic, text-level decisions the translator needs to make, bearing in mind the interconnected issues of text-type, author and reader. We also introduce the concepts of acceptability, competence and equivalence, with the aim of applying these to the strategic, text-level view of translation we have been discussing in this chapter.

Acceptability and Competence: Strategic Translation Decisions

We have already considered the notion in linguistics of 'linguistic competence', although in an oblique way. The concept of acceptability (or well-formedness) is linked to that of linguistic competence. Native-speakers have the competence in their language to distinguish and produce acceptable utterances, and reject unacceptable ones. In linguistics, an acceptable utterance means one that a native-speaker will accept or recognise as conforming to the grammar of the language: not the prescriptive grammar that tries (in English) to suppress split infinitives, prepositions at the end of sentences, etc. but the descriptive grammar that produces a sentence which, although perhaps non-standard by the rules of writing, everyone recognises as being part of their language. However, there is a social as well as a linguistic side to this question. Remember the celebrated sentence, designed to illustrate various aspects of the notion of acceptability (a query next to a sentence indicates doubtful acceptability):

(15)   ?Colorless green ideas sleep furiously

As we said in Chapter 1, the interest of this sentence is that despite its nonsensical character, we can recognise it as English because it conforms to the rules of sentence construction. It is of doubtful acceptability because the semantic content is wrong. Contrast it with the following sequence, which, on account of its defective syntax, is not an acceptable sentence:

(16)   *Sleep ideas colorless furiously green

Our linguistic competence consists in our ability to recognise and produce acceptable sentences in our native language; the process is of course more complex and approximative in any subsequent language, except in the case of multi- or bilingual speakers (those brought up to speak two or more languages from birth, or a very early age). As we said in Chapter 1, Chomsky's interest in linguistic competence has little or no reference to the social characteristics of the speaker, but a later generation of linguists, interested in studying the influence of social factors on language use, was dissatisfied with Chomsky's asocial concept of linguistic competence. The notion of competence was expanded by Hymes (1972) into 'communicative competence': the ability to produce and understand well-formed sentences, but also to ensure they are appropriate to the speaker, context, setting, etc. This latter is therefore a *sociolinguistic* concept. We have already touched on this issue without using the terminology introduced immediately above. So far, we have referred mostly to the cultural factors bearing upon translation; but 'culture' is of course a two-edged word, designating either 'high' or 'classical' culture (Mozart, Rembrandt) or 'anthropological' culture: the sum of the attitudes, practices and values that characterise a society, by no means all lofty. It should have been clear that the latter sense has been used here so far. So, knowledge of how to employ the T/V system in French counts as cultural competence, and knowledge of this type pervades every linguistic level, right down to individual sounds (missing out or leaving in the /l/ in *il y a*, depending on who one is talking to).

Communicative competence consists therefore, not only in producing sentences that conform to the grammar of one's language, but in doing so in a socially suitable or acceptable way: languages possess a non-standard as well as a standard grammar, as well as a continuum in between, allowing speakers or writers to modulate their language in response to the context. Thus a sentence may be grammatical, in the sense of being recognised as well formed by a native speaker, without being acceptable *in context* – the qualification is crucial. One way of expressing this is by referring to the notion of 'audience design', which was formulated by the sociolinguist Allan Bell (1984). Audience design seeks to explain the relationship between social and stylistic variation in language. The major assumption that is relevant here is that it is the 'audience', in the sense of a speaker's addressee(s), that is/are primarily responsible for causing the speaker to 'design' a stretch of language in response to the social characteristics of the audience, by pitching the language at a certain point on the formal–informal style continuum. The importance of context has been much stressed in the study of translation, and the relationship between social variation (prestige/non-prestige language) and stylistic (formal–informal language) is just one dimension of the many that make up the overall influence of context on language. Shared knowledge is perhaps the other most important factor. We shall refer in Table 2.1 to 'audience design' as convenient shorthand, where the term is applicable.

Hymes (1972: 58–71) summarised the components of cultural competence as shown in Table 2.1; this is the sociolinguistic 'SPEAKING' model of the constraints operating on the speaker. There is of course multiple overlap between these constraints: for instance, setting and participants are connected in that a formal setting will involve interaction with non-intimates; the ends of an interaction will determine the key, which in turn

Table 2.1 Hymes' SPEAKING model of communicative competence

Factor	Explanation	Relevance to translation
SETTING	Physical aspects of the context.	Space constraints may be relevant: sub-titles, instructions. Relevant to face-to-face translation, or interpreting.
PARTICIPANTS	Speaker/reader: hearer/writer.	The readership, as discussed in this chapter.
ENDS	Purpose or expected outcome of the interaction.	Author's intention, as discussed in this chapter.
ACT SEQUENCE	Message form and content: the topic, and how it is expressed.	The topic of the ST, considered in relation to the form in which it is conveyed; the style of the ST.
KEY	Tenor of discourse, in terms of formality.	Will in turn depend on topic under discussion.
INSTRUMENTALITIES	Linguistic 'instrument' or language variety used: standard, dialect …	As discussed in this chapter, language of ST may be formal or informal, abstract or concrete, universal or culture-specific.
NORMS	Shared expectations of behaviour.	Relationship between writer and reader; amount of knowledge presumed to be shared by the writer and reader.
GENRE	The text type concerned; technical, literary …	Self-explanatory.

will influence the instrumentalities, and so on. We have adapted this classification to the translation process by adding a third, explanatory column. The SPEAKING acronym is intended as a mnemonic, but its effectiveness depends of course on how transparent one finds the various headwords in the left-hand column – the meaning of 'instrumentalities' and 'act sequence', in particular, are not very clear at first glance. Nevertheless, the SPEAKING model does provide a quite useful summary of the issues we have discussed in this chapter. It is only one of several that attempt to summarise the constraints the translator needs to bear in mind.

The constraints that weigh on the translator are sometimes discussed in terms of what is known as 'skopos theory' (Vermeer, 1989); more specifically, the skopos surrounding an ST refers to the circumstances in which it was written, and the reasons for which it is being translated. In professional translation, this is just common sense; the translator needs to know why the ST was composed and for whom, and correspondingly, why the translation has been commissioned, and for whom. These factors will influence many translation decisions. In non-professional translation, such as takes place in departments of modern languages, the skopos surrounding an ST is often vague. The undergraduate or postgraduate student of translation is often rendering a text for reasons that have not been made sufficiently clear, in skopos terms. To take a specific example, a student presented with the translation of *préfet* needs a context that allows a rational translation decision to be made, since clearly, the lecturer who has set the text knows what the term means. So a student who translates *préfet* as 'prefect' may well attract red ink under the translation, for the obvious reason that the English term usually refers to something quite different. But in a real-world context, it is quite conceivable that a translator will use this solution, providing a brief explanation the first time round. This suggests that if an imaginary readership is specified, even in rather vague terms like 'an educated but non-specialist reader', the student can decide, in the present example, whether *préfet* should be left untranslated, translated literally as 'prefect', expanded to something like 'the government's chief administrator in the region', translated colloquially as 'the government's point-man' (heard recently on TV), and so forth. Skopos is therefore worth introducing earlier rather than later where advanced translation is being taught.

Equivalence

We have referred previously to the notion of TL solutions to SL problems in terms of 'equivalence', suggesting that in extreme cases, where linguistic and cultural material are inextricably blended, no very close equivalent is available. In these cases the translator needs to seek a solution, probably situated on a different linguistic level compared with the SL, in order to produce an effect on the reader of the TT that should be as close as possible to that produced on the reader of the ST. However, we have not yet defined exactly what 'equivalent' means in this context: equivalent to what, and in relation to whom? This is obviously a crucial issue, since we have emphasised repeatedly in this chapter that any translator hoping to render an adequate TT needs to define at the outset, and bear in mind continually, both source and target readership. When we say that two words have 'equivalent reference' we are talking about synonymy, or same meaning. We shall discuss this topic more fully in the following chapter, but we can remark briefly that even within a language, full equivalence of meaning is rare. For example, the French nouns *voiture* and *bagnole* have equivalent reference to the extent they evoke something that an English speaker will call a 'car'. But *voiture* and *bagnole* are not interchangeable in all contexts, since they differ in their socio-stylistic value, *voiture* being more formal or standard than *bagnole*. It will become clear in Chapter 3 that examples of lack of synonymy across languages are equally prevalent.

Hervey and Higgins (1992: 22) provide a useful refinement of the concept of equivalence in translation, pointing out that the difficulty associated with the notion of achieving equivalent effect in translation is that it implies the translator is attempting, in accordance with our definition above, to reproduce in the TT the 'same' effect achieved in the ST. This is problematic, clearly, since the effect varies across individuals, or even upon the same individual at different times, and in any case is unknowable without recourse to undue mentalism or psychologising; that is, speculation about other people's states of minds based on insufficient, indeed unknowable data. The only effect translators can truly know is that produced on their own minds, and therefore the only equivalence possible is what seems acceptable to each translator, perhaps after consultation. This brings us right back to the beginning of Chapter 1, when we said that adequate translation depends on a high level of competence in the two languages, both linguistically and culturally. But we have seen in this chapter that even the translator's best efforts will fail to render an ST effect if no even remotely equivalent TT effect is available.

The issue of equivalence looms large in translation studies, and because the term is a fluid one, it has been interpreted in several different ways by various scholars (see for example the discussion in Bassnett, 1991: 23–9). In the paragraphs above we have discussed equivalence from a psychological viewpoint; that of the translator who aims to reproduce in the TT the effect that the ST has produced on him or her. Other students of translation have discussed equivalence as a linguistic phenomenon, referring for example to 'linguistic equivalence' (where literal translation is possible) or 'stylistic equivalence' (where an equivalent stylistic effect is achieved without literal translation). We discuss this second, linguistic sense of equivalence in more detail when we come to consider the different translation methods in Chapter 6.

In a final section of this chapter we consider the concepts of translation 'loss' and 'compensation'.

Translation Loss and Compensation

These concepts were again formulated by Hervey and Higgins (1992: 24): the analogy they draw is with the engineering concept of 'energy loss', which is inevitable in the design of machinery and which of course is the reason why perpetual motion can never be achieved. The engineer accepts that energy loss is inevitable and the aim is to minimise it; similarly, the translator's aim is to reduce translation loss. A frequent strategy is 'compensation': accepting the loss of one element in the TT, and compensating by adding an element elsewhere. We saw this strategy at work in the English translation of *Zazie dans le Métro* above. Loss and compensation are shown in Table 2.2 and Table 2.3, but are of course irrelevant where no choice is available in the translation to be selected; this is true at least where the fragment of SL being translated is so short that no compensation elsewhere is possible. We can add that loss is a concept that lays a considerable burden of responsibility upon the translator, since the reader of a TT who does not know the SL will not know whether translation loss has occurred at any given point.

Some Genuine Examples of Loss and Compensation

It might be thought that the examples we have been discussing above are rather theoretical: is translation really so deeply fraught with the danger of failure? We saw one minor failure in the Fablon texts above, and the examples below, which are genuine and presumably all the work of professionals, show that the issues of translation loss, with or without the possibility of compensation, are real. These are genuine examples of book and film titles translated from French into English.

Table 2.2 Translation loss from French to English, with and without compensation

French	*English*
Poulet au vinaigre (Title of a Chabrol film)	'Cop au vin'
A la recherche du temps perdu	'Remembrance of Things Past'
Voilà. Le gros Lafitte qui tache (Line of dialogue from the film 'Le dîner de cons', referring to a '73 Château Lafitte that has just been adulterated with vinegar)	Subtitle: 'There. Wino's delight!'
Sous les toits de Paris (Title of a René Clair film)	'Under the Roofs of Paris'
Vivement dimanche! (Title of a Truffaut film)	'Finally Sunday!'

The first two examples illustrate translation loss and attempted compensation. The compensation strategy used in the first example seems designed to replace the rather complex word-play in the ST, which refers to a policeman, colloquially *un poulet,* who is chronically bad-tempered – *au vinaigre.* The result sounds like a recipe, and the English translation has clearly tried to echo this, while having to accept the loss of the reference in the French title to the film's plot. Loss of literal meaning is the issue also in the second example, Scott-Moncrieff's celebrated translation of the Proust title. Compensation is aimed at through the resonance provided by a fragment from a Shakespeare sonnet. The third example illustrates the constraints that operate on sub-titlers: *Le gros Lafitte qui tache* refers to the common phrase *Le gros rouge qui tache* 'rough red wine'. There seems to be no way of conveying this word-play in the limited space available – there are stringent limits on the number of words sub-titlers can display on the screen in the few seconds at their disposal. 'Wino's delight' illustrates the US English bias of much sub-titling – a translation like 'Château-bottled plonk' would probably not cross the Atlantic successfully.

Without wishing to be contentious, the third and fourth examples illustrate more or less sheer loss: 'Under the Roofs of Paris', while denotationally accurate, captures nothing of the connotation of the French phrase *vivre sous les toits.* We shall discuss denotation and connotation, and how they can conflict, in the next chapter. The last example is included to show how far up the market quite gross mistakes can occur.

Some further examples

The examples in Table 2.3 are extracts from the published French translation of Sue Townsend's *The Growing Pains of Adrian Mole.* They are a little more complex than those shown in Table 2.2, and mostly concern the difficulties of adaptation or *cultural transposition* that a translator can have to face. The accuracy and appropriateness of the French renderings are sometimes startlingly modest. Starting from the mistranslation of 'French kiss', the reader may find it interesting to see how many translation failures can be discovered. To be fair to the translator, there are certain points in the text where the translator's task is simply impossible. When translation is most successful in these extracts, the successes seem to illustrate what we have argued throughout this chapter.

Table 2.3 French translations from Adrian Mole

Character	*English original*	*French translation*
Adrian	We had a dead good half-French, half-English kiss …	Après un baiser super bon, mi-français mi-anglais…
Bert	I'd give my right ball for a week in Skeggy.	Je donnerais beaucoup pour une semaine à Skegness.
Adrian	It's a cultural desert here. Thank God, I have brought my Nevil Shute books.	C'est un véritable désert culturel, ici. Dieu merci, j'ai apporté quelques livres.
Adrian	She was full of empathy for me and said: 'never mind, pet, it'll all come out in the wash.'	Elle s'est montrée adorable avec moi: 'Vous verrez, mon p'tit chou, ça finira bien par s'arranger'.
Adrian's father	You wouldn't know proper weather if it came up and smashed you on the face.	On ne choisit pas le temps qu'il fait. Mais si tu veux mon poing dans la gueule, ça va être vite fait.
Adrian	My parents had arranged to visit some properties tomorrow and were planning to get a Chinese take-away.	Ils avaient décidé d'aller visiter plusieurs propriétés demain et de déjeuner dans un petit resto chinois.
– Adrian – Dentist	– I said: 'but I've got a gap'. – He said: 'so has Watford, and if Watford can get used to it, so can you. Bloody ignorant Poms…'.	'Mais il y a un trou maintenant', j'ai dit. 'Watford aussi en a un, et si Watford peut s'y habituer, toi, tu t'y habitueras aussi'. 'Ignares d'Anglais…'.
Adrian	I can't wait until I am fully mature and make urbane conversation with intellectuals.	J'ai hâte d'être un homme d'âge mûr pour pouvoir converser avec des intellectuels comme un homme civilisé.

Chapter 3

Translation Issues at the Word Level

In this chapter we consider translation issues as they concern the individual word, although we shall see that problems at this level quite often stem from the fact that, by their nature, words achieve meaning by combining together. Nevertheless, for convenience we separate so far as possible our discussion into the examination of words in isolation and in combination, divided respectively between this and the following chapter.

The Word and the Morpheme

The definition of the word is one of the favourite puzzles of linguistics. As pointed out in Lodge *et al.* (1997: 33), it is difficult to frame a rigorous definition of a word in phonetic terms, for example as a self-contained sequence of sounds, since in connected speech, word-boundaries are not apparent: the stream of speech is continuous. Exceptions can be found in languages that have clearly identifiable word stress, and hence word boundaries, but these seem rather uncommon. Similarly, a definition that refers to a word as a sequence of graphic symbols (in the minority of languages that have a written system) raises the question how writers make the decision to divide these sequences in the first place. Nor can we define a word in semantic terms, as a 'unit of meaning', since units of meaning exist both above and below the word level, as we shall see below. The most satisfactory definition of the word depends on its grammatical properties, and states that a word has 'internal cohesion and positional mobility', or to use the full-blown jargon in Lodge *et al.* (1997: 35), 'A word is a morpheme or series of morphemes possessing internal cohesion and positional mobility.' We discuss the morpheme below, but meanwhile, what is meant by this unpleasant jargon, and how is it relevant to translation?

When we say a word has internal cohesion, we simply mean that it cannot be interrupted, or that other linguistic elements cannot be interpolated within it. This is a property that distinguishes it from larger units of meaning like the phrase. So, *le garçon* is a unit of meaning, but in this definition we would not wish to call it a word, since an adjective can disrupt its 'internal cohesion': *le joli garçon*. Words cannot be interrupted in this way, at least in English and French, except for humorous effect: 'abso-bloody-lutely!'. The only non-jocular exception that comes to mind is 'another', as in: 'that's a whole nother question'; but we would probably wish to say that this example is marginal because non-standard, perhaps a regionalism.

The property of positional mobility distinguishes the word from the next level of meaning below it, the morpheme. Thus, a word is mobile in that it is capable of being distributed in several positions in a sentence, as in: 'the man bit the dog'; 'the dog bit the man'; 'the man gave the dog a bone', etc. These examples show that in languages where word-order reflects grammatical function, as is the case in English and French, a word can occupy different positions in a sentence in a way that reflects its grammatical role: thus, 'dog' is the grammatical object in our first example, subject in the second, and indirect object in the third. The lowest meaningful linguistic unit, the *morpheme*, is not always mobile in this way.

We need at this point to distinguish between the various types of morpheme. The basic distinction divides *free* and *bound* morphemes. In the case of free morphemes, the morpheme and word levels coincide: so, simple words like 'house', 'girl', 'beer', etc. cannot be divided into smaller meaningful units. Examples like these contrast with polymorphemic words such as 'privatise', 'redraw', 'accepting', and so on endlessly – literally endlessly, since morphemes can be combined to form an indefinite set of new words. These last three examples show the difference between free and bound morphemes. The free element forms as it were the semantic core of each word: 'private', 'draw', 'accept'. These words (and morphemes, since they cannot be analysed further) are 'free' in the sense of being freestanding; they can exist independently, are mobile, and hence contrast with the morphemes (but not words) '–ise', 're–' and '–ing'. Some words are therefore also single morphemes, not all morphemes are words, and some words are composed of sequences of morphemes. The examples '–ise', 're–' and '–ing' show that bound morphemes convey abstract information: something like 'make into', 'again' 'continuous action', in these examples. The morphemes we have been discussing are of the type referred to as *derivational* or *lexical* morphemes. Morphemes that are bound in this way are called affixes, and as these examples show, derivational morphemes can occur at the front of a word (as *prefixes*) and at the end (*suffixes*). As stated above, affixes are bound in the sense of being incapable of occurring independently; although some can stray a short distance from the word that governs them, as in:

(1)   – I'll see you at eight, then
       – ish

Derivational morphemes have the property of creating new words, as well often as shifting words from one category to another: so the adjective 'private' transforms to the verbs 'privatise', 'deprivatise', 'reprivatise', to the nouns 'privatisationist', 'antiprivatisation', and so on. We discuss the notion of the word category in a subsequent section. The computer spell-check puts red lines under the last four words in this list, but most native-speakers will recognise them as possible English words, and even if they have never seen them before will deduce their meaning instantly. This is why, as suggested above, it is impossible to say how many words there are in English, French or any other language; languages possess many resources for renewing their lexicon, of which derivational morphology is but one. Incidentally, it is also the reason why there is no 'longest word in the language'. One of the longest words in the dictionary is 'floccinaucini-hilipilification'; which means 'the state or habit of estimating as worthless'. At 29 characters, this is longer than 'antidisestablishmentari-anism', the more familiar example. The latter word has already been greatly extended by the addition of derivational affixes, but we can envisage the addition of yet more, and certainly our first example is easily capable of considerable extension: 'floccinaucinihilipilificationalism', etc. So even though in practice very long words are not a serious element in the lexicon, since they stretch our attention span unduly, in principle the search for the longest word will never be done.

Derivational or lexical morphology, which has to do with the lexicon, contrasts with *inflectional* morphology, which concerns the grammar. Inflectional morphology does not create words in the sense that deriva-tional morphology does, but is responsible for the 'inflectional para-digms' in the language, as in the following familiar example:

(2)   je suis
       tu es
       il / elle / on est
       nous sommes
       vous êtes
       ils / elles sont

We notice intuitively that the verb forms in this list are not 'words' in the same sense of the words discussed in connection with derivational morphology. This feeling is reinforced by that fact that *suis*, *es*, *est*, etc. are not given separate dictionary entries, although they may be mentioned in examples under the headword *être*. Otherwise, they may be found in verb tables in the dictionary. Similarly, if a new verb is formed, perhaps *HTLMer*, only certain forms of the verb are perceived to be new lexical words, i.e. words that refer to objects and concepts: the infinitive, present participle, past participle – for instance, *pacsé* is given a separate entry in the Oxford-Hachette. These verb forms achieve word status because they can function as other parts of speech, chiefly nouns and adjectives. But most 'inflections' of a verb – the forms that show the grammatical aspects of its function – are included under the infinitive. So French *sont* is a form of *être*, inflected to show 3rd-person plural, present, indicative, and so on, through as many of the grammatical features that the analysis requires. Inflectional morphology is responsible therefore for showing the *semantic features* of verb forms, as well as of other categories of words: to take the case of nouns, the morpheme '–s' in English indicates plurality, while in French, an '–e' often indicates feminine gender. These examples show that in English and French, inflectional morphemes are always word-final.

Word Categories

Before proceeding further it will be useful to have in mind a description of the various categories used to classify words. Discussion of word categories or word classes in language is a traditional activity in the study of grammar, as well as in modern linguistics. Terminology was developed in antiquity to describe the grammar of Latin, and in the Middle Ages these terms were applied with greater or lesser success to the description of the 'Modern Languages'. Any traditional grammar will refer to nine principal word categories, or 'parts of speech' in the old-fashioned jargon:

Nouns, e.g. *femme*
Verbs, e.g, *aimer*
Pronouns of various types:
    Personal Pronouns: *je*, *tu*, *il*, etc.
    Demonstrative Pronouns: *ça*, *celle*, etc.
    Possessive Pronouns: *mien*, *nôtre*, etc.
    Relative Pronouns: *qui*, *que*, *dont*, *lequel*, etc.
Adjectives, e.g. *belle*
Adverbs, e.g. *rapidement*, *cependant*
Articles, *le*, *une*, *de*, etc.
Conjunctions, e.g. *et*, *mais*, *bien que*, etc.
Prepositions, e.g. *de*, *jusqu'à*, etc.
Interjections, e.g. *Merde!*, *Punaise!*

Space is lacking for an extensive discussion of this system of categorisation. We can however mention briefly that it is possible to classify words according to how they are distributed in a sentence (as opposed to referring to their meaning, for example), and this distributional principle tends to be preferred in modern linguistics. A major difference between the traditional and modern systems of classification is the use of the 'determiner' category in the modern system. This is a word category that cuts across traditional ones and includes articles, possessive pronouns and demonstrative pronouns. It is easy to see the distributional principle at work here, since articles, possessive pronouns and demonstrative pronouns are all capable of occurring (being distributed) before a noun: *le / mon / ce chat*. Words of this type all 'determine' or make clear the status of the noun that follows. We shall use 'determiner' rather than more traditional terms in our discussions below.

It is useful, obviously, to have clearly in mind the various word categories, in the interests of raising consciousness generally but also because a stretch of language that is puzzling on account of its ambiguity is often so because the reader hesitates over the category of a word that is the key to understanding the sequence. So to resolve the ambiguity in a sentence like 'flying bananas can be dangerous', it can help to be able to articulate the problem. In this case the ambiguity turns on 'flying', which can be interpreted as an adjective ('bananas that are flying ...') or a noun ('the flying of bananas ...'). A further reason for having the word categories clearly in mind is that we refer to them in Chapter 6, when we look at the different translation procedures that are available.

One shortcoming of the list of word categories given above is that it implies that words belong immutably to one category only. This is of course untrue; for example; nouns in English are frequently called into service as verbs, as shown by the fairly recent examples of 'to guest' ('she guested on a chat show') and 'to trouser' ('he trousered his change'). This noun-to-verb process seems less frequent in French, where other changes of word category are more common, as shown in the examples in (3) below, taken from Battye *et al.* (2000: 301). The innovative use of a word in a different category tends to be greeted with disapproval by prescriptivists, and so the translator needs to be alert to the non-standard value of usages of the type, especially where the category change is recent.

(3) adjective as adverb: *elle a eu son bac facile*

noun as preposition: *elle a filé direction sortie*

noun as adjective: *un remède miracle*

The innovative use of a word in a new category can cause translation problems of a more complex order, as in the following example where *citoyen* is used as an adjective:

(4)   il faut donner une réponse citoyenne aux maux qui fracturent notre
       société

The Collins-Robert has *citoyen* as adjective and this use is translated as
'socially aware': clearly, the central concept refers to citizenship in its
more compassionate, sharing sense. The Collins-Robert has the example
of *une nation citoyenne*, translated as 'a nation where the notion of citizenship is central' (this incidentally is a good example of a translation that
would have benefited from one last scrutiny on the stylistic level, to
sweep away the cacophonous 'nation where the notion …').
    The translation difficulty here seems to be due to the fact of language
change tracking social change. The concept of citizenship is linked, in
France and in all countries having a highly developed sense of themselves
as a nation-state, to the relationship that citizens have to the centralising
state as well as to their fellow-citizens. This dual relationship is in turn
connected with the outward- and inward-looking aspects of nationhood;
in its outward-looking aspect, a nation defines itself in contradistinction
to other nations and this calls for a patriotic or nationalistic response from
its citizens. The inward-looking aspect implies a concern with internal
cohesion and the diminution of difference, the counterpart of external
distinction. This older conception of citizenship is expressed in the noun
civisme and the related adjective *civique*; as so often, the term becomes
contaminated by the phenomenon and a fresh term is required. The term
citoyen as adjective is therefore not interchangeable with *civique* (and of
course would not have been called into service if it had been); the innovative term expresses a modern conception of citizenship in its more
humane aspect. This has more to do with public-spiritedness, *la solidarité*,
and the attempt to combat *la fracture sociale* than the earlier, difference-
based conception.
    In other words, the issue is in part connected with codability, discussed
in the previous chapter. Nevertheless the concept of *la fracture sociale*,
implied in the verb *fracturer* in (4) above, is close to 'social exclusion', a
term frequently used in UK English, so that the compact encoding of the
concept expressed in *citoyen* adjective is not particularly culture-specific.
So the translation difficulty in (4) stems from the fact that French encodes
the new notion of citizenship in an innovative, category-changing term. A
literal translation, in the sense of the translation of the ST word by a TT
word in the same category, of *citoyen* adjective by a corresponding English
adjective like 'citizenly' does not capture this new usage. A more radical
recast seems necessary, perhaps along the following lines:

(5)   'we need to respond inclusively to the divisions in our society'

In connection with the assignment of words into categories we can mention recent research being carried out using corpus linguistics. This branch of linguistics uses computerised corpora for various research purposes; one advantage of computerisation is the ease of looking at the distribution of a word in many different contexts, as a concordancing program removes all laboriousness from the search. Thus a search for 'but' in a large text will reveal, from the surrounding text, how often the word is used in its commonest category of conjunction. Corpus linguistics has other uses in translation studies, such as the analysis of collocational patterns, which we discuss in the following chapter. One account of the subject among many is by Atkins and Zampolli (1994).

Let us now consider some translation problems connected with words, beginning in fact with the sub-word level, the morpheme.

Inflectional Morphology: Verb Inflection

As we said above, inflectional morphology changes the form of basic elements (infinitive verbs, singular nouns, adjectives, etc.) to indicate various semantic features: gender, person, number, tense, mood, aspect, etc. The translation problems caused by English–French differences in inflectional morphology are various. As indicated, since inflectional morphology has to do with the grammar rather than the lexicon, any problems they may cause are structural, and may therefore call for a radical recast if French or English exploit the grammatical feature in question in a considerably different way. The problem is often a gap in the TL. Inflection can be used idiosyncratically, as in the case of the conditional:

(6) *M. Jospin serait de retour mardi* 'Mr Jospin is said / thought to be due back on Tuesday'

Les espaces intersidéraux sont toutefois tellement vides de matière que les millions de trous noirs d'origine stellaire qui *peupleraient* la Voie lactée sont astreints à de très longues périodes de sevrage

There is a potential decoding problem here, if the translator is not aware of the possibility in French of using the conditional tense in a so-called 'epistemic' sense. That is, the writer who uses the conditional in this way is implying that s/he has no certain knowledge of the timing of M. Jospin's return. The encoding problem is to do with compactness, since a circumlocution is needed to express the underlying message the writer has encoded by using the conditional tense: 'I cannot vouch for this information'. The conditional in the second example has the same function: 'the millions of black holes which are thought to populate the Milky Way ...'. This example is even starker, since black holes exist only in theory. The translation of the conditional may depend on the degree of uncertainty, or on the ST writer's wish to be cautious, as in the following example from *Le Monde* 27 February 2002:

(7) la juge française […] aurait reconnu […] avoir favorisé le couple russe

'the French judge appears to have admitted …'

A further idiosyncratic usage in morphology is the employment of the imperfect with a conditional sense, as follows:

(8) *n'étaient les difficultés éprouvées dans la conduite de ses responsabilités...*

'were it not for the difficulties …'

un pas de plus et je tombais   'one more step and I would have fallen'

Alternation between perfect and imperfect verb forms is a problem that arises in its most acute form for the English speaker when composing in French. The tendency is to use an imperfect where a perfect form is required, and the problem is of course caused by the fact that English often does not formally mark the perfect–imperfect distinction. A French writer will occasionally go against the general rule that requires an imperfect form where a background state or continuing action is indicated and a perfect where a 'punctual' or one-off action is described. The text below provided a striking example. It is taken from the novel *Aden* by Anne-Marie Garat (1992). In this passage a character's feelings towards his provincial origins are being described, and his friendless state, consequent on his desire to conceal these origins. The author uses a perfect-tense sequence, emboldened in the passage below, as an emphatic device, where imperfect forms would normally have been expected. These unmarked forms are underlined in the passage.

(9) L'immeuble <u>était</u> au fond de la rue, une bâtisse brune, avec un couloir central qui <u>distribuait</u> deux appartements de rez-de-chaussée et <u>menait</u> à l'escalier vers les étages, <u>ouvrait</u> sur la cour arrière. Aden y avait grandi, Iana y <u>vivait</u> encore. La détestation était venue plus tard, dans la révision que permirent les années de lycée, quand il découvrit Paris, les belles demeures de la ville, l'autre planète. Pour rien au monde il n'aurait avoué de quelle province il <u>était</u> le rescapé, intuitivement instruit d'avoir à dissimuler la tare, par instinct de conservation. Il **n'eut** pas d'ami, **découragea** toute approche, en respect de son dessein solitaire. Tout cela <u>était</u> loin, mais il en

<u>conservait</u> le mal, même s'il s'était réconcilié entre temps, ayant tourné la page.

As stated above, since the perfect–imperfect distinction is often not marked in the verb form in English, there is a morphological gap here that the translator needs to fill, perhaps from lexis: 'he had not a single friend, always discouraged any friendly overture …'.

As is pointed out in Vinay and Darbelnet (1995: 150), there are a few common French verbs that express a difference in meaning through alternation between perfect and imperfect: Vinay and Darbelnet mention *vouloir, pouvoir, savoir, se taire* and *connaître*. Below is one example of each:

(10)	*Il voulait s'enfuir*	'He wanted to run away'
	Il voulut s'enfuir	'He tried to run away'
	Il pouvait le faire	'He could do it'
	Il put le faire	'He was able to do it'
	Il savait que je venais	'He knew I was coming'
	Il sut que je venais	'He heard I was coming'
	Ils se connaissaient déjà	'They already knew each other'
	Ils se connurent en 1940	'They became acquainted in 1940'
	Il se taisait	'He remained silent'
	Il se tut	'He fell silent'

The opposite case, the use of an imperfect where a perfect form is standardly prescribed for a new one-off action, has been pointed out in Byrne and Churchill (1993: 314). This use is described as follows: 'since one use of the imperfect is to present the action as in progress […], the effect of using it instead of the preterite or the perfect is to present the action as unfolding before our eyes, so to speak, and hence to heighten the effect'. The following passage is quoted:

(11)   *Il y a six ans, l'armée française débarquait sur les cotes de Provence*

   'Six years ago the French army landed on the coast of Provence'

It will be seen that no attempt has been made to reproduce the effect explained in Byrne and Churchill. It is perhaps at the limit of the translator's enterprise, since no English structure is available to reproduce it.

A further difference between French and English in the use of tenses is the far more frequent use in French of the 'historic present', the use of the present tense to recount a narrative set in the past. This is sufficiently well known not to need comment here, beyond saying that the historic present in English is confined to colloquial oral narrative ('so he says to me …') or highly literary written registers. An analogous difference is the use in French of the future where the conditional is required in English:

(12)   Il faudra attendre plus d'un siècle pour que les idéaux révolution-
        naires d'une prise en charge par l'Etat de la question sociale
        trouvent des débuts d'application concrète.

        'More than a century would have to pass before the revolutionary
        ideal of the responsibility of the State for social welfare began to
        find concrete expression'.

Note that the historic present is used here alongside the future. This use is analogous in that French looks at the situation more directly than English; where English has the conditional to look at the future in the past, French considers the situation in a less oblique way. Clearly, close attention to context is needed to identify this usage, which is not uncommon.

Inflectional morphology: The pronoun system

A gap that we have already discussed in the TL is the T/V system. Here we can look at it from the point of view of morphology, and note again that the translation problem has to do with encoding:

(13)   *permets-moi de te tutoyer*   'no formalities'

The suggested translation, from Hervey and Higgins (1992: 36) is of course not the only one available. The issue here is that an approximation needs to be found using lexis in the TL, where the SL has the relevant information encoded in morphology.

The SL inflectional system may have variation between items in a paradigm that have no equivalent in the TL. For instance, there is fairly complex variation between the French pronouns *nous* and *on*, depending on sociolinguistic factors as well as the group of people to which the pronoun refers. This is variation in a different sense to that applied to the T/V system, since in general, the choice of *tu* or *vous* is fixed, once decided between two speakers. In contrast, the use of *on* or *nous* varies from speaker to speaker and between occasions differentiated by their formality.

If we limit our discussion of *nous* and *on* to situations where the pronouns have definite 1st-person-plural (4th-person) reference equiv-alent to English 'we', where a known group of people is being referred to, including of course the speaker, it is evident that the *nous ~ on* alternation encodes social information in a way that often has no direct English coun-terpart. Consider the following examples:

(14) *nous sommes assez contents*

(15) *si on allait faire un tour?*

(16) *nous, on va aller au cinéma vendredi*

(17) *c'est nous qu'on est les plus forts*

These examples are listed in what one might call descending order of social-stylistic value. The pronoun *nous* is used with 4th-person verb form broadly by more conservative speakers, and/or in fairly formal styles of French; indeed one researcher (Coveney, 2000: 478) found that in a corpus of spoken French, only eight out of 30 speakers interviewed used *nous* in this way. This indicates that the use of *nous* with 4th-person verb form, as in example (14) above, has now a rather formal feel; the attempt to reproduce this in English might perhaps have recourse also to the pronoun system, using 'one' to render the formal *nous*. Examples (15) and (16) are 'neutral' socio-stylistically: usage that is characteristic of everyday speech, and the trans-lator's task is relatively undemanding, consisting in the selection of correspondingly unmarked forms in the TL. By contrast, the sequence of pronouns in (17) is distinctly non-standard, and its translation will perhaps exploit variation in the pronoun system also, as well as features from other areas of morphology. So, something like the following draws upon vari-ation in English morphology to produce an 'uneducated' effect:

(18) it's us what's the most strongest

Here the effect is perhaps a little excessive compared to the ST: the TT plies up non-standard 'us' rather than 'we', 'what's' rather than 'who are', 'most strongest' rather than 'strongest'.

Translation Issues at the Morphological Level: Non-Standard Forms

This issue of non-standard equivalence across the two languages is complex, because while non-standard morphology and syntax in English attract a remarkable amount of adverse criticism, there is more tolerance (and hence more variation) in France, surprisingly in a country where the tradition is particularly strong of linguistic 'prescriptivism', or laying down the law about what is and (especially) is not proper language. We need to distinguish clearly here between morphology and syntax. Recall that in the previous chapter we discussed the question of equivalence across French and English between items having sociolinguistic value that can drop or be omitted. Part of the sequence from Queneau that we discussed at that point has two examples of omission in a short sequence:

(19)   Pour le moment, elle a pas envie de le semer, mais elle se prévient
       que ce sera pas commode.

In both of the places where *ne* could have been inserted, it was not. This is
an issue to do with morphology because the negative particle *ne* is a
straightforward example of a bound morpheme that has little positional
mobility – it almost always occurs before a verb – and contributes grammatical rather than lexical information. We suggested in Chapter 2 that
reduction of the *ne*-dropping type can be paralleled in English, although
with reduction on the pronunciation level rather than the morphological:
so, *elle a pas envie* > 'she doesn't want to'. An example from English that is
comparable to *ne*-dropping is omission of 'that' as a so-called 'complemen-
tiser', or a word that introduces the complement of a verb – the element that
complements or completes it. Examples of the variable use of 'that' are as
follows, where the bracketing indicates that the word is variably inserted:

(20)   the woman [that] I saw yesterday

       he said [that] he would

The function of 'that' in the examples in (20), similarly to French *ne*, is
morphemic in the sense that the English word, when functioning in this
way, has no positional mobility and is contributing grammatical information only. There is a rough correspondence between 'that' and *ne* in
that both seem to have about the same socio-stylistic value, and we can
suggest a connection between this and the fact that both items are omis-
sible; this seems to be related to the fact that the presence of 'that' and *ne*
adds little to the sense of the sequences in which they appear. We must
however beware of establishing too direct a correspondence between the
socio-stylistic value of a linguistic item and its lack of functionality; while
'the woman I saw yesterday' is innocuous in English, the French literal
equivalent, *la femme j'ai vue hier*, is by no means so; indeed it is characteristic of marginal *banlieue* French, although more widespread in Canadian
French. A variable structure that is identical syntactically across the two
languages can have therefore very different sociolinguistic value in each.
The other relates to gaps: very non-standard, indeed stigmatised
constructions on the morphological level in English such as 'I don't want
none' and 'he don't know' have no direct French equivalent. We discuss
similar examples in syntax in Chapter 5.

Inflectional morphology: Other issues

The examples above show gaps and imperfect correspondences
between SL and TL, and this is of course the major problem the translator

has to face much of the time. Examples (7) and (8) show the conditional used to convey epistemic meaning, (9) – (13) show idiosyncratic uses of the perfect, imperfect and future, while (14) – (17) show social information encoded in the SL inflectional system in ways that need care in reproduction in the TL, whether on the same linguistic level or another. We can say that French and English differ in the efficiency with which they express certain semantic features using morphological means, and 'efficiency' relates, as so often, to codability. A further example relates to the seemingly more copious use of French of past participles functioning as nouns, as in *les sinistrés* where English will have a less concise rendering like 'the disaster victims'. We may note finally, in connection with the use of *on*, the fairly obvious point that English 'one' has a totally different sociolinguistic value to the French pronoun.

Other examples show the greater sexism of French compared to English; we have already discussed the sequence in (21) below from a different viewpoint, but the underlined pronoun suggests that in general, French (at least hexagonal French; Canadian and Belgian French are ahead here) tolerates the masculine 'generic' pronoun more readily than English. The neatest solution to this problem is often to pluralise: 'for those found guilty …'.

(21)   Au couperet des verdicts succèdera, pour celui que la justice reconnaît criminel …

The opposite case shows French able to use an 'epicene' word that has no neat equivalent in English. Epicene words are those that show no gender bias, so from the viewpoint of their morphology, the semantic feature of gender is absent. French examples are *compatriote* and *semblable*, where in the first example 'compatriot' has perhaps a rather pompous feel because of its Latin origin. There is clearly a problem of sexism with 'fellow-countryman'; 'fellow citizen' is perhaps the neatest solution, although here again 'citizen' has an administrative rather than national or patriotic connotation. In the case of *semblables*, literally 'those similar', 'fellows' has the disadvantage of evoking masculinity.

Translation Issues at the Morphological Level: Derivation

As we said above, derivational morphology creates new words by adding affixes: in French and English, prefixes and suffixes (some languages have *infixes*, affixes that insert inside a word). French has a tendency to pile up (especially) suffixes in a way that is less common in English, and this reflects the differing tendencies of the two languages. In the jargon, English is situated towards the 'analysing' end of the continuum along which languages are ranged, while French is more of a 'synthesising' language. This means that the English tendency is to express concepts using clearly separate sequences of words, while French prefers to build up complex words using affixes. French will tend therefore to look denser and more complex. A good example is the following:

(22)   *Du jour au lendemain, elle est devenue présidentiable*

Here the issue is again to do with encoding; the target form will inevitably be a circumlocution, and may or may not exist in accepted form: 'potential candidate for the presidency?' 'possible / convincing / plausible, etc. presidential candidate'? 'presidential material'?. Further examples:

(23)   *(premier)-ministrable; papable; professorable*

This is the French case corresponding to what Baker (1992: 24) points out in respect of English. Baker remarks the English suffix '–ish' is more productive (can combine with a larger set of words) than the French equivalent *–âtre*. Thus *bleuâtre* is found in French, but not the equivalent of English 'coldish', 'baddish', 'hellish', etc. The French suffix *–able*, as shown in (22) and (23), is capable of combining with a limited set of words to convey the concept 'capable of being considered for X', where 'X' is a more or less exalted post.

The possibility of using derivational morphology to create new words along the lines of the examples in (22) and (23) will perhaps one day result in the following:

(24)   *présidentiable > présidentiabilité, non-présidentiabilité*, etc.

These forms do not yet appear to exist, but consultation of native speakers suggests that it would not be too shocking if they did. Longer sequences still would be required in English:

(25)   *sa présidentiabilité* 'his/her credibility as a presidential candidate', etc.

The tendency is therefore obviously, as seen above, to 'unpack' the French words containing strings of suffixes into an English phrase:

(26)   *juridicisation*   'establishing a legal framework'

         sensibilisation   'raising awareness'

         responsabilisation   'encouraging [people, etc. to assume] responsibility'

         relativisation   'relativisation' (grammatical term) but also: 'putting into perspective'

imprévisibilité	'unforeseeable nature'
fidélisation	'development / maintenance of customer loyalty'

A notable example is *imprescriptibilité*, which foreshadows the issues of style and register that we examine in more detail below. The Oxford-Hachette translates this as 'imprescriptability', but one is tempted to wonder whether the English word would be acceptable in an equivalent register to the French. The Collins-Robert recognises this, and translates *imprescriptibilité* using an example:

(27) *l'imprescriptibilité des crimes contre l'humanité*

'the non-applicability of statutory limitation to crimes against humanity'

We discuss complex words in a separate section below, but we can point out here that the Collins-Robert translation seems to convey about as concisely as possible in English the concept that certain crimes do not carry a 'statute of limitations'; that is, a legal proviso stating they will not be prosecuted after a certain lapse of time. There is a good deal of cultural information here, conveyed quite compactly in French; in five morphemes, to be precise: im-pre-script-ibil-ité. Occasionally, a sentence containing several of these complex words will give a very dense feel:

(28) *Les banques et sociétés financiers sont conscientes que leur pérennité passe par une optimisation de leur réactivité*

The banks and financial institutions are aware that their long-term survival depends on improving their adaptability / capacity to react to market conditions

As ever, it should be emphasised that this need to unpack French complex words is a *tendency*; thus *éméritat* and *assistanat* need a circumlocution; but *lectorat* > 'readership'; *anonymat* > 'anonymity'. The general point here is that French tends quite strongly to form new words in a synthesising way. English has this resource also, naturally, but the process attracts perhaps more attention in the latter language: coinages depending on the learned, Latinate word-stock like 'meritocracy' or 'disambiguate' can be greeted on their arrival with much resistance from the more conservative-minded, and tend to be perceived as ugly. This is perhaps because such words lack the 'home-grown' feel of those that are formed from the Anglo-Saxon lexicon.

A notable feature of English is the tendency to produce jocular, non-standard suffixes like '–tastic' or '–gate' as in: 'poptastic' and 'Irangate'.

There is a rather remote parallel in French, where suffixes proper to a certain domain are attached to everyday roots to produce a comic result, as for instance with *télévore* or *téléphage* translatable as 'TV addict' or 'couch potato' (note again the English analysing tendency). Although the suffixes '–phore' and '–phage' are available in English, they are more learned than the French counterparts, so that a comparable effect will be hard to achieve in English using derivational morphology. We discuss further below some problems of style and register caused by mismatches of this type between French and English.

A further issue is the difference in function of derivational affixes across the two languages. A well-known trap is the *re–* prefix, which of course in general indicates repetition, or 'iteration' in the linguistic jargon. There are however some French words that have the prefix but, sometimes depending on context, do not convey iteration: a clear example is *racheter*; which most often means 'buy up', 'buy more' or 'buy out'. More complex examples are *revoir*, which can of course mean 'see again' but can also convey 'revise', 'review', 'overhaul'; *reprendre*, which can mean 'to take up', as in *reprendre une suggestion*. Careful attention to context is required with this set of words.

Lexical and Grammatical Words

Before looking at various translation problems on the word level proper, we examine the distinction, relevant to the word–morpheme categorisation, between 'lexical' and 'grammatical' words. This is best done using an example. The following is another extract from the *nouveaux bourgeois* text discussed in Chapter 1.

(29)   Ce sont les <u>gens</u> qui ont <u>raflé</u> la mise en <u>bénéficiant</u> de toutes les <u>évolutions</u> <u>économiques</u> de la <u>France</u> depuis qu'ils sont <u>entrés</u> sur le <u>marché</u> du <u>travail</u>

The underlined words above are 'lexical'; by this is meant that they refer to concepts outside the text. The other, 'grammatical' words have the function, within the text, of clarifying the status of the lexical words, and the relationship between them. Once again, grammatical words are akin to bound morphemes in the sense that their mobility is restricted and the information they convey is abstract: we can point to a concept 'in the outside world' that corresponds to *gens*, but words like *ce, les, depuis*, etc. are most easily defined in terms of their function (what they do) rather than their designation (what they refer to). Grammatical words are of course capable of transformation into full lexical words: Shakespeare's 'but me no buts' is a famous example of a conjunction used as verb and noun. A French example is *pour* and *contre* used as nouns: *le pour et le contre*. A well-known case where French and English differ in how they lexicalise grammatical words concerns infinitives and present participles: so, *l'être et le néant* has to translate into English as 'being and nothingness'.

Baker (1992: 84) points out that 'because a grammatical choice is drawn from a closed set of options, it is (a) obligatory, and (b) rules out other choices from the same system by default.' Thus, grammatical words are organised in closed sets: the numbers of prepositions, determiners, etc. are fixed; and there is little choice in their use. This is of course true *within* a language: a consequence for translation is that a grammatical word in the SL may encourage the translator to think that the same word is required in the TL. This is not necessarily so. Cases such as these are sometimes referred to as 'structural faux amis'. Here is an example from the definite and partitive articles in French and English:

(30) *il a mis longtemps pour gagner une reconnaissance méritée* > 'gain [zero] deserved recognition'

Similarly, Hervey and Higgins (1992: 194) point out differences between English and French in the use of 'deictic' words, those that literally 'point' to certain concepts:

(31) *la question est immense*   'this is a very large question'

     enfin, du poisson digne de ce nom   'at last, some fish worthy of the name'

These examples show the difficulty of giving a systematic account of variation across French and English in the use of deixis. Where the first example has a definite article in French but a demonstrative in English, the opposite case is true in the second. These examples show that the contrasting use of grammatical words can be idiosyncratic, or at least unpredictable, across the two languages. The choice of the TL grammatical word in each case depends on a well-developed intuition of their use in the respective languages. We can offer no principled rule here, beyond saying that the translator's intuition needs to be honed by wide reading.

Translation Issues Relating to Word Cohesion

Turning to the level above the morpheme, we stated earlier that one major criterion defining the word is its uninterruptability, to coin a new word using several derivational morphemes. Applying this test will show that sequences of letters interrupted by spaces on the printed page are words nevertheless. Thus the French sequence *chemin de fer* passes the word test, since an adjective qualifying the noun cannot interrupt the sequence: **chemin moderne de fer* is not grammatical. This illustrates the fairly obvious point that French makes very copious use of so-called 'post-modifying constructions', very often consisting of noun + preposition (most commonly *de* or *à*) + noun, and has relatively little scope for using the adjectival noun + noun sequence that is so very common in English. Thus English 'word processing' gives French *traitement de texte*, and so on endlessly (recall that the set of words having this structure is open-ended, as the process is productive). This process runs against the French tendency to compression in forming 'solid' words composed of root-word + derivational suffixes, discussed in the previous section.

The complication here however is that while sequences like *chemin de fer* and *verre à vin* are undoubtedly compound words, as indicated by the interruption test, others are more fluid: as pointed out in Lodge *et al.* (1997: 40–1), a sequence like *vedette de cinéma* can be interrupted in this way, to give *vedette (française) de cinema*, for instance. The point here is that nouns come to be combined to express a new concept, and the cohesion of the resulting compound is relatively loose until the compound either gains acceptance or drops from the lexicon as the new concept proves ephemeral. While the cohesion of the new compound is loose, it can be interrupted. There is a parallel here with English compound nouns, which start off as two-word sequences, subsequently acquire a hyphen and finally have the possibility of being written solid. For instance, in a specialised register we easily imagine the compound noun used above, 'word stock', progressing from 'word-stock' to 'wordstock'. A less marginal example is 'spacesuit', which unlike 'wordstock' does not attract red underlining from the spell-check (but not yet spellcheck!) program. The difference obviously is that English compound nouns, even when written as two separate words, cannot be interrupted, unlike their French noun + preposition + noun equivalents. It can be noted in passing that the English adjectival noun + noun sequence is almost wholly alien to French; Vinay and Darbelnet note the sole exception of *science fiction* where *science* is a noun-adjective; although *pôle position* seems to have been imported from English more recently. The noun + adjectival noun sequence is of course frequently found in French, as exemplified by *roi citoyen*, discussed in a previous section.

The italicised examples in the following extract adapted from a French logistics journal illustrate how common is the noun + preposition + noun sequence; they show also the need for the translator to analyse each sequence to see whether or nor it is a fixed compound word like *chemin de fer.* This is an extract from an interview with a manager of Toyota Production Systems.

(32)   Notre philosophie [...] est un *système de livraison* en flux tirés, basé sur un *logiciel de production* et tout un ensemble de *méthodes de livraisons* des *flux de composants.*

Logistics is concerned essentially with problems of supply and delivery, and the technical term *flux tirés* is translatable here as 'just-in-time', used as an adjectival noun. A related concept is 'just-enough'. Logisticians sometimes refer to a 'taut supply chain', meaning one that has little 'slack' or spare supply in it, so that just-in-time and just-enough relate to a supply method, commonly used by large companies, that relies on frequent deliveries, just in time, of just enough materials, components etc. to keep production rolling. A literal translation of *flux tirés* as 'taut flows' (*flux tendus* is also available as a near-synonym) brings out the idea that the supply-and-storage system is 'taut' in the sense of containing little spare capacity. The advantage of this method is that it economises storage and warehousing costs.

Aside from this technical issue, the passage is notable for the number of compound nouns consisting of post-modifying constructions used: *système de livraison, logiciel de production, flux de composants.* A reasonably smooth English translation will need to rely, as stated above, on the adjectival noun + noun sequence:

(33)   Our philosophy [...] is a just-in-time *delivery system*, based on *production software* and a whole array of methods for the delivery of *component flows.*

Here 'delivery system', 'production software' and 'component flows' are straightforward translations of the French words composed of noun + *de* + noun, using the English adjectival noun + noun. Indeed, the process can be stretched further: the sequence *système de livraison en flux tirés*, with the structure noun + *de* + noun + *en* + noun + adjective, is most naturally rendered in English as adjectival noun + adjectival noun + noun. The remaining compound noun, *méthodes de livraisons*, seems at first sight to be an obvious candidate for a similar translation: 'delivery methods'. Closer inspection shows that while the sequence: *méthodes de livraisons des flux de composants* has the appearance of a series of two compound nouns, the first sequence could be reformulated, perhaps to *méthodes destinées aux livraisons*. One point that is relevant here is that *méthodes de livraisons* appears not yet to be fully 'lexicalised' – turned into a single word like *chemin de fer* – so that a sequence like *méthodes modernes de livraison(s)* would be possible. Beyond this difficulty, the fluidity of *méthodes de livraisons* means that the translator can experience problems in identifying the word boundaries in the latter part of example (32). A first analysis, due to our familiarity with the French noun + preposition + noun sequence, might be the following, where '' indicates a word boundary:

(34)   ensemble | de | méthodes de livraisons | des | flux de composants |

The translation in (33) above shows an analysis of the word boundaries as follows:

(35)   ensemble | de | méthodes | de | livraisons | des | flux de composants |

That fact that the sentence in (32) is from an interview explains perhaps the rather 'loose' syntax in *méthodes de livraisons*. This is oral French written down; an equivalent sequence that had been scripted in the first place might well, as suggested above, have been expanded to *méthodes destinées aux livraisons, méthodes propres aux livraisons*, etc. We discuss in Chapter 5 the issue of the relative 'weakness' of French prepositions, and their tendency in writing to be accompanied by another part of speech.

The discussion in this section has again been designed to show that the intuitive knowledge possessed by native-speakers needs to be made explicit by the translator before it can be thoroughly internalised.

Complex Words

As an example of a complex word, Baker (1992: 22) gives of *arruação*, a Brazilian Portuguese word she translates as: 'clearing rubbish from the ground under coffee trees and piling it in the middle of the row in order to aid the recovery of beans dropped during harvesting'. A complex word is therefore one that packs a good deal of meaning into a small space; recall our discussion of codability in Chapter 1. Leaving aside the question whether this definition is wordier than it need be to emphasise the point being made, we can say first of all that we need not go to languages or cultures that are exotic from our viewpoint to find words that require a good deal of semantic 'unpacking' into English. It is quite obvious that in the case of *arruação*, we are dealing with the kind of culture-specific issue we considered in Chapter 1. But unpacking may be called for in cases where two cultures, otherwise fairly similar, have considerably different methods of organising a particular activity. Beyond this, the central problem seems to be what form this unpacking should take. The French 'word' *ENA*, and the words deriving from it, notably *énarque* and *énarchie*, provide examples that are pertinent to our discussion in illustrating an organisation of the training of senior civil servants that differs from the UK system. More recent medium-sized bilingual dictionaries increasingly show awareness of this issue; for example, the Oxford-Hachette translates *ENA, l'Ecole Nationale d'Administration*, as: 'Grande Ecole of public management'. The Oxford-Hachette also provides a gloss on *ENA*, as follows:

> The *grande école*, based on Strasbourg, which trains the élite force of public administrators. There are about 1,500 applicants for 150 places, drawn from the graduates of a university or another *grande école*. Entry is by competitive examination or *concours*, and requires applicants to commit themselves to ten years' work for the state.

We can point out first that for a reader who is not acquainted fully with the French higher education system, this definition points to further translation or simply comprehension problems, notably concerning *Grande Ecole* and *concours*. The Oxford-Hachette recognises this, as it provides glosses of *Grande Ecole* and *concours* of similar length to the one just quoted.

Here again we are faced with the issue of audience design as it affects the translator. We can think of a dictionary as a book consisting of translations, mostly of individual words and phrases. A dictionary is therefore unconcerned with the effect a translation may have on a more extended stretch of language. The translator, however, does need to think in these terms, since an unwieldy translation, such as that quoted above, can interrupt the flow of a text. We have said that translation of a complex word will involve semantic unpacking, in the form of a more or less wordy gloss, if the concept encoded in the complex word is not familiar in both of the cultures concerned. We need however to be more specific than this, and here our discussion of the *fleuve* issue is relevant. We suggested earlier that any translation of this word would need to be tailored to the perceived readership. From the present viewpoint, we can regard *fleuve* also as a complex word, although in a different sense. Examples like *ENA* are distinct in that although they are not invested with multiple meanings dependent on context, they are quite highly culture-specific. So while the translation of *fleuve* depends on the sense in which it is being used, the translation of *ENA* will depend essentially on the amount of cultural knowledge the translator assumes his or her reader will possess. This is fairly obvious, but the issue does raise practical difficulties that need careful consideration of the text type and readership the translator is dealing with. The present author, having occasion to use the term *grande école* in a book written for scholars of linguistics who were presumed not necessarily to know French, glossed the term as follows: 'French higher-education establishment recruiting the administrative and technical elite through competitive examination' (Armstrong, 2001: 206). There are 12 words in the TT against two in the ST, but it is hard to see how the gloss could have been telescoped further in view of the intended readership. At the same time, the readers of a monograph of linguistics will be accustomed to prose that lacks the snappiness of a newspaper article.

Examples of complex words in French come easily to hand: *alternance* in the political sense; *commune* in the administrative sense; *pantoufler* in the metaphorical sense; these may all need expansion in English because of the cultural meaning they encode so compactly in French. Other complex words seem less amenable to explanation using Sapir–Whorf. French words like *brave* and *frileux* encode a good deal of meaning and need expansion in English, but it is hard to find a cultural explanation for these examples of compactness.

It cannot be emphasised too strongly that the influence of the presumed readership is paramount. Astington (1983: 63) has several examples of the translation of the 'specific by the general'. One of these is connected with the translation of the adjective *cantonal*:

(36)   *la mort du héros était un événement cantonal*

       'the death of the hero was a local event'

The issue here clearly is that no equivalent exists in the UK or US for the *canton* as an administrative unit. A 'general' or less precise translation of the adjective may well be quite suitable, depending always, once again, on what level of culture-specific knowledge the reader is assumed to possess and require.

Denotation and Connotation

We have already referred to 'connotation', the secondary meaning attaching to words beyond their central 'denotation'. There are several sets of terms used in semantics to express this basic distinction: 'denotative' meaning is also referred to as 'conceptual', 'cognitive' or 'propositional' meaning. The sense is however always the same: the denotation of a word is its reference to the central concept it expresses, to the *signifié*, as we called it in Chapter 1 after Saussure. In this sense denotation is objective, to the extent that there is agreement across the speech community on the reference of the word in question. By contrast, connotation is subjective, and can be influenced by many factors. A simple example is 'summer'; the denotation of this word can be established in a fairly precise way, or at least one that gains widespread acceptance (period from the solstice to the equinox, for example), while the connotations of 'summer' will vary from speaker to speaker: ice-creams, beach, sunburn, relaxation, boredom, etc.

The term 'associative meaning' is used by Leech (1981: 18) to group together several types of meaning which are distinct from denotational or conceptual meaning. It is a useful term for the present discussion. Leech justifies the use of this umbrella term as follows:

> Reflected meaning and collocative meaning, affective meaning and social meaning: all these have more in common with connotative meaning than with conceptual meaning; they all have the same open-ended, variable character, and lend themselves to analysis in terms of scales or ranges, rather than in discrete either-this-or-that terms.

This quotation brings out the point that the various types of associative meaning share certain properties which distinguish them from conceptual meaning. This latter type of meaning is 'discrete' and 'either-this-or-that'; so, the denotational meaning of 'summer' is discrete in the sense that it refers to one season, without overlap with others.

Associative or connotational meaning contrasts with denotation in being subjective and fuzzy. As well as varying between individuals, connotation can of course be language-specific: a well-known example is the French *banlieue*, where connotation and denotation diverge where translation into English is in question. This term is often translated as 'suburbs', and to the extent that the *banlieues* are typically large and recent (post-war) housing developments located at some distance from their city centre, the term 'suburb' is denotationally not too inaccurate. The problem is that the term *banlieue* has been contaminated by the reality, and the English term 'inner-city' captures more accurately the English connotation of *petite banlieue*, in the measure that the term evokes inadequate housing, high rates of crime and unemployment, and large working-class and immigrant populations. The English term 'inner city', therefore, while less accurate in denotation, captures better the connotation of *banlieue*. This example is a borderline one, in that the connotation attaching to *banlieue* is no doubt very widespread in France, and the translation of the term by 'inner city' could be taken also as an example of a translation difficulty illustrating differences of social organisation across the two cultures. Other possibilities are 'high-rise estate', 'sink estate', 'council estate' each having their strengths and shortcomings.

The essential characteristic of connotation is therefore that it is secondary to the core denotation. However, the fact that connotation is secondary does not by any means make it unimportant. On the contrary, this layer of meaning is so pervasive that it needs very often to be taken into account in translation. Recall our earlier discussion of the following passage:

(37)   Au couperet des verdicts succédera, pour celui que la justice
       reconnaît criminel, un temps inédit: la possibilité, si le jugement ou
       la peine ne lui conviennent pas, de faire appel et d'être rejugé.

We remarked in Chapter 1 that *couperet* needs thought because of the needless associations it carries when translated by terms like 'guillotine' in English. Leech's terms 'reflected meaning and collocative meaning, affective meaning and social meaning' all share the characteristic therefore of evoking in the hearer's or reader's mind attributes of a concept above and beyond the 'core' meaning. We now discuss these briefly in turn.

The *couperet* problem has to do with what Leech calls 'reflected meaning': when translated by 'guillotine', as we pointed out in Chapter 1, the risk is run of interference in the reader's mind. Meaning is 'reflected' on to 'guillotine' by the concepts usually associated with it. Leech has the further example of 'The Holy Ghost'; because 'ghost' can have 'spooky' associations, the use of 'Holy Spirit' rather than 'Holy Ghost' may be preferable. Perhaps a more everyday example is 'intercourse', which by reason of its frequent collocation with 'sexual' tends now to be avoided in other contexts.

We examine collocation in more detail in the following chapter, but briefly, the problem here is the set of restrictions inherent in the structure of any language that permits certain collocations but rules out others. As Leech points out (1981: 17), the English adjectives 'pretty' and 'handsome', despite their essentially similar denotation, are restricted in how they can collocate: we can talk of a 'pretty woman', a 'pretty girl', and in some circumstances a 'pretty boy', but the collocation 'pretty man' is ruled out. This issue can be quite complex, since denotation and connotation can interact in some cases: as Leech remarks, '*handsome woman* and *pretty woman* are both acceptable, although they suggest a different kind of attractiveness because of the collocative associations of the two adjectives'. We discuss this area of the lexicon as it relates to translation in the following chapter.

The two remaining terms used by Leech, 'affective meaning' and 'social meaning', can be dealt with here, as they mostly concern the word level rather than words in combination. Affective meaning relates to the emotional content of what is said or written, and as Leech states (1981: 16), 'affective meaning is largely a parasitic category in the sense that to express our emotion we rely upon the mediation of other categories of meaning – conceptual, connotative, or stylistic'. This quotation brings out the point that there is overlap between the various categories of what Leech calls associative meaning. Thus the *couperet* problem discussed above is connected with connotation as well as collocation ('the Parliamentary guillotine'), which is itself a form of reflected meaning. Affective meaning is especially complex in spoken language; for example, the conceptual meaning of an utterance can be contradicted by the tone of voice in which it is expressed, as when an apparent compliment is conveyed with ironic intent. In writing, a straightforward example of a difference in affective meaning is 'Mother' ~ 'Mum'.

When we speak of social meaning, it is helpful to bear in mind the social dimensions along which cultures are divided: sex, age and social class are the most commonly mentioned. To take these in turn, some words are regarded as being sex-differentiated, in the sense of tending to be used by one sex rather than another. For instance, 'horrid' and 'frightful' can be regarded as rather 'feminine' words. As regards age, it obvious that the generations are differentiated by the vocabulary they use. Corresponding to this is the fact that some words are 'older' than others, or archaic in the terminology. Some are so archaic as to be rare in speech: 'steed' ~ 'horse', for example.

All of these connotational factors raise problems of decoding and subsequent encoding for the translator. The central problem here relates to style: 'steed' and 'horse' mean the same thing as regards their denotation, and the essence of stylistic variation is the possibility of saying the same thing in denotation while selecting the suitable connotation. To do this, the translator needs keen awareness of the various stylistic choices available. For instance, a younger translator may be in the habit of saying 'Tell me about it!' to express heartfelt agreement with something that has just been said. But for translation purposes, other, older variants that may be more suitable in context need to be borne in mind: 'You're telling me!'; 'I'll say!'; 'You can say that again!', etc., etc.

We mentioned social class as the third important factor influencing style variation. The issue of social-class differentiation as it influences socio-stylistic language use is a complex one, so that we discuss it in a separate section.

Style and Register

Closely connected with denotation and connotation, and especially with social meaning, are the issues surrounding style and register. To deal at once with the venerable register–style terminological issue, some linguists use the term 'register variation' to refer to linguistic variation that is conditioned by situational context, that is broadly along the formal–informal dimension, though of course many other factors, both functional and social, also come into play. It is regrettable that usage should differ among linguists between style and register, although one can usually tell what is meant. Where some writers have 'register', others use 'style', reserving the former term to refer to the dimension of linguistic variation that responds to subject-matter: the register of law, of medicine, of linguistics and so forth; in other words, the technical vocabulary or jargon. In what follows we adopt what is perhaps the commoner term in UK usage and refer to 'register' in connection with the formal–informal axis of variation. We will however use the adverb 'stylistically' where this seems more suitable than 'register' or 'register-based', etc.

Register variation relates to what Leech calls 'social meaning'. We referred briefly in the previous chapter to the relationship between social variation (prestige versus non-prestige language) and register variation (formal versus informal language). It is worth pointing out that the relationship between social and register variation in language reflects a more far-reaching relation, one that affects many aspects of social behaviour. It can be summarised in the following way. In any society above a given level of complexity, division of labour becomes necessary, and social groups come to be (perceived as being) ranked hierarchically, some occupational groups enjoying more overt prestige, deriving from a perceivedly greater access to power and wealth than others. (In contrast to overt prestige, some social groups enjoy 'covert' prestige, the frequently unacknowledged prestige accorded on account of toughness, non-conformity, lawlessness and other non-mainstream attributes.) The social behaviour (including of course non-linguistic as well as linguistic) of the more highly-ranked groups, who are in a position to define the standard language and behaviour generally, comes to be highly prized by all social groups; the next step is that the social behaviour of the higher groups is associated with more formal situations. Thus, the more formal the speech situation, the more prestigious will be the speech variety used, just as for instance more prestigious forms of dress are worn on formal occasions: the tailcoat may on the one hand be worn by members of all social classes at weddings, and on the other forms part of daily dress only at prestigious establishments such as certain British 'public schools' (endowed fee-paying boarding schools).

The translator must of course keep a close watch on the ST to monitor its level of formality. By and large, texts that are public and non-intimate call for formal language, and a wide range of reading is necessary in the two languages to sensitise the translator to nuances of register. So much is obvious; what is less obtrusive is the fact, referred to several times so far, that the different lexical structures of French and English can hinder the achievement of equivalent stylistic or register-based effect from ST to TT. The classic example, from Vinay and Darbelnet, is the trap set by the compound noun *exposition canine*; here, the Latinate words may evoke in the translator's mind the need for a formal equivalent in the TT. But the French term is in fact of a neutral register, and 'dog show' is an acceptable rendering. This is a simple problem of efficient decoding and encoding.

A further point worth mentioning is the need for consistency in the selection of register. Astington (1983: 120) gives the example of the translation into French of the sequence 'I can't speak to that person'. He points out that a very formal rendering would be *Je ne puis parler avec cette personne*, where formality derives from the *puis* variant and the omission of *pas*, which is a stylistic possibility with a restricted range of verbs. A much more colloquial formulation is *Causer à ce mec? Pas question!* What is to be avoided is a mixture of styles within the same sentence: *Je ne puis causer à ce mec* combines in a stylistically inconsistent way the very formal *je ne puis* with *causer à ce mec*, which is non-standard on account of the use of *mec* and of the preposition *à* where the standard language prescribes *avec*. It can be added that Astington's discussion needs refinement by pointing out that one would not normally wish to translate the formal 'I can't speak to that person' by *Causer à ce mec? Pas question!*, since formality should be translated by equivalent formality so far as is structurally possible. So *Causer à ce mec? Pas question!* would translate by 'It makes me sick to talk to that bloke' or something similar. That said, the point that styles should not be mixed is a valid one, at least within a short utterance like the one just discussed.

More complex problems arise where the SL or TL have a wider range of socially and stylistically coded synonyms that are lacking in the other language. To take the example of French, a striking feature of the informal lexicon is the social (and hence register) variation it shows. Table 3.1 provides a list of lexical pairs taken from a study by Lodge (1989), who was interested in French speakers' attitudes to non-standard vocabulary. This list shows a sample only of the pairs of non/standard words available to speakers; one researcher (Armstrong 2001, Chapter 7) counted 237 pairs of this kind in a corpus of spoken French.

A comparison between English and French highlights the fact that although there are of course plenty of slang terms in English, the extent of the phenomenon seems wider in French, both in the number of casual or informal terms used and the number of people who use them. Very many French speakers will refer to their car as *la bagnole*. Is there an equivalent

Table 3.1 Sample of lexical pairs selected by Lodge, 1989

Non-standard	Standard
baffe (pop.)	gifle
bagnole (fam./pop.)	automobile
bahut (arg. des écoles)	lycée
se balader (fam.)	se promener
baratin (pop.)	'discours abondant'
blague (fam.)	farce
bosser (pop.)	travailler
bouffer (fam.)	manger
boulot (fam.)	travail
bouquin (fam.)	livre
piaule (pop.)	chambre
pieu (pop.)	lit
pif (pop.)	nez
pognon (pop.)	argent

term in English that is so widespread socially? Similarly, is there a non-standard synonym in English for 'eat'? The point here is that although *bouffer* is of course a more casual term than *manger*, it seems to mean very much the same thing. Instead of 'eat' we might say 'scoff', but this seems to add something as well as casualness – 'scoff' implies greed of the eater as well as informality of the speaker.

As so often, the problem here is the lack of correspondence in the TL to this range of variants in the SL. In the other direction, we have mentioned in passing the mismatch between the word-stocks of French and English: largely Greco-Latin in the one, Greco-Latin plus Anglo-Saxon in the other. The consequence is obviously that in English there are often available learned and everyday synonyms to express the same concept. This is social variation in that one term may be archaic, the other current. One cannot furthermore predict which will be which. We have already mentioned the case of *exposition canine*. This example illustrates the problem neatly, but there is of course no choice in the rendering of this term, since 'canine exhibition' sounds hopelessly pompous. Similar examples are very numerous: the Latinate *animalerie* translates as Anglo-Saxon 'pet shop'. Problems arise where choice is available. To take the French example of the adjective *innombrable*, the *Petit Robert* gives the Latinate synonyms *infini, nombreux* and *considérable*, not all of which, like all synonyms, are interchangeable ı every context; a point to which we will return in the following chapter. English has Latinate 'innumerable', as well as the everyday 'countless' and the less common 'uncounted'. Corresponding to French *immortel* (French near-synonyms *éternel* and *impérissable*) are English 'immortal' and other Latinate synonyms, but also the poetic 'deathless'. The only general strategy can be to pay close attention always to the register of the ST; this can be difficult, since only long immersion in a culture can promote anything like near-native sensitivity to the socio-stylistic value of every word and phrase.

Nominalisation

The issue of nominalisation is well documented in the translation liter-ature: both Vinay and Darbelnet and Hervey and Higgins discuss it at some length, so that an extended treatment is not needed here. We mention it now because it concerns the individual word; in Chapter 5 we examine the problem on a different level, that of syntax. Examples of the French tendency to express a concept using a noun, where English will have another part of speech, are very numerous. Some taken at random are:

(38)	*au plaisir de vous rencontrer*	'looking forward to meeting you'
	l'unité fait la force	'united we stand, divided we fall'
	il a expliqué la façon dont il fallait procéder	'he explained how to proceed'
	le gel des terres	'set-aside'

The last example shows obviously a noun in English; the point is that this noun is composed of verb-form + preposition, whereas the French has noun + noun. The Fablon texts in Chapter 2 contain the following examples:

(39)	*prendre des mesures*	'measure'
	selon les instructions	'as instructed'
	le mettre en position	'position the Fablon'
	éviter la formation de bulles	'avoid bubbles'
	une fois l'eau séchée	'when the water has dried out'

Once again, it needs to be pointed out that this is a tendency, and so admits of exceptions. So, *au plaisir de vous rencontrer* can also be expressed as: *je me réjouis de vous rencontrer* in a more formal register. Similarly, the example in (38) above, *il a expliqué la façon dont il fallait procéder*, could less formally be *'l a expliqué comment il fallait procéder.* Furthermore, English have a noun where French has another part of speech as in le taken for the Fablon instructions:

 le Fablon   'cut the Fablon to size'

Nevertheless, from the viewpoint of French–English translation, the strategy of denominalisation is one to be borne constantly in mind.

False Friends

This is a very large subject, and we can only try to sketch out here some principles that distinguish the various types of false friend. The subject is so large that several books have been devoted to it, either partially or wholly: for example, Koessler and Derocquiny (1928), Kirk-Greene (1981) and Van Roey *et al.* (1998) are dictionaries wholly devoted to false friends, while Thody and Evans (1985) also give many examples, often accompanied by a discussion of the cultural context behind the particular problem. Batchelor and Offord (2000) have a substantial section devoted to the problem. Kirk-Greene lists about 3000 words, but the frequency of certain words is a more important issue, which we discuss below. The false-friend phenomenon again reflects the essentially arbitrary assignment of the signifier to the signified; it is also of course in part a product of the long common history that French and English share. These two factors can pull in various directions, sometimes with quite complex results. So for instance, despite their similar etymologies, the English adjective 'terrible' is a term of negative evaluation, but 'terrific' is positive. The English adjective 'wicked' is an even more striking example: while retaining its pristine sense, in formal English at least, of extreme moral disapproval, it is also a term of approval for younger speakers. The fact that the French adjective *terrible* is a positive term illustrates the operation of the same principle, this time across two languages rather than within one: *pas terrible* 'not very good'.

Kirk-Greene (1981: v) points out an important distinction within the large category of false friends: between on the one hand, those words whose form is wholly misleading; and on the other, those whose form gives some guide to their meaning but which have more than one meaning, only one of which will fit in a given context. The first type should not really give trouble to the advanced translator: so, the French words *ballot* 'parcel', *bribe* 'fragment', *verger* 'orchard' have forms that are in a sense less problematic, because, although their form gives totally misleading information if unfamiliar, they are less likely to lead astray the translator when seen in context. Thus, the phrase: *elle portait un lourd ballot* should not send the advanced translator's mind searching in the electoral semantic field.

Batchelor and Offord's categorisation (2000: 31) of what they call 'deceptive cognates', the technical term for *faux amis*, is similar to that of Kirk-Greene; they distinguish between deceptive cognates proper, where the meanings of the word in either language are quite unconnected, and partial deceptive cognates, in which 'only part of the meanings of the words coincides'.

Examples of deceptive cognates proper seem quite rare, unfortunately; Batchelor and Offord list about 160. To supplement Kirk-Greene's two-way distinction, we can establish a further, intermediate category of false friends that have a similar surface form in the two languages, but refer to more or less subtly different concepts: for example, French *jaquette* means 'morning coat'. English 'jacket' is rendered by French *veste* or *veston*. UK English 'vest' corresponds in turn to the French *gilet de corps*. Many entries in dictionaries of false friends have this rather rambling structure, exploring the various correspondences around a group of related lexical items until these are exhausted. The difference between the *ballot* type of false friend and the *jaquette* type is connected to the relation between surface form and meaning across the two languages. Whereas the English learner of French is given no clue from English as to even the approximate meaning of French *ballot*, since English 'ballot' is totally unconnected in meaning, the learner is pointed in *more or less* the right direction in the case of *jaquette*.

Some words of the *jaquette* type, especially abstract words, can present difficulties depending on the word with which they collocate. For example, the French adjective *abusif* fairly famously (perhaps not famously enough) does not mean English 'abusive', though its meanings relate clearly enough to one sense of English 'abuse'. Thody and Evans have the example of *les coups de téléphone abusifs*, not telephone calls that are abusive or insulting, but those made without authority, perhaps at an employer's expense. The connection with one sense of English 'abuse' is quite transparent: one is misusing or abusing a privilege by making *des coups de téléphone abusifs*. This concept needs always to be borne in mind when translating *abusif*. Kirk-Greene has the example of *les parents abusifs*: not abusive, but overprotective parents. Again the concept is of a right or privilege exercised beyond its proper limits. Alongside this concept, the translator needs to be aware that French *abus* and its derivatives never refer to physical or verbal abuse.

A third type of false friend is the word that has several meanings in French; the translator's task is to render the correct one. Some are well known: French *important*, as well conveying English 'important', can also mean 'large', as in *Marseille est une ville importante*. As ever, the context needs to be studied carefully. More serious mistranslation can occur in the case of *arrêter*, which can of course mean 'stop', but has also a near-opposite sense: *elle a arrêté sa decision* 'her decision has been fixed / settled upon'. The difference between words of the *abusif* type and those like *arrêter* is that *abusif* always has the same sense, or one that is only subtly different from the central concept of abuse in the sense of misuse, and the translator must find the correct collocation in the English translation. By contrast, a word like *arrêter* has at least three core meanings, these always overlap, but the sense *in context*, and therefore its translation, can require some thought. It is also a frequent word, and no doubt most often does mean 'stop' or 'arrest', so that the translator is at risk of imposing one of the more frequent senses of the word in the wrong context. This problem tends to arise in highly abstract texts, although in principle the surrounding context should make clear that the sense of the word in question is not the everyday one, as in the examples below.

(41)   *après sept ans il y a prescription*   'after seven years the statute of
                                                limitation applies'

(42)   *la Cour de Cassation a été saisie du dossier*

       'the Court of Appeal has been notified of the case / the case has
       been referred to the Court of Appeal'

To summarise, some false friends are more dangerous than others, in the sense that an opposing or very different meaning can be rendered if care is not taken. Beyond the elementary level, words like *bribe* and *verger* should not give trouble, because they will give an obviously nonsensical rendering if mistranslated. Words like *abusif* are more dangerous, because a mistranslation of *les coups de téléphone abusifs* or *des parents abusifs* can seem plausible.

The most dangerous false friend is the one that looks innocuous because one of its senses does in fact correspond to what the translator might think is meant. The only general strategy in the case of false friends is to exercise caution wherever a French or English word bears a resemblance to another in the corresponding language. This means constant caution in view of how common false friends are. The only completely certain method, if not very practical, is to look up every such word every time, and even then a general dictionary will not always help. A dedicated dictionary of false friends needs to be within reach, and ideally should have provided quite intensive spare-time browsing material at one stage in the translator's career. As ever, the price of accuracy is eternal vigilance. A final example shows two of the more insidious kind of false friends in a short stretch of text, taken from *Le Monde*:

(43)   Les syndicats français [...] dénoncent un système abusif d'évaluation, assorti de quotas, pouvant conduire au licenciement pour insuffisance professionnelle. Saisie du dossier, l'inspection du travail s'inquiète de pratiques qui pourraient être illégales.

Here, *abusif* could be translated as 'unjust' or 'unfair', while *saisi* has the same sense as in (42).

Chapter 4

Words in Combination

In Chapter 3 we considered words in isolation, although we saw that when we try to study words in this way, translation problems become apparent, resulting from the relationships that words contract with each other; the cases we saw in the previous chapter were reflected and collocational meaning. In this chapter we consider in more depth the way in which word-sets are structured so as to achieve meaning in combination, as usual of course from the viewpoint of the translation problems caused.

The Structural Organisation of Meaning: Paradigms and Syntagmata

We shall consider the organisation of the lexicon again from the viewpoint of Saussure's structural, or difference-based, view of language. From this perspective, we can look at lexical structure along two dimensions: the 'vertical' paradigm and the 'horizontal' syntagma (plural: syntagmata). We have already considered briefly the paradigm in the previous chapter. The fact that grammarians usually organise paradigms in lists seems to reflect an assumption about the mental organisation of the lexicon. By this latter term we mean something like 'the mental dictionary'. An axiom of linguistics is that speakers possess a lexicon and a grammar; this second term means here a set of rules internalised by the speaker and allowing the combination of elements from the lexicon into acceptable sentences along the syntagmatic or syntactic level, as shown in Figure 4.1:

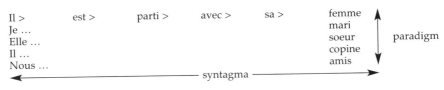

Figure 4.1 The interaction of paradigm and syntagma

Figure 4.1 expresses the idea that items from the various paradigms (the lexicon) are slotted into syntagmata (phrases and sentences, following grammatical rules) to form meaningful sequences. The first syntagma, *il est parti avec sa femme,* has been filled in; it would not be difficult to fill the others similarly, as *je suis sortie sans mon mari,* and so forth. The paradigm and syntagma are therefore two interlocking dimensions, corresponding respectively to the lexicon and the grammar as defined above and combining in speech or writing to produce sequences that conform to the grammar of the language concerned. We now consider in turn the paradigmatic and syntactic levels of lexical structure.

Grammatical Paradigms

Within the broad paradigmatic dimension, speakers appear to operate, on the one hand with 'grammatical paradigms', and on the other, with 'lexical paradigms'. This reflects the distinction between lexical and grammatical words discussed in the previous chapter. We can represent grammatical paradigms in quite a simple way, as they are shown in grammar books:

Table 4.1 Some grammatical paradigms in French

Part of speech	*Verb*	*Object pronoun*	*Subject pronoun*	*Disjunctive pronoun*
Paradigm	suis	me	je	moi
	es	te	tu	toi
	est	le / la	il / elle / on	lui / elle / soi
	êtes	vous	vous	vous
	sommes	nous	nous	nous
	sont	les	ils / elles	eux / elles

The examples shown in Table 4.1 demonstrate the obvious point that grammatical paradigms can concern parts of speech other than verbs. Latin is the most familiar example of a language that is rich in inflections; one whose verbs, nouns and other parts of speech change their form to reflect their grammatical role. Inflection at this level of complexity has been lost from French and English, where for the most part, word order rather than word inflection indicates grammatical function. Highly inflected languages like Latin can therefore have a certain degree of flexibility in their word order, in contrast to French and English whose word order is to a large extent fixed. Nevertheless, pronouns and other grammatical words continue to inflect in French and English, as well of course as verb forms. We have relatively little evidence of how the brain organises language, but it makes sense to assume that groups of words such as those shown above are associated fairly closely together in the mental lexicon in a non-random way, to make possible their ready selection and insertion into a string of words arranged along the syntagma, the 'horizontal' unit of syntax.

We examine now the principal lexical relations that are commonly distinguished, attempting subsequently to provide an integrated view of how words are situated in these relations, namely: polysemy, synonymy and hyponymy.

Lexical Paradigms and Polysemy

Just as it makes sense to assume that grammatical words are organised in the mental lexicon in such a way that they can be easily retrieved and inserted into a syntactic sequence, so we can assume that sets of lexical words are grouped together similarly. However, whereas grammatical paradigms are closed sets (for example, Table 4.1 shows all of the French subject pronouns, a set that admits of no further additions in the foreseeable future), lexical paradigms are more complex and open-ended, since more layers of meaning are involved, words have multiple meanings, and the meanings of lexical words are susceptible to processes of change. So, the difference between *suis* and *es* in Table 4.1 can be expressed quite simply, in terms of a bundle of fairly abstract semantic features: *suis* = *être* as 1st-person present indicative, while *es* = *être* as 2nd-person present indicative. If we wish to represent one small part of the lexical structure of French in a similar way to that shown in Table 4.1, we can represent a set of lexical words as shown in Figure 4.2:

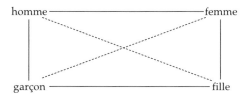

Figure 4.2 A lexical paradigm

Here the lines between the various words represent different types of lexical relation: *homme* and *femme* are differentiated here by the single semantic feature of sex, so that we could oppose the two terms by saying that whereas *homme* is +human, +adult, +male, *femme* is +human, +adult, +female. Similarly, while *homme* is +human, +adult, +male, *garçon* is

+human, –adult, +male. A solid line in our diagram shows therefore a close relationship, one differentiated by only one feature, while a broken line shows a less close relation: *garçon* is +human, –adult, +male, while *femme* is +human, +adult, +female.

The problem with this simple representation is that it ignores the often quite complex webs of overlapping meanings in which words are situated. The relevant term in linguistics here is *polysemy*, which comes from the Greek and conveys the sense of 'many meanings'. It seems that speakers prefer an organisation of the lexicon that adds multiple meanings to words, with each meaning more or less closely related to the others, rather than an organisation that has many words each having a single meaning. This seems to be true at least so far as fairly common lexical words are concerned: we saw in the previous chapter that infrequent and complex words like *imprescriptibilité* have a single sense, even if the way they are translated depends on the intended reader.

One result of polysemy is that a given word can have differing combination possibilities across languages. Lodge *et al.* (1997: 55) show the example of the various senses of the French word *garçon* in Figure 4.3.

(1) *enfant mâle*: 'Ils ont trois filles et un garçon' = 'boy'
(2) *homme celibataire*: 'A cinquante ans il est toujours garçon' = 'bachelor'
(3) *jeune ouvrier travaillant chez un patron artisan*: 'garcon épicier', etc = 'boy', 'apprentice'
(4) *[jeune] homme* 'Il est sympa, ce garçon' = 'lad', 'bloke', 'chap' …

Figure 4.3 The different senses of *garçon*

The obvious translation issue here is the need for close attention to the accurate sense of the word of interest; the sense is to be deduced from the unit of syntax in which it is found. We can illustrate this problem by using the very simple example discussed in Lodge *et al.* (1997: 62), where the one overlapping sense of the French words *pas* and *marche* are contrasted with the polysemic senses possessed by each word. In the following example, the symbol '≈' signifies 'is more or less equivalent to'. The near synonyms have been taken from the 1986 *Petit Robert*:

(1) pas ≈ marche; étape; enjambée; démarche; danse …
     marche ≈ pas; chanson militaire; moyen; fonctionnement …

As pointed out in Lodge *et al.* the meaning of *pas* and *marche* is dependent on the surrounding context. Obviously therefore, in the following sequence the two words are interchangeable, since they both convey the sense of English 'step' or 'gait':

(2) Elle s'avançait d'une marche / d'un pas hésitant(e)

Near-synonymy occurs therefore when the sense of two words that are polysemic overlap in one semantic area. Near-synonymy is also dependent on linguistic context and results in *selectional* restrictions, as in (3), where the context permits *marche* in its *chanson militaire* sense, but not *pas*, since this is not one of the senses of the latter word:

(3)   La musique jouait une marche / * un pas militaire

We have already looked at this question in relation to *faux amis* in the previous chapter, although without alluding directly to the concepts of polysemy, near-synonymy and selectional restrictions. Recall that a phrase like the following (taken from Kirk-Greene, 1981: 9) needs care:

(4)   il a arrêté ses plans

If we consider the case of *arrêter*, we see that the various senses of the word are related, just as with *garçon*. The basic sense of *arrêter* is 'stop', 'fix', but a suitable translation will depend on the word with which *arrêter* collocates in each case. Kirk-Greene translates example (4) as 'he drew up his plans'. The sense of *arrêter* in this sequence is akin to the others, in the measure that one draws up or fixes plans, to a point where they are decided and the process is then stopped.

The selectional restrictions of a language can be thought of as rules that alert speakers to the combination possibilities of the lexicon on semantic grounds. The celebrated 'colorless green ideas sleep furiously' sentence discussed previously was in fact originally devised to illustrate this. The translator's problem is clearly that selectional restrictions differ across languages, on account of the polysemic combinations that are specific to each. Example (3) illustrates an elementary English–French encoding problem, and is included to show the relation between polysemy, near-synonymy and selectional restrictions in a very straightforward way. French–English decoding problems, as in example (4), stem from the same cause, and they can and do cause difficulty at an advanced level.

The consequences of polysemy and near-synonymy beyond the word level are therefore obviously that each language has different combination possibilities for each of its words from those occurring in other languages. This in turn is because the polysemic relations in which words are involved differ across languages. At the same time, less frequent words are relatively context-independent, and hence less likely to cause decoding problems of the type that stem from polysemy.

Lexical Paradigms and Synonymy

The lexical relation of synonymy relates to *sameness* of meaning. When discussing polysemy above, we suggested that languages seem to reflect the desire of speakers to economise mental processing by assigning more than one meaning to certain words, so avoiding the storage and retrieval problems associated with a one-word–one-meaning system. Languages seem to prefer to add new meanings to the lexicon by extending the function of existing words: so for example, 'air' in English, as well as *air* in French, has had its pristine, literal meaning extended to mean 'tune', 'appearance', etc. As mentioned above, translation problems arise where languages extend the meaning of a word in different directions.

From this functional point of view we can suggest that complete or absolute synonymy is rare because it is not needed; why have two words to designate a concept in precisely the same way, where one will suffice? If not totally absent, complete synonymy is said to be very rare: an example sometimes mentioned is the French pair *désinence* ~ *inflexion*, translatable as English 'accidence' ~ 'inflection'. These are learned terms, both referring to the phenomenon shown in Table 4.1, where words inflect or change their form to express their grammatical function. Complete or absolute synonyms are words that are interchangeable in every context. One can question whether even the terms cited above are absolute synonyms in this sense, since both *désinence* and 'accidence' seem rarer than their synonyms, and the use of a rare word in place of its more frequent synonym will add a different stylistic colouring to a text. A more everyday example is the English pair 'almost' and 'nearly', but even these differ in their distribution, as 'almost' in poetic language can qualify a noun, as in Philip Larkin's 'our almost-instinct', and 'nearly' can have a literal spatial sense, as in to 'to approach more nearly'.

We saw in Chapter 3 that pairs of French words like *vélo* ~ *bicyclette*, despite having the same reference, are differentiated by their social-stylistic value. In the definition of complete synonymy given above, we would therefore wish to exclude them as absolute synonyms. Similarly, near-synonyms in English like 'begin' and 'commence', 'finish' and 'terminate', like countless other pairs, are differentiated by their formality, as we saw in the previous chapter, which in turn depends on their Anglo-Saxon or Greco-Latin origin. Complete synonyms, if they exist at all, seem to come more easily to mind in formal French and English, and in linguistics one can point to the example of *schwa, e caduc, e muet, e féminin, e latent*, etc., the terms that refer to the French vowel found in sequences like *jE mE lE dEmande* (schwas indicated in the orthography are in capitals). Even here, however, the use of one term rather than another can depend on the theoretical intent of the author of the text. So, 'schwa' is a descriptive phonetic term, while labels such as 'mute e' or 'latent e' imply a more theoretical, phonological level.

So, near-absolute synonymy in highly formal French or English seems easier to explain, given that there is in general less variation across informative texts along the register dimension. At the same time, as was pointed out above, the very fact that one term is preferred over another can reflect the author's theoretical intention, or their wish to impart an archaic flavour to a text, for whatever reason. It may be then that complete synonymy, in the strict definition given above, does not exist.

As was pointed out in the previous chapter, the rarity of complete synonymy is due either to simple differences of denotation (tart, pie, flan, etc.); or to differences of connotation (stylistic level, affective meaning, reflected meaning, etc). Wide reading in the SL, as well as systematic ransacking of reference books, especially perhaps the thesaurus, are needed to ensure the correct synonym or circumlocution is selected.

Lexical Paradigms and Hyponymy

When we consider the lexical relation of hyponymy, we are once again in the domain governed by Sapir–Whorf where translation problems are concerned. Hyponymy is the lexical relation of dominance or inclusion: an umbrella term, or *superordinate*, expresses the broad meaning of each of the *hyponyms* governed by the superordinate. In its turn, each of the hyponyms expresses a more detailed area of meaning within the general sense expressed by the superordinate. Differing numbers of words cover or encode particular sectors of experience in each semantic field, as shown in the examples below. The examples are again taken from Lodge *et al.* (1997: 58–9). The example in Figure 4.4 is purely illustrative, and of little interest so far as French–English differences are concerned, since the two languages have the same hyponymic system regarding terms for trees. It is however worth pointing out the synthetic tendency at work in French here: *cerisier* as against 'cherry tree'; *abricotier* for 'apricot tree', and so forth. Similarly, the examples in Figure 4.5 show that French encodes hyponyms for specific types of harvest in a more compact way than English. Some languages are relatively concise in the way they express sets of hyponyms, others less so. The issue here is again therefore codability. Clearly, however, French *vendange* can very easily be expanded in English to 'grape harvest', and so on with the other hyponyms.

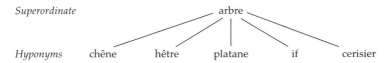

Figure 4.4 Terms for trees in French: the superordinate and its hyponyms

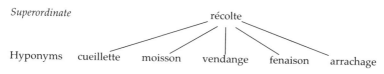

Figure 4.5 Terms for harvests in French: the superordinate and its hyponyms

Subtler examples of differences in hyponymic systems occur where languages categorise experience using different grids; for instance, the French superordinate *fonctionnaire* has a wider range of hyponyms than its English equivalent, so that a rendering of the term by 'civil servant', in a discussion of the French public sector, may cause the English reader to impose an unsuitable interpretation on the term. Depending on context, *fonctionnaire* is often better translated as 'state employee' or 'public-sector worker', since the French term also comprises teachers, police officers and others.

A more purely linguistic difficulty is caused by the assignment of different superordinate meanings to related words in the two languages: *soldat* translates as 'private soldier' in English, while the superordinate French term is *militaire*. Correspondingly, English 'soldier' comprises, at least in some contexts, every rank from private to field marshal; 'sailor' has an analogous scope, equivalent similarly to French *marin* rather than *matelot*. This is yet another manifestation of the omnipresent *arbitraire du signe*.

As we saw in Chapter 1, from the viewpoint of the Sapir–Whorf theory of the influence of socio-cultural factors upon language, we can suggest that some differences of hyponymy or near-synonymy may or may not be explicable in socio-cultural terms. The *fonctionnaire* example clearly is, since it reflects an organisation of the public sector that is different across the two countries. The harvest example is no doubt related to the French tendency to synthesise, discussed previously. The English distinction between 'sheep' and 'mutton' where French has only *mouton* can be explained by reference to the histories of the two languages: after 1066, the massive influx of Norman French words created the dual English word-stock we have already referred to. Similarly, an explanation of the French distinction between *savoir* and *connaître*, where English has only 'know', would need a fairly detailed examination of the development of French from Latin. Other examples are harder to explain in socio-historical terms: French has no superordinate corresponding to the English 'aircraft', for example. Correspondingly French has no compact term for the subordinate term 'toddler'.

From the practical translation point of view, it is profitless in some cases to speculate why French has a different encoding system from

English, as in the case of harvest terms or the *savoir–connaître* distinction; in other cases, *fonctionnaire* for example, knowledge of the socio-cultural situation is essential. But in all cases, it is the surrounding context that determines meaning, whether or not a translation problem is lying in wait. This way of looking at word-meaning can be called *distributional*: as pointed out in Lodge *et al.* (1997: 65–6), rather than searching for fine differences of meaning between pairs of near-synonyms like *lieu ~ endroit*, it is more profitable to examine the contexts in which each is distributed. In this example, it will be noticed that *endroit* is more freely distributed, while *lieu*, the older word, tends to occur in fixed locutions like *arriver sur les lieux* 'to arrive at the scene [of the crime]'. Other examples listed in Vinay and Darbelnet (1995: 59) are the following:

(5)   *poêle – fourneau*   'stove'

      ruines – décombres   'ruins'

      écharpe – cache-col   'scarf'

      éclair ~ foudre   'lightning'

We can regard these as examples of (limited) hyponymic sets in French where English has none; clearly, we can also say that the meaning of a word is determined by its surrounding context, since the type of stove, ruins or scarf in question will be made clear by what precedes and follows. In other words, where hyponymy exists in French in the examples in (5), it is matched by polysemy in English. Corresponding examples (Vinay & Darbelnet, 1995: 55) can be shown where English differentiates in a hyponymic way between sounds of different kind, while French has to make do with the noun *bruit*:

(6)   'the slam of a door'   *le bruit d'une porte*

      'a dull thud'   *un bruit mat*

      'the clatter of dishes'   *le bruit de vaisselle remuée*

In the following section we explain how this context-based view of word meaning unifies the lexical relations of synonymy, polysemy and hyponymy. Again from a practical viewpoint, we can mention that differences of hyponymy across French and English are more acute, for an English native-speaker, where French–English translation is operating: English 'seat' translates, depending on context, as French *chaise*, *siège*, *fauteuil*, etc.; English 'room' as French *pièce*, *chambre*, *salle*, etc. For the English native-speaker translating into French, problems caused on the hyponymic level will be subtler, and will involve encoding issues of the type exemplified in the third example in (6), where *le bruit de vaisselle remuée* needs to be conveyed by compression into the verb 'clatter'.

The Interaction of Synonymy, Polysemy and Hyponymy

Although we have treated the lexical relations of synonymy, polysemy and hyponymy separately in the preceding sections, it should be plain from the examples used above that the three dimensions in fact intersect in many cases. To look once again at the *fonctionnaire* example, a passage from *Le Monde* shows surrounding context used to select the relevant sense:

(7)   la France est dans l'Union européenne l'un des Etats qui comptent le plus grand nombre de *fonctionnaires de la sécurité, gendarmes compris,* par habitant

Here a suitable translation into UK English of the italicised phrase would simply be 'police officers', since the UK has no *agent de police ~ gendarme* distinction. What is notable for the purposes of our present discussion is that *Le Monde* transforms the superordinate *fonctionnaire* into one of its hyponyms using the post-modifier *de la sécurité*. One could at first sight take this as an example of the circumlocutionary style typical of *Le Monde*, but in fact it is hard to see how the sense could have been expressed otherwise, since the hyponym *agents de police* excludes *gendarmes* by definition. A hyponymic system is therefore one which encodes, in the superordinate term, the near-synonymy of the hyponyms; or to put it another way, where the superordinate may have compressed within it the polysemic senses that the hyponyms encode in more explicit form. What brings the meaning out fully is the context: the syntagma.

A further example may illustrate this point more fully. The term *voie* (from the Latin *via*) has the basic sense of 'road', or more abstractly 'way'. According to the adjective that qualifies it, as well of course as the surrounding context, the term may have a different translation: straightforward examples are *voie ferrée* 'railway track', but also the abstract 'railway (system)' as against *voie navigable* 'waterway'. Here we have polysemy expressed by qualifying adjective.

On a more abstract level still, we see *voie* used a near-synonym of *moyen*, as in the following expressions:

(8)   *la voie hiérarchique*   'the proper channels' (administrative jargon)

     la voie diplomatique   'the diplomatic channel'

     la voie de droit   'legal means'

The habitual involvement of a word with other, related words through polysemy, hyponymy and near-synonymy, as well as with yet other words on the syntagmatic level, is implicitly recognised in the way in which compilers of dictionaries organise each article, grouping the closely related senses of a word in proximity to one another. Dictionaries like the *Petit Robert* also give glimpses of the involvement of a word in other synonymic and hyponymic systems by listing near-synonyms, for instance by giving *moyen* as a synonym for *voie* in the sense shown in (8).

It will be apparent that our discussion of *voie* has been much to the same effect as the points made in connection with the multiple senses of *garçon* earlier in the chapter. The remarks made concerning *voie* are intended to present the same issue in a more theoretical light, from the viewpoint of the three lexical relationships discussed above. It hardly needs to be said that these remarks apply to countless other French and English words; once again, translation difficulties arise where an SL word is involved in synonymic, polysemic or hyponymic relations that differ from the equivalent TL terms. Figure 4.6, adapted from the diagram shown in Germain's *Sémantique fonctionnelle* (1981: 79) illustrates the interaction of synonymy, polysemy or hyponymy. Taking the word *canapé* as the central element, Germain shows how the word is '*susceptible d'être le centre d'une constellation de mots*', each one of which is involved in its own '*champ associatif*' or 'associative field'. The term 'field' is used in lexical semantics to refer to a set of related words. One could therefore shift the focus to each of the words shown in the network in Figure 4.6; in each case, a different fragment of the whole associative network would be revealed.

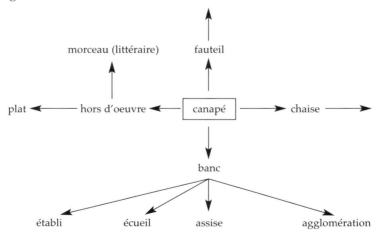

Figure 4.6 A network of 'associative fields' (adapted from Germain (1981: 79))

Figure 4.6 represents a 'functional' view of how groups of words might be associated in a French speaker's mind. Functional linguistics lays stress on efficiency of communication, and tends to discuss linguistic phenomena in terms of a tension between the desire for economy on the one hand, and for clarity on the other. So for example, a functional explanation of the omission of *ne* in sequences like *je sais pas* would suggest that speakers omit the first negative element because two are not needed, and that *pas* is retained because it is capable of receiving stress in phrase-final position, and therefore conveying the negative message clearly. Similarly, a functional view of semantics is concerned with efficient storage and retrieval, and from this viewpoint the semanticist assumes that sets of words will be grouped in 'associative fields'. If we accept the theory that word-sets may be grouped in the mental lexicon in this way, we can suggest that the advantage of such an arrangement is that it makes possible the ready selection of near-synonyms.

Germain points out that it is unclear to what extent we are justified in accepting a representation like that shown above as typical of what goes on in the mind of a French speaker. But from a translation point of view this does not matter, because the important point is that an English native-speaker's mental organisation of the comparable part of the lexicon organised around 'canapé' will differ from a typical French equivalent in several important respects, if the mental lexicon of the speaker of any language is organised even remotely like the way shown above. In this example, the French associative chains break up very soon when mapped onto English; if we accept that French *canapé* and *banc* are near-synonyms, these terms translate obviously as English 'canapé' and 'bench'. At this point the French and English chains diverge totally, since whereas French *banc* has the polysemic value indicated in the diagram and translatable by English 'reef', 'stratum' etc. (French *écueil* and *assise*), these have only a remote connection with English 'bench', being allied rather to 'bank' – which can translate French *banc*, but only in compounds like *banc de vase* 'mud-bank'. Similarly, the associative link between 'canapé' and 'hors d'oeuvre' may well exist in the minds of many English speakers (although fewer English than French), but again the next link will break down for an English speaker, whereas the connection between *hors d'oeuvre* and *morceau* is well established for a French speaker. The next steps are quite clear, since yet again, polysemy exists in French in the form of the multiple senses of *morceau*: 'piece', 'bit', 'cut', 'fragment', '(literary) passage / extract'.

To reiterate, an English network centred on 'canapé' will look very different because of the dissimilar associative links between the elements that make up the network. This explains why the English native-speaker is at a disadvantage when searching for near-synonyms to translate a French term; the associative networks lead in quite different directions. The French and English networks centred on 'canapé' provide a very crisp example of a word that in both languages has similar senses. To take a more complex (and perhaps more representative) example, if we were to construct an associative network with at its centre a word like *voie*, which has a broader range of polysemic meanings, we can imagine that near-synonyms leading off in various directions would include *route*, *moyen*, *train*, *passage*, etc. If we assume that the primary meaning of *voie* is that given first by the *Petit Robert*, that is *'espace à parcourir pour aller quelque part'* we might select 'road', 'path', or 'way' to translate this sense. Depending on which term we select, the English associative field would show a different fragment of the overall lexicon. We shall see below how these differences of associative organisation put difficulties in the way of translating collocations.

The network shown in Figure 4.6 resembles in graphic form the list-based organisation of a thesaurus, where words are associated on the basis of relations of polysemy, near-synonymy and hyponymy, subtle or gross. The aim of the monolingual thesaurus is to enhance word-power, promote elegant variation, or expressed less positively, to compensate for temporary or permanent memory deficits. Another way of putting this is by reference to passive as against active linguistic competence; in our mother tongue as well as our second languages, we have far more words as it were in storage than in live memory, and the thesaurus aims to help overcome retrieval problems. The thesaurus is clearly an essential tool in helping to overcome problems of the *voie diplomatique* type discussed above; in conjunction with a dictionary, near-synonyms can be worked through and checked against the dictionary for actual attestation as collocational sequences. The thesaurus, especially the classic *Roget*, has the obvious advantage of the cumulative effect of its many editions, whereby gaps in associative fields are filled in gradually. In this sense it resembles a large collective memory; a more efficient version of the near-totality of the lexicon, organised similarly to the fragment shown in Figure 4.6. The disadvantage of *Roget* is of course that which it shares with all dictionaries – it cannot show the latest coinings and collocations. A corresponding advantage is that *Roget* contains a good number of archaisms that can be suitable in formal texts.

Lexical Paradigms and Antonymy

For completeness we mention briefly the lexical relation of antonymy, or oppositeness, which has more interest from a theoretical than a practical point of view in translation. Few studies of translation mention this aspect of lexical structure, perhaps simply because antonymy presents relatively few problems. Of the various types of opposites, 'comple-mentary' antonyms, of the 'male' ~ 'female', 'alive' ~ 'dead' type, seem uniform across English and French, as do 'converse opposites' like 'husband' ~ 'wife' or 'buy' ~ 'sell' (cf. Lodge *et al.*, 1997: 60).

In contrast, so-called 'true' or 'gradable' antonyms may vary in their cross-cultural reference. These opposites are not absolute in the same way as those mentioned above. An example of a pair of gradable antonyms is 'large' ~ 'small'. These are clearly relative concepts that can vary in response to many factors. So, a house that an aristocrat describes as 'tiny' might seem surprisingly large to one who is less well situated. Similarly, the 'left' ~ 'right' political opposition by no means implies the same elements in the two countries of interest here, and such terms may need qualification in translation. For instance, all Rightist political parties in France take for granted the legitimacy of state intervention to a greater extent than their UK and US equivalents.

There are opposites in English that are expressed less compactly in French – *profond* ~ *peu profond*, for instance – and oppositional systems can vary across languages or dialects in the fineness with which they calibrate antonymy. Baker (1992: 23) mentions differences in how languages express physical or interpersonal perspective; an example from Scots English is the threefold distinction of distance 'this ~ that ~ yon', which is lacking in standard English. English 'fetch', opposed to 'bring' or 'take', often has no compact equivalent in other languages. The well-known translation trap connected with 'fetch' is that the French equivalent, *aller chercher*, is in danger of being 'over-translated' to 'go and find'.

Table 4.2 Antonymy dependent on context; the example of yes–no in French

Polarity of question	Polarity of situation	Examples		English	French
+	+	Did you?	I did	yes	oui
−	+	Didn't you?	I did	yes	si
+	−	Did you?	I didn't	no	non
−	−	Didn't you?	I didn't	no	non

Source: Adapted from Catford (1965: 41)

Table 4.2 illustrates the principle of the context-dependence of the meaning of common words through a comparison of the 'yes–no' antonymic systems in English and French. The difference is clearly that where a question in French has 'negative polarity', i.e. expects a negative answer, French has *si* where the answer is positive, against the questioner's expectation. As stated above, the interest of this is theoretical rather than practical, although the fact that English will have a different intonation for 'yes' equivalent to *si* poses an interesting challenge for the translator where dialogue is being rendered from French into English.

In connection with antonymy, we may mention briefly variation in some 'default' settings featured in the two languages. In Chapter 2 we discussed the concept of 'marked' language. Markedness finds expression in various ways, and can also reflect quite deep-seated psychological tendencies; for example, the fact that we assume the good as the normal state of affairs is built into language, so that when we say 'I was impressed' we mean by default we were favourably impressed. Other 'unmarked' settings vary across English and French, however. Where measurements are in question, English assumes the large as the default: 'how big is it?', while French has a neutral perspective: *combien il mesure?*. Similar English adjectives concerned are 'long', 'heavy', etc. Literal French–English translation is obviously unacceptable here.

Homonyms

These are words that look or sound alike, but have different meanings. Words having the same written forms but different pronunciations are *homographs*, words sounding the same but spelt differently are *homophones*. As an example of homographs, the *Petit Robert* has *nous portions* 'we were carrying' against *les portions* 'the portions': same spelling of *portions*, but different pronunciation and of course meaning. Homographs give rise to puzzle sentences like *nous portions nos portions* and *les poules du couvent couvent*. Homophones seem more common: *vers, verre* and *vert*; *sot, sceau, saut, seau*, etc. The two categories may of course coincide, with, as in the French *vers* 'towards', 'verse', worms', all words pronounced and written identically. Homonymy is distinguishable from polysemy by distance of meaning. We noted above the example of 'air' in English and *air* in French, which as well as the literal meaning, have fairly closely related figurative senses like 'tune', 'appearance', 'ambience', etc. The relative closeness of these polysemic senses is often reflected in dictionary entries, so *air* in its literal meaning and some of its figurative meanings are listed under the same article in the *Petit Robert*. Correspondingly, French *pas*, representing both the lexical word 'step' and the grammatical negative particle 'not', although etymologically both the same word, have diverged so much in meaning that they must now be regarded as homonyms. Again, the *Petit Robert* reflects this by defining the two words under different articles.

Homonyms are common; they provide grist for the mill of punsters and crossword compilers, and of course are the source of elementary howlers like translating English 'list' as *inclinaison* (list of a ship) instead of *liste*; or the other way round. They should not cause translation problems at an advanced level, but may cause momentary puzzlement, as in the following example:

(9)   A noter que les flux de matière accrétée par les trous noirs super-
      massifs *tapis* au coeur des galaxies ne se structurent pas toujours sous
      la forme d'un disque mince […]

Here *tapis* is the past participle of *tapir*, and no reference to carpets is in question. We discuss this passage further in the following chapter, in connection with the reinforcement of French prepositions.

Collocation: The Tendency of Words to Co-Occur Regularly

While selectional restriction has to do with the constraints that prevent words co-occurring in ways that produce nonsense, collocational restriction operates to produce largely arbitrary variation between near-synonyms, as in the following examples, again taken from Lodge *et al.* (1997: 65):

(10)   toucher / percevoir / * recevoir son salaire

       prononcer / * donner un discours

       essuyer / * rencontrer un échec

These restrictions are arbitrary in the sense that there is no strong semantic reason why one should not *recevoir son salaire* in French. The language has selected *toucher* and *percevoir*, for no very readily apparent reason. Although in principle rather different, selectional and colloca-tional restrictions can in fact shade into another. We used the example of 'rancid' in Chapter 2 to illustrate collocation, remarking that the adjective collocates with 'cheese', 'butter' and perhaps 'milk'. 'Rancid aluminium' (the title of a recent film) breaks the collocational pattern to achieve a certain type of stylistic effect. Clearly therefore, 'rancid' collocates most closely with certain dairy products. Baker (1992: 47) suggests that the collocation 'rancid eggs' is unacceptable or at least unlikely. Consultation of a large corpus of spontaneously occurring English would be needed to check this[1], but as Baker points out, collocation has to do with 'semanti-cally arbitrary restrictions which do not follow logically from the propo-sitional meaning of the word'. We can perhaps push the semantic scope of 'rancid' further, suggesting that it can collocate with 'socks' or 'bedroom', to illustrate the point that while to some extent fuzzy at the edges, the scope of 'rancid' essentially qualifies part of an organic, perishable area of experience capable of producing unpleasant smells when attacked by bacteria. But the scope cannot be extended very far, and the large arbitrary element of collocation has important consequences for language-learners. Because it is largely arbitrary, it is not capable of reduction to a system of rules; so for example, one must simply learn that in English one 'toasts' bread, even though its brief exposure to fierce heat differs in no essential way from grilling.

The difficulty for the translator is not so much to recognise an SL collocation as to find an acceptable TL equivalent, taking care not to be led astray by the TL form into a literal translation that might be stilted or even misleading. Astington (1983: 121) has the following example:

(11)   *Notre civilisation est tout simplement incapable de résoudre les problèmes qui nous préoccupent*

       'Our culture simply doesn't have the answers to our problems'

Astington makes the point that while English has the possibility of combining 'problem' with 'answer' and 'solution', French has a narrower scope, being limited to the related terms *résoudre* and *solution*. This breadth or narrowness of expressive possibility may of course work in either direction between TL and SL; that is, the TL may have more than one collocative option where the SL has only one, as in the preceding example, or the converse may be true.

The following passage is noticeable for the number of collocations in a short space. It is from *L'Alsace Lundi*, a regional newspaper, and concerns a fire in a restaurant:

(12)   … tel est le triste bilan du très *violent incendie* qui, à la suite d'une *forte explosion* de gaz, a entièrement *ravagé un restaurant* …

This example illustrates quite vividly the different combination patterns across the two languages: a 'violent blaze' seems less idiomatic than an 'intense blaze'; an explosion is 'powerful' rather than 'strong' in English; and the verb 'ravage' in English collocates with nouns like 'face' and 'landscape'. A more idiomatic rendering would perhaps be: '… entirely gutted the restaurant'.

The following examples are disparate in type, but they each show the need for the translator to get away from the SL collocation and engage in consultation; whether of their intuition, reference works, or colleagues. Some cases are more difficult than others:

(13) *portable scotché à l'oreille*	with a mobile glued to his / her ear'
ces délicieuses enfants	'these delightful children'
d'une importance capitale	'of paramount importance'
l'exégèse dominante	'the prevailing theory / hypothesis / explanation'
les dents qui se chevauchent	'snaggle teeth'
un mois creux	'a slack / quiet month' (for business)

The first three example are very straightforward illustrations of combinations that are permissible in the SL but not in the TL: 'with a mobile taped to his / her ear' reads very oddly, while 'these delicious children' is at best extremely affected, and 'of capital importance' totally unidiomatic. The fourth example relates to the Latinate bias of French: clearly, although 'exegesis' exists in English, the term is not characteristic of an everyday register, while English 'dominant', at least to the present writer, looks unidiomatic alongside 'theory / hypothesis / explanation', etc. The fifth example simply shows the need to ransack works of reference for the suitable English collocation, and to resist the influence of the SL structure by writing 'overlapping teeth' or something similar. The last example in (13) illustrates what Baker (1992: 53) calls 'collocational meaning'; the phenomenon whereby (in this case) an adjective needs a different translation according to the noun that it qualifies. Many collocations of this type are of course in the dictionary, while some less frequent ones may need independent thought or research. In many cases, success in finding the right collocation seems simply to depend on an adequate range of reading.

To illustrate the concept of collocational meaning, Baker has the example of the English adjective 'dry', which would require a different English–French translation in each of the following collocations:

(14)   dry voice dry book dry humour dry wine dry bread dry run

Translation in the opposite direction is capable of causing difficulties due to SL influence; for example, *répondre d'un ton sec* translates as 'to reply sharply' rather than 'drily'. A further example, among many others, is the adjective *blanc*:

(15) *une nuit blanche*	'a sleepless night'
une colère blanche	'a towering rage'
un jeu blanc	'a love game' (in tennis)

The example of *une colère blanche* illustrates the need for the translator to develop his or her own reference tools: the collocation is not listed in any of the standard dictionaries. More frequent collocations are *une colère noire* and *une colère bleue*. Again, independent research might be needed here to establish whether more or less subtle differences are expressed by these metaphorical colour combinations. A further colour term that may be translated variously is *noir*: *une noire journée* can be rendered 'a disastrous day', etc. The placing of an adjective before the noun, where it is usually found post-posed, is of course a stylistic device used for emphasis; an English adverb may be needed to reproduce this emphasis. Other adjectives of the type where meaning depends on collocation are discussed in the following section.

It is worth noting finally the difference of meaning produced by the position of certain adjectives. Byrne and Churchill (1993: 106–9) provide a full list; some are well known, such as the following:

(16)   *une ancienne église*   *une église ancienne*

Others, such as *méchant* and *mauvais*, by reason perhaps of being more frequent and hence less 'visible' are more likely to lead the translator into error. No general strategy governing the translation of collocations can be recommended beyond eternal vigilance.

We may note finally that the false-friend and collocational problems can sometimes coincide, as in the following example:

(17)   *un délai de décence*   'a decent interval'

Attitudinal Adjectives

Following on from adjectives whose meaning depends on their position, we mention those whose collocational meaning can differ quite strikingly from their literal meaning when found in other contexts. The most extreme examples are those like English 'old', which when qualifying a noun in attributive position – placed before it – can convey meaning that is rather hard to define precisely, but is connected with the communication of warmth or interest on the speaker's part, as in: 'how's the old leg?'. The French term for this phenomenon is *les adjectives en position affective*, where 'affective', in French as in English, means 'relating to the emotions'. Thus the use of 'old' here adds nothing in conceptual terms, but conveys the concern of the speaker for the leg of the hearer. The selection of 'old' to do this task is clearly quite arbitrary, as shown by a possible translation following another noun:

(18)   'how's the old book?'   *et ce fameux livre?*

This example clearly shows that *fameux* is capable of being used in this 'affective' sense, apart from its core meanings of 'famous' and 'splendid'. Another French adjective that can be used in this way is *petit*, as in the following examples:

(19)   *je boirais bien un petit scotch*   I could do with a nice whisky'

   il courait d'un groupe à l'autre, [...] *avait un petit mot pour chacun*

   'he would hurry from one group to the next [...] with a kind word for each'

Sometimes the use of *petit* can convey not warmth but disapproval, as in the following example taken from a review of the David Mamet film *State and Main* (French title *Séquences et conséquences*):

(20)   *David Mamet semblait tout désigné pour exécuter cette satire du petit monde du cinéma*

   David Mamet seemed the ideal person to make this satire of the cosy little world of the film industry

Depending on the translator's interpretation of what precisely *petit* is intended to convey here, the translation could perhaps be expanded or transposed to 'small world' (to evoke the English cliché), 'claustrophobic', 'inward-looking', 'self-regarding', and so forth.

   The characteristic of the adjectives discussed above is that they precede the noun; they are gradable (as in our discussion of antonyms: 'old', *petit* and *fameux* can all be thought of in terms of more or less); and they provide as it were a passing comment on the noun, rather than extending its meaning in any real sense. By contrast, an adjective that does extend the meaning of a noun needs a literal translation: *une table hexagonale* is one distinguished objectively from round, square, etc. tables. In the jargon, adjectives like *petit* and *fameux* provide 'intension' rather 'extension' of meaning, and apart from these examples, whose translation can be quite free in some cases, other gradable adjectives can be translated in a way that does not lay too much stress on the literal sense, as in the following cases, taken from Jones (1996, 321–2); the second one is adapted:

(21)   je vous remercie de cet excellent repas

   cet extraordinaire résultat a suscité un tollé général

Jones calls adjectives of this type 'attitudinal', quite clearly because again they do not qualify the noun in a truly objective sense, but simply express the speaker's attitude towards it. They are capable of a fairly free translation, although not so free as *petit* and *fameux*. Adjectives like these cause no substantial translation difficulties; they are fairly common in arts journalism where writers, composers etc. may be referred to using epithets like 'major' and 'distinguished'. These also are adjectives of intension with little objective meaning, but can usually be closely matched across the two languages.

The examples in (21) also illustrate the French tendency towards the use of more intense attitudinal adjectives where English tends to show more reserve. Some further examples, from Fuller (1973: 15):

(22)   le brillant discours de M …

        brillament exposé par …

Fuller comments: 'the translator must remember the tendency in certain languages to use superlatives, and the consequent need to tone down the [TL] language so as to reproduce the meaning rather than the words'. For *brillant* Fuller suggests that '"excellent", "able" will often sound less fulsome; similarly, "skilfully", "ably" for *brillament*. At the same time, of course, "brilliant(ly)" is sometimes just the word needed.'

A further striking example of an attitudinal adjective is *sacré*, another term whose rendering depends on the following noun, and on the translator's understanding of the surrounding context; or both:

(23)   *c'était une sacrée piscine*   'it was a really good pool'

        c'est un sacré mensonge   'that's an outrageous lie'

The general rule therefore is to be wary of attributive gradable adjectives which in both languages are used to describe the speaker's or writer's attitude: extreme cases may require a very free translation. The situation is more complex in French, because the normal position for an attributive adjective is after the noun rather than before. So, some French adjectives of the attitudinal type placed after the noun can also have what Astington (1983: 26) calls 'multiple equivalence' in English; that is, they may need to be translated variously, again of course depending on the noun they qualify. We discuss multiple equivalence more fully in Chapter 7. The issue of attitudinal adjectives brings us back to collocational meaning, although of a specialised type. A further example is the adjective *fou*, which needs to be translated by a suitable equivalent according to the noun qualified:

(24)   *un prix fou*   'a ridiculous price'

        un charme fou   'extraordinary charm'

        un mal fou   'incredible difficulty'

We can note finally that some English nouns used adjectivally have this affective sense: 'family baker', 'executive housing', etc. The same principle of non-literal translation applies: *boulanger artisanal, des immeubles de grand standing*.

Word compounds

We discussed in the previous chapter the composition of the very frequent noun + preposition + noun sequence, at that point from the angle of an analysis of the internal structure of such sequences, with a view to determining their status as words. As with the collocations discussed above, we can consider the meaning of compound nouns or adjectives from the viewpoint of potential mistranslation caused by the influence of the SL structure. An interesting example is the compound *prêt-à-porter*; the literal meaning is of course 'ready-to-wear', and indeed bilingual dictionaries have the translation 'ready-to-wear', 'off-the-peg' (UK) and 'off-the-rack' (US). However, a look in the English side of the recent Collins-Robert one-volume bilingual dictionary (1999; 5th edition) gives *de confection* for 'off-the-peg' – and *prêt-à-porter* for 'ready-to-wear'. Consultation of native-speakers suggests that *prêt-à-porter* is perhaps more suitably translated as 'designer' when an adjective ('designer suit', etc., depending on context), perhaps as 'designer wear' when a noun. Certainly 'off-the-peg' is now slightly pejorative in English, and is far removed from the glamorous *prêt-à-porter*. In a discussion of the fashion industry, the literal translation 'ready-to-wear' may be suitable, in contradistinction to clothes that are made to measure. Context is all; in this particular context, a literal translation will often be suitable. But at first approach, a literal rendering needs to be regarded always with scepticism. Another general conclusion is to beware of (especially bilingual) dictionaries, even ones that otherwise are of proven worth.

As Vinay and Darbelnet (1995: 126) point out, the noun + preposition + noun structure, very common in French, will often not translate literally in English, as the following examples show:

(25) *un drôle de type* 'a strange fellow'

  un Américain de naissance 'a native American'

  espèce de crétin 'stupid idiot'

Idioms

Ketteridge (1956: v) expresses the difference between an idiom and a figurative expression as follows: 'An idiom is an expression the meaning of which cannot be deduced from its component parts. [...] In a figurative phrase, the words have their ordinary connections and relation, but are used metaphorically.' One can add that many idioms are metaphors whose figurative force has been lost, since they refer to cultural practices long vanished. Thus, whereas the figurative phrase *porter de l'eau à la mer* 'to carry coals to Newcastle' is still transparent, *être sur les dents* 'to be done up' (with tiredness) is not; a little research into the history of the language would be needed to establish the figurative reference of the latter phrase. The *Dictionnaire des Locutions françaises* by Rat (1957) is a useful guide to the origin of idioms such as this, and indeed consultation of a dictionary of this type may help to fix the meaning of an idiom in the mind of the translator, on the principle that a phrase whose meaning is transparent will be more easily retained – studies have shown that subjects of psychological tests memorise meaningful sequences of sounds more easily than mere gibberish.

This is especially true where the reference of an idiom is so thoroughly archaic that any figurative force is lost: an example is *l'échapper belle* 'to have a narrow escape', where the feminine inflection of the adverbial is obscure. A monolingual dictionary will quite often provide the historical source. Such collocations are of course capable of causing decoding problems, again since their meaning, by definition, is not readily apparent from their surface structure, or can be misleading. They may lack an equivalent in the TL. Two examples are the following, which Scott-Moncrieff famously mistranslated from *Un amour de Swann*:

(26)   une beauté de diable

        mener une vie de bâton de chaise

The difficulty attending the first example is clearly the surface structure; Scott-Moncrieff mistranslated it as 'devilish pretty', while in fact the phrase translates suitably as 'the bloom of youth'. The second, translated by Scott-Moncrieff as 'a cat and dog life' (implying constant quarrelling, often between husband and wife), in fact conveys the sense of 'to lead a fast life', in the sense of a frenetic pursuit of pleasure – 'to have a hectic social life' would perhaps be the most current translation.

Incidentally, the English phrase should have been written 'a cat-and-dog life', because where a noun phrase functions as an attributive adjective, the noun phrase is conventionally hyphenated. Correspondingly, a noun phrase functioning as a 'predicative adjective' – placed after the noun – is not hyphenated. So, one should write 'fair-haired children', but 'children who are fair haired'; 'over-familiar examples', but 'examples that are over familiar'. This rule can be called arbitrary or conventional, since ambiguity is unlikely – supposedly ambiguous examples like 'a man-eating tiger' as against 'a man eating tiger' are for amusement only. Nevertheless, adherence to this rule is an aspect of 'communicative competence', as discussed in Chapter 2. The rule is conventional, but a translator who fails to observe the rule potentially causes the reader to pause unnecessarily, if only to register irritation. Like other types of conventional behaviour, the hyphenation of noun phrases used as attributive adjectives needs to be observed at a formal level; it allows the reader to concentrate on the message contained in the text without the distraction of speculating on the competence of the translator. It is one of the many aspects of the need to adhere to the norms of the standard language where these are required.

Returning to the translation of idioms, the English–French example below shows a translator taken unawares by an English idiom that needed just a little more research for a satisfactory rendering. The passage is from *The Boy who Followed Ripley*, by Patricia Highsmith; in French, *Sur les pas de Ripley*. The phrase 'to sleep like a top' seems likely to be analysed by an English native-speaker as referring to the 'spinning top' sense of the word, puzzling as this may be. But consultation of the dictionary shows the relevant sense to be 'top' as a sort of mollusc, akin to a limpet, from whose shape the 'spinning top' sense was perhaps coined. Limpets are clearly rather inert creatures, and the comparison to the fact of sleeping like one is vivid, although now no longer transparent in English. This example shows again an idiom whose earlier reference has been lost. What is unfortunate in the example below is that the translator has chosen to interpolate an element not present in the ST, perhaps to amuse a French reader with one of the oddities of English. A more convoluted interpretation might be that the translator wished to attribute to Tom Ripley, the principal character in the novel and rather an unpleasant one, a misinterpretation of the idiom in order to show him in a ridiculous light, but this seems unnecessarily fine-spun. It seems safe to assume that the mistranslated interpolation is simply the product of inadequate research; it is particularly gratuitous since no expansion was needed from SL to TL.

(27)   Tom, taking off his sweater, realized that he was going to sleep like a top tonight, but he didn't want to get into an etymological discussion of sleeping like a top, in case Eric was interested in the phrase, so Tom said nothing [...]

Tom, en enlevant son pull à col roulé, se rendit compte qu'il allait dormir comme un loir cette nuit, ce qui en américain se disait *to sleep like a top* (dormir comme un sommet!); mais il se retint de prononcer l'expression, qui ne manquerait pas d'intéresser Eric, car il ne tenait pas à entamer une nouvelle discussion étymologique.

The interference produced by this type of error in the mind of the English reader of an English novel translated into French is of course unlikely to be representative, but the example does show the need for thorough research into TL idioms on the part of the non-native translator.

Idioms may be confusing because of their close surface resemblance to each other, as in the following pairs:

(28)   *mettre sur pied*   'to set up,   *mettre à pied*   'to lay off' (workers)
                            establish'
       à poil   'naked'   *au poil*   'excellent'
       mettre à jour   'to update'   *mettre au jour*   'to bring to light'

The first phrase of the first of these three pairs is so transparent as to be figurative rather than idiomatic, while the second needs a little more imagination; it is perhaps useful to set up a mnemonic with 'give someone their marching orders'. The difference between the members of the second and third pairs is harder to rationalise; the underlying linguistic difficulty is that the use of prepositions is often arbitrary. That is, while a phrase like *le livre est sur la table* shows a non-arbitrary or 'motivated' use of a preposition, the choice of preposition in a sequence like *à poil* gives no transparent indication of the meaning. As with false friends, a specialised dictionary of idioms needs to be at hand, for browsing as well as consultation.

Other idioms carry culture-specific information and may need expansion:

(29)   *les trente glorieuses* 'the thirty-year boom period after World War II'

The translation above is from the Collins-Robert, and is about as compressed as possible while remaining clear; but (as ever) depending on context, the translator may feel that a further expansion, gloss or even footnote is required to explain to an English reader why this socio-historical concept is so compactly encoded in French.

Figurative Expressions

As stated above, an idiom is often an image whose figurative force derives from an earlier state of the language and is no longer clear. Similarly, Ketteridge (1956: v) suggests that: 'many similes, lost in current English, are still preserved in French'. This seems true of metaphors as well as similes. A simile is an explicit comparison, often using 'like': 'My love is *like* a red, red rose'; while a metaphor suppresses the explicit element: 'The Iron Duke'. The example of *mener une vie de bâton de chaise*, if representative, seems to endorse the impressionistic observation made by Ketteridge; perhaps the closest equivalent expression in English is 'to live the life of Riley', but this suggests enjoyment and freedom from want

rather than a hectic social round. The following example su̧
an adherence to the classic literary canon that is less noticeab.

(30)   *une année de vaches maigres*   'a lean year'

The reference is from the Old Testament. The issue of interest her
if contemporary French prose tends still to draw upon its literary h   ₋ge
to a greater extent than English, problems of close equivalence may result.
For example:

(31)   *qui sent morveux se mouche*   'if the cap fits, wear it'

Intuition suggests that the French expression is more current than its
English equivalent. If the translator feels that an expression like 'if the cap
fits, wear it' is so outmoded as to be obscure, then a rendering into plainer
language may be the answer, although in this case the gloss might well be
rather wordy: the meaning is something like' 'if you feel the general
remark just made applies to you, then that indicates your guilt'.

   Other English idioms appear to undergo updating, as in the following
example:

(32)   *être sur son trente et un*   'to be dressed up to the nines'

If the English idiom in (32) is felt to be a little archaic for the context, then
'to be in one's Sunday best' is also available. Some dictionaries have 'to be
dressed to kill' as an alternative, but this seems slightly different. As
always, one needs to be prepared to match one's intuitions against those
found in the dictionary; the matching of the phrase to the context is of
course also paramount, since an innovating phrase in an old-fashioned
text will read incongruously, as we pointed out in the previous chapter in
our discussion of style.

Clichés

   These are tired expressions that through overuse have lost their
vividness; indeed it is the very freshness and vividness of a phrase, and
hence its attractiveness, that dooms it to clichédom. We latch on to an
expression like '24/7' and over-use it so much that the freshness quickly
fades. Clichés can cause encoding problems if the SL structure is slavishly
adhered to, as in the English cliché 'to *sit down* and do something'.
Judging by some speakers and writers, one can do little in the English-
speaking world without first sitting down. An equivalent cliché may be
available, as follows:

(33)   'he sat down and wrote the report'   *il prit la plume pour rédiger le
                                             rapport*

The fundamental problem here however, if we concentrate on French–English translation, is twofold. First, the translator needs to be sufficiently versed in the SL to recognise a cliché when it occurs. An English-native-speaker translator certainly needs to be aware of the hackneyed nature of English locutions like 'at the end of the day', 'the fact of the matter is', 'leave no stone unturned', etc., etc., etc. In any case, Eric Partridge's *Dictionary of clichés* is available as a reference tool. There seems unfortunately to be no close equivalent French compilation; although, to the extent that many idioms and figurative expressions are also clichés, handbooks by Ketteridge (1957), Duneton (1978) and Rat (1957) provide some guidance.

The more radical problem still is how to deal with the cliché, when it has been spotted. One can argue against carrying over lack of vividness from SL to TL; for example, the French tag *on peut affirmer sans crainte d'exagération*, rather than rendered by the equivalent 'we can state without fear of exaggeration' could perhaps be improved to: 'we can confidently state', or something similar that does not seem too hackneyed. Against this view, it is possible to argue that the translator should attempt to reproduce the tone of the ST for good or ill, and that a truly faithful translation will convey the 'feel' as well as the sense of the original. This is a fairly complex issue, as the translator who carries over lack of vividness from ST to TT will bear the responsibility for the dullness of the text.

As ever, keen sensitivity to what one is writing is needed, as well as the ability to resist, or at least to consider resisting, the obvious word or phrase. Some writers are acutely aware of the prevalence of clichés, and use them as a source of humour, as shown by a diary-writer in *The Guardian* ('Smallweed', 1 June 2002) at a time when a government minister was being harassed (the clichéd term would be 'hounded') by the press. At such times a public figure, in clichéd terms, is either 'embattled' or 'beleaguered', and the diary-writer tried to amuse his readers by tabulating recent press use of the two terms (see Table 4.3):

Table 4.3 Clichéd terms

	March	*April*	*May*	*Total*
Beleaguered	19	4	15	38
Embattled	17	7	12	36
Total	36	11	27	74

A further, perhaps deeper reason for the prevalence of clichés is that we appear to some extent to store language in 'pre-formed sequences': that is, very common combinations of words that are perhaps stored in their entirety rather than being built up from the individual units they comprise. So speakers are operating to some extent with pre-formed sequences held in the lexicon in the same way as the individual lexical items that are combined to form sentences in the Chomskyan 'creative' sense. Recall that we discussed earlier a basic axiom of linguistics, namely that speakers have a mental dictionary and grammar, and that they use the grammar to combine words from the dictionary and so produce sentences, some of which may never have been heard before. This is the sense in which the language faculty is said to be 'creative'. This idea is plausible for the obvious reason that speakers cannot possess in their minds all the possible sentences of their language, since these are infinite in number.

We can perhaps think of the notion of the pre-formed sequence (PFS) as being complementary to that of the creative linguistic faculty, rather than opposed to it. The PFS concept is also allied to Germain's idea of associative lexical fields: if sets of lexical items of related meaning are stored in associative paradigms for ease of retrieval, they may also be stored in limited syntagmatic sequences for a related reason, ease of combination. Ellis (1996: 118–19, cited in Wray, 2002: 24) has the amusing example of a discussion of PFSs, or what she calls 'formulaic language', which is itself expressed in PFS form:

In-a-nutshell / it-is-important-to-note-that / a-large-part-of-communication / makes-use-of / fixed-expressions. / As-far-as-I-can-see / for-many-of-these-at-least / the-whole-is-more-than-the-sum-of-its-parts. / […]

The sequence quoted by Wray goes on for much longer than this excerpt, suggesting the relative ease with which passages of this kind can be constructed, and hence the extent of the phenomenon. Many of us have seen lists of clichés jocularly provided as padding for essays and reports. As Wray (2002) points out, despite their seeming readiness to talk in a clichéd fashion by reaching for these ready-made chunks, speakers nevertheless show awareness of clichés by using phrases such as 'sleeping like the proverbial' – itself a cliché, of course.

The subject of clichés is a difficult one, since the conscientious writer is presented with a tension between the need, on the one hand to achieve vividness by the avoidance of clichés, and on the other to produce idiomatic prose that conforms to the collocational patterns we have been discussing in this chapter. Cliché-ridden prose is at worst irritating, at best unmemorable, while its opposite runs the risk of conveying an affected, over-worked feel. Personal taste, which is in part the product of the extent and type of the translator's reading, is a further conditioning factor. The most we can safely say is that the translator cannot afford to ignore this issue.

Note

1. Ready consultation of the very large volume of English and French now available on the Internet, to verify whether a collocation is idiomatic, is possible by entering a sequence into a portal such as Google and checking the number of 'hits'. I owe this observation to Aidan Coveney.

Chapter 5

Translation Issues at the Syntactic Level

Definition of Syntax

In linguistics, the grammatical level customarily includes *morphology* (the formation of words from morphemes) and *syntax* (the formation of sentences from words). We considered the morphological level in Chapter 3, as it seemed to make sense to do so when examining problems at the level of the word. In this chapter we consider syntax; as with morphology, translation problems in syntax occur, obviously, where French prefers syntactic arrangements that differ from the equivalent English mode of expression. As before, we shall in this chapter concentrate mostly on French–English translation problems, to do with decoding and especially encoding.

The term syntax is from the Ancient Greek, and means approximately 'arranging together'. It is: 'the branch of grammar dealing with the ways in which words […] are arranged to show connections of meaning within the sentence' (Matthews, 1981: 1). When considering translation difficulties at the syntactic level, we are therefore concerned mostly with how French and English exploit different word order; a further important issue is the toleration of gaps in the SL that have to be filled in the TL, or which require a recast or even an equivalent on another linguistic level. Before looking at specific problems we define some key terms in syntax.

Syntactic Units

We shall have occasion in this chapter and the next to refer to the basic units of syntax: sentence, clause and phrase. Definitions of these are provided below, along with comments on English–French differences.

The Sentence

Various definitions of the sentence have been proposed. For instance, a sentence has been defined in relation to its size: a definition of this sort would run along these lines: 'the sentence is the largest unit recognised in the analysis of syntax'. The problem here is that we can easily construct sentences that are shorter than some phrases or clauses: 'She went', for example. Recall that the word is equally hard to define, and when trying to define the sentence we are faced with the same problem, namely that of establishing an accountable point of view from which the definition is attempted; in other words, one that is justified by the evidence. A more useful definition of the sentence refers to its structural autonomy: this states that a sentence is independent of other sentences for the purposes of description or analysis, even though reference to other sentences in the surrounding text may be necessary for full understanding. The example given above fulfils this condition.

A further way of defining the sentence is from the viewpoint of 'functional analysis', or what the various components of the sentences are doing. Thus we can say that a sentence has minimally to have a subject and a predicate. This latter term means something like 'an element in the sentence that says something about the subject'. Again, the 'She went' sentence above works from this point of view, while an element like 'she' on its own does not.

Yet another way of considering the sentence is by reference to its structure. Using this approach we can say that a sentence consists indispensably of a phrase containing a verb, either transitive (taking an object) or intransitive, and with or without other elements like adjectival, adverbial and noun phrases. We define the phrase below. A sentence can be quite complicated if it contains a 'ditransitive' verb – one that takes both a direct and indirect object, like 'she gave me a pencil'. But at the least complicated level, Julius Caesar's famous summary of one of his military campaigns satisfies the verb criterion used to define the sentence: 'Came, saw, conquered'. This example is of course translated from the Latin *veni, vidi, vici*, and in English illustrates ellipsis, a phenomenon that is quite frequent in both formal and informal language. An English translation that attempts to convey the compression of the original needs to suppress the personal pronouns which Latin can do without in any case. We discuss translation problems connected with ellipsis in a section below, but briefly, it is the omission of easily recoverable elements from a sentence. The omission of pronouns from the translation of Caesar's pronouncement does not damage its status as a sentence, and shows that the verb is the irreducible core of the sentence. We can even imagine the 'She went' example reduced to 'went' in a situation where the context makes the sense plain. From the structural point of view therefore, a verb or verb phrase is the core around which the rest of the sentence is organised. Sentences that seem to lack a verb usually turn out to have one that is underlying, as in: *(il est) excellent, ce vin,* '(this is a) true story'. This structural view of the sentence is compatible with the functional view if we assume that the subject is capable of being elided, while remaining recoverable.

We need to tighten the structural specification further and say that a sentence must contain a 'finite' verb form, defined in Crystal (1991: 137) as 'a form that can occur on its own in an independent sentence or main clause'. In other words, a sentence must contain a verb form of the type capable of occurring in a sentence. More usefully, finite verb forms can be defined negatively: they are verb forms that are not infinitives ('to go') or participles ('going', 'gone'). So according to this specification, 'To sleep; perchance to dream' is not a sentence. More everyday examples are quite often seen in translations from French done by inexperienced translators, such as the following:

(1) *Aveux de provinciaux vieux jeu, sans doute*

'These being admissions from the old-fashioned people of the provinces'

We can quite easily transform the French sequence under (1) into a sentence by undoing the ellipsis. Most obviously, this involves tacking on to the front a 'presentative' construction like *ce sont*; one which presents or leads into the focus of interest in the sentence. To make the English rendering under (1) into a sentence, the non-finite 'being' needs to be replaced by 'are'. This second transformation seems more radical than that performed on the French sequence, since the first merely involves addition (of *ce sont*), as opposed to substitution (of 'are' for 'being'). This example shows that the translator needs to have internalised a rigorous definition of what a sentence is, most crucially in English. The rendering under (1) suggests that the translator has in mind the popular definition of the sentence: 'such portion of a composition or utterance as extends from one full stop to another' (OED). We may recall such a definition from the schoolroom, but it is not adequate as a guide for advanced composition, and is especially misleading in French–English translation. This is because clauses quite often extend from one full stop to another in French, but rather more rarely in English. This brings us to the definition of the clause.

The Clause

The clause is a unit in syntax that is intermediate between phrase and sentence. Some clauses can function in a syntactically independent way, similarly to sentences, as for example *Marie quitta la maison*. A 'main' clause like this can be supplemented by a 'dependent' or 'subordinate' clause, such as *lorsque le taxi arriva*. So quite obviously, a main clause is also a sentence, and thus can function independently, while a subordinate clause cannot, so that the reader needs to keep in mind the main clause to complete the sense of the sequence. Put another way, there is a one-sided relationship between main clause and subordinate clause, such that the former can function without the latter, but not vice versa. This is another reason that explains the fact that the English 'sentence' in (1), 'These being admissions from the old-fashioned people of the provinces', is a subordinate clause. A further relationship possible between clauses is one of coordination, where clauses are of equivalent status rather than one depending on the other: 'June walked and John ran'. Here two sentences are joined by a 'coordinating conjunction' like 'and' or 'while'. The other type of subordinate clause of interest here is the 'relative', one that is introduced by a relative pronoun like 'that', 'which', 'whose', *qui*, *que*, *dont*, etc. From the functional point of view, the basic distinction is between coordination and subordination. Within this latter relationship there is in turn a difference between subordination of the type introduced by conjunctions, and the type that is contained in a relative clause.

Since the problem we are considering centres on the frequency of subordinating and coordinating clauses between two full stops in French compared to English, it seems important to be aware of the linguistic clues (as opposed to common sense or intuition) we can use to recognise a subordinate clause as opposed to a main one. We have already discussed this issue in relation to the 'These being admissions …' sequence, which neither contains a finite verb nor possesses autonomy, and so is not a sentence in the strict definition used here. If the 'These being admissions …' sequence is transformed into a sentence by the substitution of a finite verb, the sentence is then autonomous in terms of its syntax: even though, as stated earlier, reference to another sentence in the text will be needed to make sense at the semantic level. This is of course made plain by the linking word 'these', which points back to the previous sentence. In Chapter 7 we look at issues to do with links between sentences – problems of coherence and cohesion at the wider level of the text.

To resume the example of the *lorsque le taxi arriva* sequence, it is plain that the clause contains a finite verb, but the conjunction *lorsque* shows very clearly the relation between main and subordinate clauses. This latter type should not give trouble, although we discuss in a later section, under 'Structural False Friends', cases where a French conjunction, if translated literally, gives the wrong dependency relationship in English.

An example of the possibility in French of putting a clause between full stops, and even at the beginning of a new paragraph, is the following, taken from a *Le Monde* passage on political *cohabitation*:

(2) Quant à François Mitterrand puis Jacques Chirac, [...] ils ont continué d'incarner le pays, notamment sur la scène internationale.

Au point que les Français ont longtemps paru non seulement s'accommoder de ces deux légitimités concurrentes mais y trouver leur compte [...].

A translation of the second 'sentence' (actually a dependent clause) that runs as follows is unsatisfactory in at least two ways:

(3) 'To the extent that the French have long since seemed, not only to have got used to these competing sources of authority, but also to find some advantage in them'

The French–English translator needs to consider carefully before making a clause of this type 'extend from one full stop to another'. Firstly, the connecting sequence 'to the extent that' leads the eye forward in search of the main clause, then probably back to check that what has been read is in fact a dependent clause that looks superficially like a sentence. As a consequence, time is lost and the reader may experience irritation. This ambiguity can be avoided by using a sequence like 'so much so that' which does not point forwards, but this brings us to the second, more fundamental problem. Dependent clauses that extend from one full stop to another run into problems of acceptability in English; this is a matter of acquired intuition, but a dependent clause presented as a sentence using the OED definition that refers to punctuation has *broadly* a rather pretentious, literary feel in English, while being more widespread in journalistic French and other everyday text types, as the example in (2) shows.

The example above shows further that a feel for sentence identity and punctuation are related. The translator has the choice of rendering the French sequence in (2) as a long sentence separated by a semi-colon, or by two sentences separated by a full stop:

(4) 'As to François Mitterrand and then Jacques Chirac, they continued to symbolise the country, especially on the international stage; so much so that the French have long since seemed, not only to have got used to these competing sources of authority, but also to find some advantage in them'

or 'As to François Mitterrand and then Jacques Chirac, they continued to symbolise the country, especially on the international stage. This was so to the extent that the French have long since seemed, not only to have got used to these competing sources of authority, but also to find some advantage in them'

In summary then, when we consider how French and English distribute stretches of language between full stops, we see a pattern that is familiar on other linguistic levels: an everyday or journalistic tendency in French which looks more literary in English. This is by no means to say that clauses between full stops are unknown in English: a relative clause like: 'None of which …' is not uncommon in journalism. We have been considering a *tendency* whereby full sentences are more frequent in English.

The translator needs therefore a highly developed sense of what the basic sentence is, defined in relation to its syntactic properties, as well as a sense of when it is possible to deviate from this basis in English. Two common deviations in French seem to be the dependent clause between full stops, exemplified above; and the sentence that has undergone ellipsis. We provide further examples of this latter type below, taken from *L'Express*:

(5)   Le 4 × 4 de la godasse

Il existe des traditions familiales. Combien de fois avons-nous, mes filles et moi, entrepris l'escalade de la colline de Chaillot en Range Rover climatisée? <u>Exploit digne de Camel Raid</u>. Partageant nos gènes aventureux, ces délicieuses enfants ne craignent pas la traversée des Halles, trekking d'enfer dans un lieu sauvage aux heures indues, les petons à l'abri – sinon au frais – du fabuleux Pataugas. Son chic se mesure à l'élégant délacement des lacets et à la longueur de la jambe dévoilée entre le haut de la chaussure et le bas de la jupette minimale à l'insolence iridescente. Papa les préférait en escarpins? Elles argueront que le Pataugas, lui, dérobe la cheville aux regards; les jeunes filles d'aujourd'hui sont du dernier pudique. <u>Conflit des générations?</u> <u>Certes: et historique</u>. A leur âge, nous préférions les Clarks. <u>Ces «desert boots» qui ont vaincu Rommel et l'Afrikakorps.</u> Le Pataugas, lui, n'a que tenté de «pacifier» l'Algérie.

The text in (5) is about 150 words long, and the four underlined sequences are elliptical sentences (the first three) or a dependent clause (the last) that would probably require expansion if translated into English. We discuss ellipsis more fully below.

The Phrase

The smallest of the three units of interest here is the phrase. The phrase is a word (*Marie*) or word group (*le type que j'ai vu hier*) functioning as a building block, or constituent in the jargon, of a larger unit (a clause or sentence). A phrase does not have the subject-predicate structure typical of the clause or sentence, and hence is not autonomous. Phrases are of different types, and are defined by reference to their 'head'. This is the indispensable core element in a phrase. The heads are in capitals in the following examples: *le BOURGEOIS provincial*; *le TYPE que j'ai vu hier* (noun phrases). In linguistic terminology, a noun phrase (NP) is a general term covering three types of linguistic item: pronoun; proper names; and what is more usually thought of as a noun phrase, that is determiner + noun, with or without adjectives or other modifying elements (like *que j'ai vu hier*). This is once more a structural description, relying on the linguistic categories of the elements contained in an NP: we shall see below that a functional analysis reveals other types of NPs. The other phrase types are: verb, prepositional, adjectival, adverbial, defined below.

To look briefly at how sentences are composed of phrases, we can consider the following straightforward example:

(6)   Le grand homme mord le chien

In this example it is intuitively plain that, apart from the fact that it is a string of words drawn from different grammatical categories, some of the words are more closely associated than others. If asked to analyse the sentence in (6), at the top level we will arrange the words into two main groups:

(7)   [Le grand homme] + [mord le chien]

Obviously, these groups correspond to what we have so far called 'phrases'. On closer inspection we see that the second of these phrases can be subdivided further:

(8)   [mord] + [le chien]

Having undergone long and gruelling hours of sentence analysis at school, most native speakers of French are quite good at breaking down sentences into their constituent phrases. But even without this training, no native French speaker, or indeed anyone who has an advanced knowledge of the language, would want, for example, to say that the phrase *mord le chien* breaks down into [mord le] + [chien]. One knows intuitively that the definite article *le* 'belongs to' the noun *chien* more closely than to the verb *mord*. We are back once again in the Saussurean realm of structure, this time at the level of the study of the relations between elements of a stretch of language. The study of the structure of sentences tells us that they are not put together in a linear fashion;

elements are arranged hierarchically, in the sense that some elements depend on others and that some elements are more important than others.

To reiterate the definition of the noun phrase given above, we can label phrases like *le grand homme* as noun phrases (NPs) because the head of the phrase is the noun. Similarly, phrases like *mord le chien* are verb phrases (VPs) because the essential element in the phrase is the verb. Other phrasal categories we find in French are:

- prepositional phrases (PPs) which contain a preposition such as *à, de, dans, sur* etc. plus an NP, e.g. *dans la maison, après vous, à six heures*;
- adverbial phrases (AdvPs) which contain an adverb and any elements which qualify it such as *très lentement, tout bêtement*;
- adjectival phrases (APs) such as *complètement stupide*.

Phrases are not limited to any particular length. Depending on the type of phrase, they can be anything from one word to many words long, such as the two NPs, *Marie* which consists only of a proper noun (PN), and *le type qui m'a demandé de lui donner des sous* which contains a noun followed by a relative clause, but which nevertheless can be analysed as an NP as a whole.

A phrase can contain a number of words and indeed other phrases: the head of the phrase can be modified by other elements in the phrase. This is to say that some other element in the phrase can serve to give extra information about, or help identify the head of the phrase. However, the elements that are capable of appearing in different phrases are limited by the category of the phrase in question. Within an NP, nouns can be modified by adjectival phrases (e.g. *le **très petit** garçon*), by prepositional phrases (e.g. *les chaussures **de Marie***) or by a relative clause (e.g. *le type **dont j'ai parlé hier***). Within a verb phrase, verbs can be modified by adverbs, but not by adjectives (e.g. *Il mange **lentement** / *lent*). Words or phrases that modify other words and phrases are always optional, at least to the extent that the omission of a modifying word or phrase will still leave a grammatical sequence, even if the sense is damaged. Other elements in a phrase are not necessarily optional: NPs in French, for example, nearly always contain a determiner, and, if the verb in a VP requires an object or an indirect object, then this must be present in the phrase itself.

As at the levels of the sentence and the phrase, it is useful for translation purposes to understand the distinction between the grammatical category of a phrase and its function in a sentence. In other words, we are looking once again at the difference between a structural and a functional view. In the sentence *J'ai vu Marie **au moment prévu*** the phrase in bold belongs to the category prepositional phrase, because it contains a preposition and an NP. At the same time it functions as a 'time adverbial', giving information about when the action took place. Note that we use the term 'adverbial' when expressing this functional point of view, not 'adverbial phrase', which refers to the structural definition.

There are several issues connected with the phrase level in the context of translation. Firstly, for recognition purposes, it is useful to have a clear idea of the structure and function of the various types of phrase in the two languages, since in the following chapter we will be discussing various translation procedures that involve operations of the phrase → clause type (in this and the following chapter, the symbol '→' means 'can be translated by'). A clear idea of what a phrase can consist of will also help with idiomatic translation. If we consider the example of the noun phrase, we can point out that not all NPs have the clear structure exemplified by *le bourgeois provincial*. So, a French noun phrase having this clear structure may be translatable in English by a noun phrase that has a less 'nouny' or nominal feel. In other words, we are considering again, this time at the phrase level, the issue of nominalisation. One example will suffice to illustrate this:

(9) <u>*sa réaction*</u> *m'a étonné* 'I was amazed at <u>how he reacted</u>'

It makes sense to analyse the underlined elements in these two sentences as NPs, in view of what their function is. This is in spite of the fact that the English NP contains no noun. We can note then that the English translator has sometimes the option of translating a French NP in this way; and also that a literal translation gives a more formal feel:

(10) *sa réaction m'a étonné*   'his reaction amazed me' or 'I was amazed at his reaction'

For some reason, concepts expressed as sentences containing nouns give a formal impression compared to other modes of expression, as in the following examples:

(11) 'Your performance in the test made a good impression on us'

'You performed well in the test and that impressed us'

These two sentences are quite closely equivalent in meaning, but the second is more colloquial. We mentioned in Chapter 3 the well-known fact of the two word-stocks that are available to the translator into English, one learned or 'conceptual' and one colloquial or 'affective': 'large' ~ 'big', etc. etc. Example (11) shows an additional source of alternation, between expression based on nouns and one based on other parts of speech. Again, noun-based expression seems more frequent in French.

Translation of Phrase Function Rather than Structure

We referred above to phrases that have an easily recognisable structure; in phrases of this type, the head or central element is clearly apparent and we can see that a reduction of the phrase to this element would be straightforward. In other cases, there is a mismatch between form and function, and from the translator's point of view some phrases are more conveniently defined in this second, functional way, as in the English example discussed above, 'how he reacted', which functions as a noun phrase even though structurally it is a verb phrase. Other NPs may be ambiguous because an identification of the head is less easy. We gave the example above of *le bourgeois provincial*; here the structure is clear because noun and adjective are plainly identifiable. Molière's title *Le Bourgeois gentilhomme*, at first encounter, may lead to misinterpretation because of the juxtaposition of two nouns, one of which very frequently functions as an adjective. The first noun is in fact the head of the phrase, so that the title would translate as 'The noble bourgeois', not the other way round.

Other cases of noun phrases that are better defined, for the purpose of translation, by their function are adverbials such as the following:

(12)   *respirer avec joie*   'to breathe in exultantly'

     les avions sont arrivés à bon port   'the planes arrived safely'

     un coup d'état conduit en   'a military coup smoothly carried
     douceur   out'

     le Président leva les bras d'un   'the President raised his hands
     air solennel   solemnly'

     on a parlé sans périphrase de   'they spoke uninhibitedly about
     la censure   censorship'

     il ne faut pas s'affoler outre   'we must not get too excited'
     mesure

     il a été séquestré par erreur   'he was wrongly detained'

In these examples we have a prepositional phrase functioning as an adverbial; once again the translation issue is denominalisation, since the English rendering is done most idiomatically through an adverb rather than a phrase containing a noun. These examples are adapted from Astington (1983: 10–13) who makes the point that 'to avoid "heavy" adverbs ending in *–ment*, phrases are used in French'. We can add further that some French adjectives do not have an adverbial form. The fact that

Astington devotes four pages to this issue reflects the frequency of the translation procedure. Astington calls the process 'Adverbial phrase → Adverb', but in our terminology it is 'Adverbial → Adverb'.

In connection with the 'Adverbial → Adverb' process, it is worth adding that a few of the adverbials mentioned by Astington fall into the category of idioms, in the definition given in the previous chapter: 'an expression the meaning of which cannot be deduced from its component parts'. Two examples are as follows:

(13) *je n'ai jamais agi à la légère*　　　'I have never acted rashly'

　　　la decision a été prise à la sauvette　　'the decision was taken hurriedly'

These idiomatic adverbials contrast with others like *sans périphrase*, where we can easily imagine other nouns combining with the preposition to form an adverbial with a different sense.

The opposite case of 'Adverb → Adverbial' seems less common, where a French adverb translates as an English adverbial prepositional phrase. This lesser frequency is shown by the fact that Astington has only four examples, one of which is shown below:

(14) *les routes sont difficilement praticables*

　　　'the roads are passable, but only with difficulty'

The general point we are making here, then, is that an idiomatic translation will often concentrate on the function rather than the structure of a phrase. Procedures that result in a category of word or phrase in the SL being rendered by a different category in the TL are known in the translation terminology as 'transpositions'. A further example from Astington shows a French adjective translated by an English prepositional phrase:

(15) *la production romanesque*　　'the production of novels'

Here again there is a mismatch form and function: the English PP 'of novels' has adjectival force, so that on the analogy of the adverbial we might call it an 'adjectival' (not an adjectival phrase). We discuss further transpositions of this kind in the following chapter.

Having looked at preliminaries and discussed some translation problems located at the sentence, clause and phrase levels, we look now at some disparate issues that concern syntax more generally. Firstly we examine apposition, an area of syntax where French prefers a terser mode of expression than English.

Apposition

Apposition is the placing side by side of two noun phrases that have the same reference, i.e. refer to the same person, thing or concept. There is however a relation of dependency between the two phrases, such that one can be omitted without much damage to the sense. So, with *Paris, [la] capitale de la France*, both noun phrases have the same reference, and the second could be removed without compromising the core meaning. One well-known difference between French and English is the absence of a definite article in the following type of apposition, consisting of proper name + noun phrase:

(16)   *Guillaume Depardieu, (le) fils de Gérard …*

The situation is rather complicated here, because while there is the possibility of variation in French and English, the various renderings of (16) have different stylistic characteristics. Clearly, English can simply use an apostrophe – 'Guillaume Depardieu, Gérard's son …' – but the omission of the definite article gives a slightly old-fashioned flavour to the sequence where 'son of Gérard' is chosen. Omission of the definite article seems commoner in French. It is debatable whether the retention of the definite article emphasises that the child in question is an only son:

(17)   'Guillaume Depardieu, [the] son of Gérard …'

Other cases of apposition may have the potential to cause decoding problems, or at least stand in the way of an idiomatic rendering:

(18)   Système de messagerie polyvalent embarqué, le terminal *Marie* est destiné à exploiter le trafic opérationnel du bord échangé lors de liaisons navire/navire, navire/terre et terre/navire […].

        'An on-board multi-functional messaging system, the *Marie* terminal is designed to manage operational traffic sent during ship-to-ship, ship-to-shore and shore-to-ship exchanges' […]

Or perhaps more idiomatically:

(19)   'The *Marie* terminal is an on-board multi-functional messaging system designed to manage operational traffic sent during ship-to-ship, ship-to-shore and shore-to-ship exchanges' […]

Here the length of the first phrase in apposition, *système de messagerie polyvalent embarqué*, seems to be the factor hindering ease of translation. Note that the indefinite article is indispensable in the TL in this apposed phrase: 'an on-board multi-functional messaging system'.

Absolute constructions

These are defined by the OED, as 'standing out of the usual grammatical relation or syntactical construction with other words'. As so often, the linguistic terminology is unhelpful; the COD gives 'independent' as one of the synonyms of 'absolute', and incidentally defines an absolute construction as 'noun and participle used as adverbial clause'. They seem commoner in French than in English. Fowler's rather daunting definition of an absolute construction is that 'it consists in English of a noun or pronoun that is not the subject or object of any verb or the object of any preposition but is attached to a participle or infinitive'. The difference between apposition and an absolute construction is therefore that the subject is different across the two phrases in the latter construction. The issue, as often, is that French uses the absolute construction fairly copiously in a way that seems archaic in English. Thus, Fowler gives as an example:

(20)   *he a scholar*, it is surprising to find such a blunder

This construction is elliptical, the participle 'being' having been omitted. The French equivalent is more acceptable as an everyday sequence:

(21)   *lui savant*, on s'étonne de trouver une telle bévue

Other examples in English are however perfectly current, such as:

(22)   let us toss for it, *loser to pay*

(23)   *breakfast over*, they left

Other examples are intermediate between currency and archaism, as for example:

(24)   *beard removed*, I did not recognise him

As Hervey and Higgins point out (1992: 230), in certain cases the tense of the verb in the phrase following the absolute may influence how it is translated. In the following example, the absolute phrase may be translated 'As Prime Minister', 'When s/he was Prime Minister', 'When / if elected Prime Minister', etc., depending on the sense of the phrase following.

(25)   *Premier ministre, son rôle dans l'affaire a été / sera / serait …*

On a point of English, it is worth re-emphasising finally that a respectable absolute construction has a subject that is different across the two phrases. The trap to be avoided here is the construction of a sequence which looks superficially like an absolute, to the extent that it consists of a clause + comma + sentence, but which can only be united by a common subject since no other interpretation is syntactically possible. Obviously, the conscientious writer should be incapable of producing a howler like the following (reputedly from an instruction leaflet accompanying a cricket bat):

(26)   'As a new cricket bat, you will want to keep it in good condition ...'

An example that is less glaring, while still providing amusement, is as follows:

(27)   'They [Japanese whiskies] do not imitate Scotch but are very much whiskies in their own right. Drunk in this way, you will discover their true excellence.'

The golden rule is always to ensure that the subject in the absolute cannot be interpreted as being the same as that in the following sentence.

The discussion above may seem to imply that an absolute is always found at the beginning of a sentence, but Hervey and Higgins (1992: 234) have the following example:

(28)   *on célébra Rocroi délivré*   'we celebrated the relief of Rocroi'

This seems to be an absolute in the sense that it can be turned around to look like the type of construction we have just been talking about: *Rocroi délivré, on célébra*. The problem with this analysis is that Rocroi seems to be the direct object of *célébra* in (28). The sentence seems better interpreted as an example of an elliptical construction, along the lines: *on célébra [le fait que] Rocroi [avait été] delivré*. We now discuss ellipsis more fully.

Elliptical Constructions

As stated above, ellipsis is the omission of elements that are present in the fullest version of the sequence in question, and can be reconstructed by the hearer or reader. The spoken language makes much use of ellipsis, often by omitting pronouns and other elements like auxiliary verbs: 'got any suggestions?', *viendra? viendra pas?*, and so on. Ellipsis is however also found in formal prose and verse: one example from many is from Pope's 'Essay on Criticism': 'Authors are partial to their wit, 'tis true, / But are not critics to their judgment too?'

The device is frequent in French, and an English translation will often have to reverse the process. A useful strategy can be to expand the ellipsis mentally in the SL before translating it. Comprehension may sometimes be a problem, as in the following example:

(29)   *Paysan, il se trouve abasourdi par le rythme de la ville*

not   'The peasant is dumbfounded ...'

but   'As a peasant, he is dumbfounded by the pace of life in the town'

Here, *paysan* can be interpreted as an ellipsis of *en tant que paysan*. Other examples are less likely to produce decoding problems than to provide the potential for awkward translation. The general principle is that the elliptical construction needs expansion when translated from French into English.

(30)   *Jeunes, ils couraient des manifs ...*   'When they were young, they joined in the demos ...'

   Devenus des quadras ...   'Now they have become forty-somethings ...'

   Cosmopolite, il appelait de ses voeux la mondialisation

   'As a cosmopolitan, he hoped and prayed for globalisation'

The examples above show that, as is the case with some absolute phrases, the way in which certain elliptical constructions are expanded will depend on what follows. A further example (from Astington, 1983: 7) shows this very clearly. Incidentally, Astington refers to the use of the structure in (31) below as an example of 'adjectives in apposition', but it is more accurately described as ellipsis:

(31)   *Pragmatiques, les Américains ont tiré la leçon de l'expérience brésilienne*

   'Pragmatic as they are, the Americans have drawn a lesson from the Brazilian experiment'

The following passage shows the difference between apposition (italicised) and ellipsis (underlined). The apposition seems to need quite a radical recast here:

(32)   *'Séquences et conséquences', transcription française* sous forme de titre de comédie ringarde de l'appellation originale du film, 'State and Main', raconte un débarquement un peu particulier : celui, dans une paisible bourgade du Vermont, d'une équipe de cinéma, <u>lunettes noires et portable scotché à l'oreille</u>, venue tourner un film.

   'Séquences et conséquences' is the rather corny French-comedy version of the English title, 'State and Main'. The film features a slightly odd sort of invasion: the descent on a sleepy Vermont small town of a cinema crew arriving to shoot a film, complete with dark glasses and mobiles glued to their ears.

We have so far looked at ellipsis at the beginning of a sentence, but of course it occurs elsewhere. We mentioned above that it makes sense to think of the *on célébra Rocroi délivré* sequence as ellipsis rather than a sort of inside-out absolute. If it is ellipsis, the expanded version might be something like *on célébra le fait que Rocroi avait été délivré.* Clearer examples are as follows, the first one taken from Astington (1983: 50):

(33)   *tout donne à penser que, consulté, il souscrirait à ce verdict*

'everything suggests that, were he consulted, he would agree with this verdict'

le clonage perd une part de son intérêt puisque incapable de produire autre chose que des animaux « nés vieux »

'cloning loses some of its interest, since it can produce only animals "born old"'

In these examples, it is easy to reconstruct what has been missed out, and the English translation needs to include the reconstructed element.

Emphasis within the Sentence

We discuss the question of emphasis for two reasons: first, because French and English achieve emphasis differently in speech, and so the subject is directly relevant to the translation of dialogue; and second, because emphasis in speech is mirrored in writing other than in dialogue in the two languages. The influence of stress upon the selection of words and upon word order stems from the contrasting ways in which syllables are stressed in French and English.

The way in which stress works in the two languages is one of the most striking differences between them. Stress can be defined as the degree of force with which a speaker produces a syllable, relative to neighbouring syllables. The degree of force may find expression in increased pitch, length or loudness. The functioning of the stress system is very different in spoken French and English, and is of course reflected in writing in both languages. English puts stress to a variety of uses to which French does not. First, English makes use of stress to distinguish between the grammatical function of many pairs of words whose spelling is identical: for example, between 'increase' (noun) and 'in'crease' (verb) (the symbol ' placed before a syllable indicates it is stressed). Secondly, stress is used in English to indicate contrasts beyond the level of individual words: compare 'blackbird' and 'black 'bird', for example. Thirdly, many English grammatical words have both stressed (or strong) and unstressed (or weak) forms: speakers may use a strong rather than a weak form of a word in order to emphasise what they think is the important element of information in an utterance, as in 'I think John and June should go' (unstressed 'and', pronounced [n]) as opposed to 'I think John 'and June should go' (stressed 'and', pronounced [ænd]).

French is often called a 'syllable-timed' language, while English is described as being 'stress-timed'. In syllable-timed languages, the rhythm of speech is measured in syllables of roughly equal weight, whereas in stress-timed languages it is measured in stressed syllables occurring at regular intervals, regardless of the number of unstressed syllables occurring in between. This has important implications for the way in which poetry is written in the two languages. A more day-to-day consequence of this is that, since every French vowel receives more or less equal stress, the vowels do not reduce to schwa as do those of English. Compare for instance the pronunciation of the vowels in English 'monopoly' and its French equivalent *monopole*.

More significant, however, is the fact that stress in French is relatively fixed, while English has the possibility of displacing stress if need be. This may be illustrated by comparing the following equivalent French and English sentences:

(34) 'Elle 'y 'a 'ache"té 'un 'nouv'eau 'livre "hier

She 'bought a new 'book there 'yesterday

(The symbol '"' indicates the main or 'primary' stress.) Whereas in English the main stress is free to range over the various words in the sentence as emphasis requires, in French the main stress tends to fall in a predicable way on the last syllable of the word-group (phrase or sentence). As a phrase is expanded, the stress is displaced to the last syllable. This can be illustrated by comparing the following French phrases:

(35) une sou'ris

une chauve-sou'ris

une chauve-souris 'brune

Stress is therefore more flexible in English than in French, in the sense that English speakers may choose to emphasise a normally unstressed syllable by displacing stress, provided that in the sentence as a whole stresses continue to be timed at approximately regular intervals. French speakers on the other hand tend to employ additional lexical items or different grammatical constructions to emphasise elements they wish to convey as being important in informational terms. Thus for example, an English speaker may contradict a declarative by using the strong form of a word, as follows:

(36)   You're not going tonight!

Yes I am going! (Weak form: Yes I'm going)

Contrast this with the way a French speaker would contradict the equivalent declarative:

(37)   Tu ne sortiras pas ce soir!

Si, je sortirai! (Unstressed form: Oui, je sortirai)

French uses a different word for 'yes', while English uses a stressed form. To look again at the example of John and June, while English, as we have seen, uses the strong form of 'and' to highlight what is considered to be the informative element of the sentence, i.e. that both John and June should go (and not just John), French would tend to add words:

(38)   Je crois que John devrait y aller, et June aussi

French does however use what we may call contrastive stress to clear up ambiguities, as in the following example:

(39)   J'ai dit ˈrécrire, pas ˈdécrire

Here again the symbol indicates that a greater degree of stress has been applied to the following syllable than to neighbouring ones.

The examples above show how French and English differ in how they emphasise elements within a sentence. The result often is that a French writer will reorganise the syntax of a sentence to place the stressed elements in phrase-final position, since this is where stress normally falls in French. The following example, taken again from the review of 'Séquences et conséquences' discussed above, illustrates this quite neatly:

(40)   *Ces clichés, Mamet ne cherche pas à les éviter …*

'In no way does Mamet seek to avoid these clichés …'

or   'Mamet does not by any means seek to avoid these clichés …'

The unmarked French sentence corresponding to the stressed version in (40) is obviously:

(41)   Mamet ne cherche pas à éviter ces clichés

Here the order of the syntax is basically that which is said to be most frequent in French (and English), namely subject-verb-object (SVO). Clearly, the structure in (41) has a syntax that is slightly more complex than straightforward SVO, but we can ignore this for the purposes of the present discussion. The syntax in (40) is unusual because the object (*ces clichés*) is placed first, then resumed in the form of an object pronoun. The result is to displace the focus of the sentence to what is now found at the end, i.e. the verb group *cherche pas à les éviter*. The obvious way of rendering this in English is to emphasis the element in the sentence that conveys negation, expanding it from 'does not' to something like what is suggested under (40) above.

The issue of emphasis is complex, and we have hardly done more than scratch the surface here. The examples discussed above show that differences in the choice of words in the SL, as well as unusual word order, can be employed to achieve emphasis. Perhaps the commonest indicator is deviation from SVO in formal prose. Astington (1983: 88–9) suggests that 'the use of *c'est* is the commonest way of bringing an element into prominence'. Two of his examples show this use quite clearly:

(42) *ce n'est pas moi qui ai fait cette*   'it was not a discovery of my own'
      découverte

      c'est ainsi que s'écoulaient les   'in such a manner did life pass by'
      jours

In these examples we see again that SVO word order in the French is disrupted for emphasis, and the English translations reflect this. Other devices listed by Astington are the use of *c'est que*, as in:

(43) *c'est que flâner était difficile, dans ce Paris inconnu*

      'you know, strolling was difficult, in this unknown Paris'

In addition, Astington lists repetition, ante-position and post-position. We discuss these last two below; repetition is easily illustrated:

(44) *je voudrais maintenant parler*   'now I'd like to talk of real politics'
      politique, politique

Concerning ante-position and post-position, it is important to point out that in speech (or its representation as dialogue in novels), the use is very frequent of so-called 'NP-doubling', which results in two subjects, as in the following example, or two objects, as in (46) below:

(45) *mon père il a une voiture de service*

      'my Dad's got a company car'

The term 'NP-doubling' covers both the sequence shown in (45), which comprises subject noun phrase + pronoun, and sequences composed of two object NPs (recall that an NP can be a proper name, pronoun or full noun phrase – determiner + noun with or wthout other modifying elements). Terms used to describe this structure proliferate, as shown by Astington's use of 'ante-position and post-position'; but NP-doubling is the most accurate term syntactically. The phenomenon occurs seemingly because French speakers in everyday speech, as well as more formal varieties (as we shall see below), prefer often to operate with subject pronoun + verb form as a single unit, which they do not like to separate if they can avoid doing so. This is not an emphatic device; it merely reflects the quite strong tendency of French speakers to treat subject pronoun + verb form as if it were in fact the verb form. It is logical therefore to wish to use a noun phrase in a sentence where it is needed, alongside the subject pronoun + verb form sequence that often found. This kind of non-emphatic sentence, containing pronoun and noun phrase with the same reference, needs to be distinguished sharply from emphatic sentences of the type shown in (40). Sentences of the type exemplified in (45) are fairly frequent in everyday speech, somewhat less so in more formal speech; they concern the translator therefore where dialogue or interpreting are in question.

In prose, resumption of a noun phrase with a pronoun or relative pronoun does however convey emphasis and should therefore be translated suitably. This is true of some formal speech also. The following examples are both from Astington (1983: 19):

(46)   *ce sens, voila ce que nous allons tenter de mettre en lumière*

'it is this meaning that we shall attempt to make clear'

l'idéologie la plus typiquement française, je ne la crois ni libérale ni socialiste

'if you ask me which is the most typically French ideology, I think it is neither liberal nor socialist'

These examples both show 'ante-position', i.e. of the noun phrase. The second phrase shows, as stated above, that the 'doubled' NP can be an object, although it is usually resumed as a subject. We can point out incidentally that Astington has been misled by a false friend: *libéral*, in a political context, is very often most suitably translated by 'free-market' or 'laissez-faire', and this is the sense that contrasts most plausibly with *socialiste* here. The French politico-economic term *liberal* rarely translates as 'liberal' in the UK or US political senses, unless the term is expanded to make clear what is meant, along the lines of 'economically liberal'.

The conveying of emphasis through 'ante-position', as shown above, seems commoner than 'post-position', where noun phrase follows pronoun. It is not however clear from Astington's two examples that emphasis is in fact the aim:

(47)   *alors, il était inéluctable qu'ils s'affrontent, ces groupes armés*

'so there was bound to be a confrontation between these armed groups'

elle sera longue et dure, la lutte contre l'inflation

'the fight against inflation will be a long and hard one'

Astington's 460 French examples, as he states in his Preface, are taken from 'modern novels, "L'Express" and the news broadcasts of "France-Inter"' This rather vague statement shows the importance of clearly attributing every ST sequence where a discussion of translation procedures is in question; we have of course repeatedly made the point that the translator needs crucially to be aware of the provenance of an ST. It is not made plain whether the sequences in (47) are from a spoken or written source. However, even if they were gathered from *France-Inter*, which clearly is a source of fairly formal speech, there is plenty of evidence to show that even in careful speech styles such as those heard in serious radio and TV discussions, speakers are often operating, as we suggested above, with subject pronoun + verb form as a single unit. This is one reason why the negative particle *ne* is rather rarely heard in everyday speech; speakers are often reluctant to interrupt the subject pronoun + verb form sequence by inserting *ne*. At the same time, the use of *ne* as a marker of formality remains important, so that it is still heard at high levels in formal speech in the spoken media.

What remains unclear is whether the subject doubling seen in the examples in (47) is due to the wish to convey emphasis, or simply to present the subject pronoun + verb form without interruption while the rest of the utterance is being organised 'on-line', as it must be in speech – assuming these examples are drawn from speech. It is perhaps significant that Astington's English translations are not marked by any very noticeable emphatic device. In any event, NP-doubling for emphasis using 'ante-position' of the noun phrase, as in (46), seems commoner than post-position as in (47); if indeed these latter examples show the wish to mark emphasis.

Prepositions

There is a strong tendency for prepositions in French to be 'supported' or replaced by a part of a verb, or another part of speech. As so often, the issue is the avoidance of too slavish an adherence to the ST, as in the following example:

(48)   *des délégations de tous les pays ont adopté un protocole visant à limiter nos émissions de gaz à effet de serre*

'delegations from all countries adopted a protocol to limit our greenhouse-gas emissions'

The translator can consider translating *visant à* in this context, perhaps by 'designed to' rather than 'aiming to', if it felt that what needs stressing is the intention of the protocol rather than its function. But equally, the French tendency to reinforce a preposition should be borne in mind, and as a result the simple omission of *visant*, as shown above, is also worth considering.

The following passage is notable for the number of reinforced or substituted prepositions, which have been italicised:

(49)   A noter que les flux de matière accrétée par les trous noirs supermassifs *tapis* au coeur des galaxies ne se structurent pas toujours sous la forme d'un disque mince, tandis que le transfert de matière *au sein d'*un système binaire s'opère en général *par le truchement* d'un disque d'accrétion.

'It is worth pointing out that flows of matter attracted by supermassive black holes found within galaxies do not always have a thin disk structure, while the transfer of matter in a binary system generally works through an accretion disk.'

The first italicised example, *tapis au coeur des galaxies* is perhaps capable of causing a decoding difficulty: the author has chosen to represent black holes, in a literal translation, as 'crouched in the heart of galaxies'. A part of a verb is necessary here to make clear that black holes and not flows of matter are associated with the heart of galaxies. Nevertheless, a similar image in English reads oddly ('lurking'?), so that a more neutral translation seems to suffice. The second two examples, *au sein d'un système binaire* and *par le truchement*, are very straightforward instances of the French preference for more linguistic material where English is content with a preposition.

Mistranslation can happen where the translator is insufficiently unaware of this tendency. Hervey and Higgins (1992: 239) discuss the translation of prepositional constructions from an English–French point of view, and have the following example:

(50)   'The book can only be sold through a book seller'

Le livre ne peut être vendu que par l'intermédiaire / par l'entremise d'un libraire

Where there is a preceding referent the prepositional phrase *par l'intermé-diaire de* can of course, like others such as *à propos de* and *à l'intention de*, transform as follows:

(51)   Le livre ne peut être vendu que par son intermédiaire

Transformation of this kind can lead the translator into error, as in the following phrase, taken from a book about Eleanor of Aquitaine translated from French:

(52)   'it was through her intermediary that ...'

It seems very likely that this is a misinterpretation of *ce fut par son intermé-diaire*, deriving from *par l'intermédiaire d'Eléonore d'Aquitaine*. The translator, perhaps unaware of this derivation, seems to have translated the French too literally. A rendering such as 'it was through her agency' would convey the correct sense, since 'it was through her intermediary' implies animate agent rather than abstract influence. This is not a case where very formal English could have 'intermediary' synonymous with 'agency'.

Idiomatic Constructions

While dictionaries of idiomatic phrases are available, what we might call idioms at the syntactic level, or idiomatic constructions, are more likely to cause difficulty, since while they are the object of comment scattered through grammars and other textbooks, no compilation appears to exist. A further problem is that such constructions may be difficult to find in dictionaries and grammars, because they are often composed of frequent grammatical words, as is the case of the construction:

et + [subject] + *de* + infinitive

The following example shows *et* + subject + infinitive:

(53)   *La France a demandé un délai de réflexion. Et le Royaume-Uni de faire de même*

        'France has asked for time to reflect. And the United Kingdom has done likewise'

Both the Oxford-Hachette and the Collins-Robert have examples of this construction under the *et* article, although both use pronouns rather than full noun phrases. The Oxford-Hachette example is as follows:

(54)   *et lui de sourire*   'whereupon he smiled'

A sequence without a noun phrase is also possible:

(55)   Durand sourit. Et de répondre doucement …

In Chapter 4 we mentioned the use of the conditional in an 'epistemic' sense, to convey the writer's state of knowledge of the subject of discussion. A further idiosyncratic use of the tense is with the sense of *même si*, as follows:

(56)   *On aurait voulu échouer qu'on ne s'y serait pas pris autrement*

Even if we had wanted to fail, we wouldn't have gone about it differently

A further construction replacing *même si* is the following, using *quand même* + conditional:

(57)   *Quand même n'existeraient pas des raisons d'opportunité, il faudrait essayer de négocier*

'Even if negotiations could not be justified on grounds of opportuneness …'

Incidentally, this example shows the pristine sense of French *opportunité*. The rather learned 'opportuneness' could perhaps be replaced here by 'timing': something is opportune when the time is right for it to happen. This is unfortunately a case where *glissage* is occurring in French under English influence, so careful attention is needed every time to determine whether a use of *opportunité* is translatable in the original sense of 'timing', or in the newer sense of English 'opportunity'.

Inversion

We referred very briefly in Chapter 1 to the relative prevalence in French of inverted constructions compared to English. This issue should not normally cause problems of decoding or encoding, although the first encounter in French with a verb at the very beginning of a sentence tends to be disconcerting; it must be excessively rare in English outside of poetry. A little thought is needed to produce an English rendering that is not clumsy. The following example is taken from a fairly technical document on taxation, but verb-first constructions are not too uncommon in formal non-technical French of the type found in *Le Monde*.

(58)   Sont exclues du champ d'application de la taxe, les personnes morales dont:

– les immeubles situés en France autres que ceux affectés à leur propre exploitation, industrielle, commerciale, agricole ou à l'exercice d'une profession non commerciale, représentent moins de 50% de leurs actifs français (c'est-à-dire les sociétés, dont le siège est situé hors de France, qui ne peuvent être considérées comme à prépondérance immobilière).

'The following legal entities are exempt from the tax:

– those whose real property situated in France, other that reserved for the industrial, commercial or agricultural use of the legal entity, or for non-commercial use, represents less than 50% of their French assets (that is, those companies whose head office is outside France and which cannot be considered preponderantly a property company).'

Inversion of the type shown above seems motivated by the desire to place the information of interest where it is more likely to gain attention. The frequent, less meaningful word *sont* is therefore placed first so that the reader is led to focus on the important information. This conforms to the so-called 'end-focus' principle that places information of interest at the end of a sequence. We shall have more to say about this in Chapter 7, in connection with issues at the text level.

Inversion is sometimes simply called for by the syntax of French, as in the case of certain adverbs and adverbial phrases like *à peine, sans doute, peut-être* (Byrne & Churchill, 1993: 468 give a full list). Another item in this list is *aussi*, which of course commonly means 'also', but conveys 'therefore' in the sequence below. The clue (apart from the sense of the passage) is the inversion after *aussi*:

(59)   Les résultats bruts d'exploitation ont fortement augmenté grâce à la bonne orientation générale de l'activité tandis que les besoins en fonds de roulement évoluaient peu dans l'ensemble. Aussi, la demande de crédits à court terme s'est-elle inscrite en repli pour le sixième trimestre consécutif.

'Gross operating results have improved substantially thanks to the good general tendency of economic and industrial activity, while overall the need for liquid assets showed little change. Therefore, the demand for short-term credits has gone down for the sixth quarter running.'

The Passive

As all French grammars written for English speakers point out, passive constructions are less common in French than in English. This is due partly to the possibility of using *on* in French, and partly to the use of pronominal constructions such as the following, which we discuss in more detail in the next chapter:

(60)   les pommes se vendent à dix francs le kilo

It is worth pointing out here the possibility of using in English the so-called 'middle' construction, that is an apparently active sentence that in fact has passive force:

(61)   'apples are selling at ten francs a kilo'

Another example:

(62)   *ce genre de texte ne se traduit pas très facilement*

        'this type of text does not translate very easily'

We discuss further examples of French equivalents to the English passive in Chapter 6, when we look at the translation procedures of modulation and tranposition.

Structural False Friends

These are *faux amis* on the level of syntax; they can be harder to spot than their lexical equivalent. The best known concerns the use of *si* in a non-conditional sense. The following example is adapted from the *Le Monde* piece on human-rights legislation already discussed:

(63)   Concrètement, si les premiers condamnés de l'année bénéficieront automatiquement de la nouvelle loi, tout condamné par arrêt prononcé postérieurement au 15 juin 2000 sait d'ores et déjà qu'il pourra lui aussi faire appel de sa condamnation, pour peu que son avocat ait régulièrement formé un pourvoi devant la Cour de cassation.

        'In concrete terms, those sentenced early in 2001 will automatically benefit from the new law, while all those pronounced guilty after 15 June 2000 know already that they can also appeal against their verdict, so long as their lawyer has lodged a valid request for a stay of judgement in the court of appeal.'

Here the use of *si*, as indeed the future-tense form in the following verb implies, does not establish a conditional relationship between the two clauses of interest, but merely a relation of synchronicity: the two events described are taking place more or less over the same period.

A further complication is that English 'if' can translate French *si* with this non-conditional sense, but generally in a higher register of English than the French equivalent, as in the following example (Amis, 1991: 273):

(64)   But if there are disastrous Conservatives, there are also […] sensible men on the political left

A further example from *The Guardian* (8 January 2002) confirms that the construction tends to be found in formal prose:

(65)   But if the tie was fiercely contested, it was no worse than many matches in Britain […]

In both of these examples, 'if' is used in the so-called 'concessive' sense: the author concedes a point, then takes the argument further in the light of the point just conceded. In examples (64) and (65), 'if' could be replaced by 'while' or 'whereas' without damaging the sense. The tendency seems to be that the non-conditional use of *si* / 'if' is commoner in formal registers of English, so that if in doubt, *si* used in this sense should be translated as in (63), or with an equivalent rendering.

A potentially misleading use of *pour* + infinitive can also be thought of as a structural false friend, as in the following example:

(66)   *Un tel système, pour être équitable, comporte des risques*

        'Although such a system might be equitable, it involves some risks'

or   'However equitable such a system might be...'

A further construction that may cause problems of recognition is *que* + subjunctive translatable as 'the fact that ...':

(67)   *Qu'il faille passer pas ces obligations est un scandale*

        '[The fact] that one must submit to these conditions is scandalous'

or   'It is scandalous that one must submit to these conditions'

We can extend the category of structural false friend to include constructions that are highly characteristic and are in need of a basic recast if an idiomatic rendering is sought, such as the following, discussed by Fuller (1973: 30):

(68)   *Ce n'est pas parce qu'un traité a pu être signé ... que les efforts doivent se relâcher*

There is little risk of miscomprehension here; the issue is the need to avoid the influence of the SL syntax. Fuller expresses the matter very strongly:

'Avoid translating this typically French construction by "It is not because … that we can afford …", which sounds nonsensical in English.' It certainly sounds unidiomatic. Fuller suggests:

(69)   'We cannot afford to sit back just because a treaty has been signed'

or   'The fact that a treaty has been signed does not mean that we can afford to …'

Verbs used Intransitively

It is quite common for French to use a transitive verb in an intransitive construction. Translation into English may or may not require a radical recast. Hervey and Higgins (1992: 228) have the following examples, which seem to need nominalisation into English:

(70)   *au risque de scandaliser …*   'at the risk of provoking a scandal …'

         les chiffres rendent morose …   'the figures have produced gloom …'

Other cases may simply require the insertion of an object where the ST has none, as follows:

(71)   *Marie permet d'émettre et de recevoir tous types de messages …*

         '*Marie* allows users to send and receive messages of all types …'

         Vous trouverez sous ce pli un plan du centre ville, pour permettre d'orienter vos premiers pas à votre arrivée

         'You will find enclosed a map of the town centre, to allow you to find your bearings as soon as you arrive'

Non-Standard Syntax

The issue of non-standard syntax is relevant to interpreting and the translation of dialogue and non-standard language in fictional narrative, as well as in some journalism: for instance, *Libération* caters for a younger readership and this is reflected in its sometimes quite informal language, even in discussions of serious subjects. We pointed out in Chapter 1 that syntactic variation is a feature of French that seems more prominent in French than in English. This is true in the sense that variation in syntax, and indeed in grammar generally, is employed by all French speakers to greater or lesser degrees, while in English the use of non-standard grammar polarises groups of speakers. This seems to be because some non-standard grammatical constructions are perceived in English as betraying lack of education, and even of the capacity to think straight. So speakers who use non-standard multiple negation, as in 'I don't want none', often attract stigmatisation, expressed in this case through the argument that multiple negation is illogical on the analogy of mathematical formulae, where two negatives express a positive. This type of argument is of course inapplicable to natural languages, and multiple negation is frequent in Shakespeare and his contemporaries. What has happened is that the standardising process has fastened on features like multiple negation and put them beyond the pale of the standard language. French differs sharply from English in this respect, tolerating a good deal of variation in its grammar.

A striking example is so-called 'WH-interrogation', that is the formulation of questions using a 'WH word' like 'who', 'what', etc. (*qui*, *quoi*, etc. in French). As Gadet (1997: Chapter 12) points out, French speakers potentially have available a considerable array of WH interrogative variant structures, although not all speakers use all of the variants available. The four most common are listed below under (a)–(d), in descending order of socio-stylistic value.

(72) (a) quand venez-vous?

(b) quand est-ce que vous venez?

(c) vous venez quand?

(d) quand vous venez?

Gadet lists 14 variants in total, some surprisingly convoluted, like the following:

(73) (e) c'est quand que c'est que vous venez?

(f) quand que c'est que c'est que vous venez?

Variant (a), realised through inversion of subject pronoun and verb, is now rather formal in everyday French, although still the standard construction in formal writing. Variants (b) and (c) might be called more or less 'neutral' in their socio-stylistic value, while (d) is rather colloquial. Variants (e) and (f) illustrate again the point that socially-coded language is conditioned by input from several social dimensions: sex, age and class are the most frequently studied in sociolinguistics, but others factors like region and ethnicity can also influence language use. The examples under (73) seem to convey somewhat of a rural flavour, perhaps hard to render in English without resorting to exaggerated 'hayseed' stereotypes of the kind found in Thomas Hardy.

As was mentioned briefly in Chapter 1, constructions in English equivalent to those under (45) and (46) are virtually absent, since there is very little optionality in the use of interrogatives. A marginal example is the following:

(74)   When used you to see him? ~ When did you use to see him?

The first variant in (74) in now characteristic of an old-fashioned variety of English. We may point out in passing the quite common mistake of writing 'When did you used to see him?' in sentences like the second one in (74). This is perhaps due to the fact that the verb form 'use', when employed in this 'be accustomed to' sense, is always followed by the infinitive of the verb, and hence by 't', so that it is indistinguishable from 'used' in speech. But writing 'When did you used to see him?' is like writing 'When did you went?': in interrogative sentences like the one in (74), as well as in negative sentences like 'I didn't use to go', the form of 'use' is not in the past after the auxiliary verb 'do'. The ability correctly to manipulate 'use' in this way is one of the shibboleths of English.

To return to questions in English generally, apart from the example in (74) and a few other cases, variation is simply not found in the English interrogative system. As we mentioned in Chapters 1 and 2, translating the French examples in (72) and (73) above will require the use of resources from other linguistic levels or elsewhere in the grammar. As stated previously, this is a problem largely connected with the translation of dialogue, although as we saw in Chapter 2, some French novelists have used the device of importing non-standard language into narrative.

Some other features of non-standard grammar are listed in Table 5.1.

Translation Problems and Procedures in Syntax

One conclusion that emerges from this chapter is that the translation problems that arise in syntax are very disparate. This contrasts with the word level, where we saw that a systematic approach can at least be attempted using concepts like synonymy, hyponymy, collocation, etc. At least within the compass of the present volume, anything like a comprehensive account of syntax is harder, because the combination possibilities at the sentence, clause and phrase levels are so very numerous. Therefore in Chapter 6 we complement the problem-based approach we have adopted in the present chapter by considering a procedure-based approach; looking, as it were, at the remedies available rather than at the various ailments. We supplement this procedure-based view by looking at all of Astington's 57 subject areas, some of which of course overlap with the translation procedures discussed in the standard texts and presented in the following chapter.

Table 5.1 Some French grammatical variables

Variable	Standard variant	Non-standard variant(s)	Comment
auxiliary *avoir/être*	*je suis venu*	*j'ai venu*	Quebec French; Northern France (Lille)
pronouns	*nous allons* (definite reference) *on va* (indefinite reference)	*on va* (definite reference) *vous allez/tu vas* (indefinite reference)	Universal where French is spoken; not highly stigmatised
subject-doubling	*mon père a une voiture de service*	*mon père il a une voiture de service*	As above
omission of complementiser *que*	*je pensais que c'était bien*	*je pensais c'était bien*	Quebec French; very non-standard *banlieue* French in the Hexagon
use of indicative where subjunctive is required standardly	*il faut que j'aille au marché*	*il faut que je vais au marché*	Very non-standard
stranding of prepositions where fronting is standard	*les assiettes sur lesquelles il y avait des crasses*	*les assiettes qu'il y avait des crasses dessus*	Very non-standard
non-standard subject-verb concord in a cleft sentence	*c'est moi qui suis le plus fort*	*c'est moi qu'est le plus fort*	Very non-standard
use of the conditional in conditional clauses where the imperfect is standard	*si ça m'avait intéressé*	*si ça m'aurait intéressé*	Very non-standard
use of *que* instead of *dont*	*mon frère dont je suis toujours sans nouvelles*	*mon frère que je suis toujours sans nouvelles de lui*	Very non-standard

Chapter 6

Translation Types and Procedures

Introduction

In this chapter we attempt to draw together the threads of what has been said so far from a different perspective. We have seen in previous chapters that the linguistic operations performed during translation are very disparate: expansion, contraction, (de)nominalisation, abstraction, and so forth. Whereas previously we have looked at procedures that take place on the various levels of linguistic analysis, here we look at translation devices from the viewpoint of the classification of the types and methods mentioned in the standard texts. This will involve looking at some of the operations discussed in previous chapters, under broader, less disparate headings like 'transposition' and 'modulation'. Firstly however we consider the continuum that runs from literal to free translation.

Everyday discussion distinguishes between 'literal' and 'free' translation. From the more technical viewpoints of textbooks like Hervey and Higgins and Vinay and Darbelnet, we have a similar distinction, and sometimes the same terms: thus, Hervey and Higgins also have a classification of translation types with 'literal' and 'free' at either end of the spectrum, while that used by Vinay and Darbelnet ranges from 'borrowing' to 'adaptation'. Newmark distinguishes between 'semantic' (literal) and 'communicative' (free) translation. Taking account of these various categorisations, we shall attempt to classify the principal linguistic and cultural operations that translators perform, and the different motivations in each case. Concepts that are also useful here are again equivalence, translation loss and compensation, introduced in Chapter 2, as well as the issue of choice: the translator may be obliged by the structures or idioms of the TL to render an SL sequence in a certain way, so that no choice is available. Whether or not choice is available, loss and compensation need often to be borne in mind.

Vinay and Darbelnet's categorisation into 'seven methods' (1995: 30–42), from which some of Hervey and Higgins' types derive, has been adopted by other scholars of translation. For example, the book by Chuquet and Paillard, '*Approches Linguistiques des problèmes de traduction*'

Table 6.1 Vinay and Darbelnet's seven methods of translation

Method	Example
Borrowing	*C'est un must* > 'It's de rigueur'; *commune, parlement* left untranslated
Calque	*Conseil d'Etat* > 'Council of State'
Literal translation	*Quelle heure est-il?* > 'What time is it?'
Transposition	*Traverser en sautant* > 'Jump across'
Modulation	*Complet* > 'No vacancies'
Equivalence	*Quelle heure avez-vous?* > 'What does your watch say?'
Adaptation	*En un clin d'il* > 'Before you can say Jack Robinson'

(1989) takes the sevenfold typology as its starting point. We present the Vinay and Darbelnet categorisation in abbreviated form in Table 6.1, concentrating on French–English translation. For completeness we give all of the seven methods, although we shall see that not all are directly relevant to straightforward translation of the sort we having been looking at so far. Vinay and Darbelnet were perhaps captivated by the mystic significance of the number seven. We shall see in any case that other translation procedures are available. All of the examples below concern French–English translation: or non-translation, in the case of borrowing.

Below we look in more detail at these seven categories.

Borrowing

The process of 'borrowing' is one of the ways in which a language renews its lexicon. As is frequently pointed out in linguistics, this term is inaccurate, because the 'borrowing' of a word is permanent if the term proves its worth in the borrower language. Sometimes the borrowing may prove ephemeral. It makes sense to assume that bilinguals, or those who have a good knowledge of a language other than their mother tongue, are responsible for bringing borrowed words into their native language. The reasons for doing this will be various: for example, the bilingual may feel that a borrowed term expresses a meaning that only a circumlocution can express fully in the mother tongue. If this device is used in translation, the first use will obviously have to be accompanied by an explanation or gloss. Hervey and Higgins have the examples in English of the German words *Zeitgeist* and *Weltanschauung*; these words translate literally as 'spirit of the times' and 'world-view', and are perhaps perceived as expressing the relevant concept more compactly than an English gloss, since German often has 'solid' words that give the impression of concision. A further example is *Schadenfreude*, now well established in English but still very perceptibly a German borrowing. We may note in passing that borrowings most often undergo a shift in meaning: *Zeitgeist* now means in English something like 'latest trend' rather than the more philosophical 'spirit of the times'.

Regarding the process of borrowing from a French–English translation perspective, we can look at the problem in two ways. Firstly, the translator may be confronted with an English word that has recently been 'borrowed' into French. We said above that bilinguals may import a foreign word into their mother tongue because they feel a semantic gap is thereby filled, if only in a more compact way. French has a very large stock of English borrowings – 'loan-words' – that are no longer perceived as such: *budget, club, ticket* are three taken at random. These were borrowed centuries or decades ago and are now fully integrated into French, in the sense of no longer being perceived as English words. They present no substantial translation problems. French examples borrowed into English are Saussure's terms 'langue' and 'parole'; the first word especially is still very transparently French. The terms have however found a niche in a specialised register of English ('parole' has of course common currency in a different sense). Others that are recognisably French reflect aspects of the culture that are perceived as prestigious in the UK and US; the most obvious examples, such as 'à l'américaine', 'à la maître d'hôtel', 'haute couture' 'prêt-à-porter', etc., refer to cooking and fashion. Others are more properly structural, like the use in English of 'à la' to mean 'in the manner of': 'à la James Joyce'. Yet others seem useful because of compact expression: 'noblesse oblige', for example, is crisper than 'privilege entails responsibility'. There are of course countless other French loan-words in English which are now fully integrated into everyday English, having been imported over the centuries since 1066.

More recent English borrowings into French such as *standing, look, must*, have been imported into French as a result of the fascination felt by some French people for certain aspects of Anglo-American (especially American) culture. This fascination is matched by a revulsion felt by other French people, so that the influx of Anglicisms into French has been the object of much debate and even legislation in France. The *Loi Toubon* of 1994 obliged French state employees to use, when composing oral or written state documents, officially approved alternatives to UK and US English terms. Clearly therefore, Anglicisms are attractive to some French people, but threatening to others. By the term 'Anglicism' we mean here a UK or US English word still transparently recognisable as such. The issue here is of course not linguistic, but socio-cultural and political, and the debate reflects the sense of cultural uniqueness that is quite prevalent in France at the political level and elsewhere, and is summed up in the phrase *l'exception française.*

A French writer who uses an Anglicism is perhaps motivated by snobbery of a kind, similarly to an English writer who uses a term like 'au contraire', which can be found in any good English dictionary, but which, like schadenfreude, is still patently a foreign word and is by no means fully integrated into English in the sense of being part of everyone's 'normal' or core vocabulary. In cases like 'au contraire', there exist also perfectly current English alternatives, in contrast to French examples in English like 'folie à deux'; these latter have the genuine advantage of compact expression. Snobbery of the former kind is summed up in the joke: 'Pretentious? Moi?' The translator, when confronted by an Anglicism in a French text that still has a certain exotic value and whose use seemed to be motivated by this type of snobbery, may choose to reproduce the effect produced in the ST by trying to match the exoticism through use of an equivalent French term, as in the example given in Table 6.1, where the effect of the arguably snobbish use of English *must* in French could to some extent be reproduced by the French 'de rigueur' in English. There is of course an equivalence problem here, since the exotic effect produced by the use of borrowing in the two languages conveys an impression of prestige or snobbery that is quite different in each language, so that the connotations of French and France for English speakers differ from the reverse case. Broadly, things French connote 'high' culture for an English speaker – cookery, fashion, art, and so forth, while for the French, Anglo-American artefacts and concepts generally connote popular culture.

A slightly more complex example of borrowing is the following, where a French sociologist discussing the linguistic situation in Quebec (in Labsade, 1990: 96) uses some English words that will have the effect of direct borrowings for a speaker of standard (non-Canadian) French:

(1) La modernité était anglaise. Le français rural s'y est perdu en vains efforts. Il a pu servir encore à exprimer le cercle des souvenirs, des amours, des loisirs, de la colère et de la résignation. Pour le reste, des mots vagues et interchangeables. [...] Du dash à la factorie, du boiler des lavages du lundi matin au grill du samedi soir, la précision venait d'ailleurs.

The writer is contrasting here the social functions of French and English at a certain point in the history of Quebec. The English translator of this text would need to make explicit the fact that 'dash', 'factorie', 'boiler' and used by the author as exotic borrowings. This could be done ͺ typographical emphasis or a footnote. The idiosyncratic spelling of ͺctory' would of course be a help to the translator. The issue here is obviously that the English words in the French text have exotic value simply by reason of being English; when transferred into a translated English text, their exoticism in the original must be indicated by other means.

The second type of borrowing, less marginal but perhaps of less theoretical interest, occurs where a translator chooses to import an SL word directly into the TT. The word will be culture-specific, and the advantage of direct borrowing is compactness. A gloss or footnote will have to accompany the first occurrence of direct and temporary borrowing; so for example, the translator may decide to retain in the original French a word or phrase like *Conseil d'Etat, commune* in the sense of lowest French administrative unit, or *parlement* in the sense of pre-Revolutionary law court. It will be necessary to gloss the term first time round, while retaining the original form on later occasions. The danger is perhaps that look-alikes such as these can lead the reader astray, or simply cause irritation if the original gloss is forgotten. A further possibility is to include a glossary of borrowings that are frequent in the text, if the length of the translation warrants it. Care has to be taken to show that the borrowings are clearly marked as such, using typographical emphasis such as italics. Borrowing of this type is worth considering where the ST word has already been imported into the TL with a different sense, as in the case of English 'commune', or where the ST word resembles an existing TL word, as with *parlement*.

Calques

Calques or semantic translations are common in the English–French direction as a means of expanding the lexicon of the latter language, rather than as a translation procedure as such. The concept is translated word-for-word while the translation conforms to the syntax of the borrowing language. For instance, the concepts underlying French words like *col-bleu* and *gratte-ciel* have been borrowed from English ('blue-collar' and skyscraper') and adapted to conform to French word-structure. These examples illustrate borrowing at one remove. The translator may choose to calque a French term like *Conseil d'Etat, Conseil constitionnel, Palais Bourbon*, etc. by giving the renderings 'Council of State', 'Constitutional Council', 'Bourbon Palace', and again a gloss will be needed at the first occurrence. One advantage is again compactness; a further advantage is that the calque will be transparently recognisable as such if the SL phenomenon referred to is culture-specific, as are the examples given above.

Literal Translation

Literal translations concern the syntax rather than the lexicon. Vinay and Darbelnet suggest that they are usually impossible, and indeed the existence of so many textbooks that attempt to systematise translation procedures makes this seem very likely. We can even suggest that the discussion of translation difficulties starts when the decision has been made in any given instance that literal translation is ruled out. However, we discuss below a broader interpretation of literal translation. A sequence like the following is a good example of literal translation in the sense of word-for-word equivalence:

(2) *Le livre est sur la table* 'The book is on the table'

The example given below (from Vinay and Darbelnet) illustrates the opposite case. A word-for-word rendering of this kind is sometimes known as 'interlinear translation':

(3) 'He looked the picture of health' *Il paraissait l'image de la santé

Interlinear translation is used in linguistic description to illustrate the structure of an unfamiliar language compared to one's own. Strict literal translations can also be used for special effect: the word-for-word rendering into French of English phrases like 'Well I never' *Bien je jamais* are exploited for humorous purposes in publications like *Astérix*. Similarly, a French novelist may portray an English character as speaking French in a more or less literal word-for-word translation from English, to show the character's imperfect mastery of French. So the motivations for using literal 'translation' in this sense are either the wish to produce humour or an exotic effect; or both. The following example, translated literally from the Irish by the humorist Brian O'Nolan ('Myles na Gopaleen') (1968: 276) is typical:

(4) A time after that my brother Paddy moved towards me from being over there in Ameriky. There was great surprise on me he is coming from being over there the second time, because the two sons who were at him were strong hefty ones at that time; and my opinion was that they were on the pig's back to be over there at all.

Here much of the syntax differs considerably from what is idiomatic or indeed grammatical in English, although the sense is clear enough. Again, this example does not relate directly to the translation procedures as discussed in this book, and observation as well as common sense suggest that literal renderings as shown in the preceding examples are rare in everyday translation.

We mentioned in Chapter 2 that a looser interpretation of the term 'literal' is also possible. We suggested that a sentence like 'functions play an important role in science' was translatable 'literally' as *les fonctions jouent un rôle important dans les sciences*, concluding that literal can mean 'word-for-word' translation, if we leave aside basic structural features of the SL and TL, in this case definite and indefinite articles and TT plural where the ST has singular. In this broader interpretation, a literal or 'semantic' translation (using Newmark's term) may be performed to convey what Newmark calls the 'phonoaesthetic' aspect of the ST. Newmark gives the example (1988: 243) of a translation of the famous opening passage from de Gaulle's 'Mémoires de Guerre'. We quote the first two sentences below, along with Newmark's translations, which he calls 'semantic' or 'at the author's level', and 'communicative' or 'at the reader's level':

(5)   Toute me vie, je me suis fait une certaine idée de la France. Le sentiment me l'inspire aussi bien que la raison.

Semantic translation:

'All my life, I have devised for myself a certain idea of France. Feeling inspires me with it as well as reason.'

Communicative translation:

'All my life I have created a certain idea of France for myself. My feeling, as well as my reason, inspires me with this idea.'

One could argue that a semantic translation is worth considering here because of the author's status. The text is 'authoritative' (Newmark's term) in view of the fact that de Gaulle is regarded as a good prose stylist, so that the form of the text as well as the content is of interest. Authoritative texts may be so either on account of the message being conveyed (sets of instructions, from which little or no deviation is advisable) or of the status of the writer. In the case of de Gaulle, both conditions are satisfied – he is considered to be an accomplished writer, and his memoirs are authoritative because written from a privileged position. From the linguistic viewpoint, an English reader of de Gaulle's memoirs may be judged to benefit from a translation that reads like the French in some respects. What respects are these? Newmark's semantic translation has selected English renderings of French words that are not literal: 'devised' for *fait*; 'feeling' for *sentiment*, for example. What gives the literal feel here is that the translation adheres quite closely to the syntax of the original: most notably, *je me suis fait* is rendered as 'I have devised for myself'. The translator who decides that a semantic rendering is suitable will no doubt need to say so in a preface.

This is a fairly complex issue, because any attempt by a translator to convey the phonoaesthetic feel of the ST – an auditory impression of how the syntax of the ST runs compared to a more idiomatic TT – will tend to be vulnerable to slippage as the written language evolves over time. The semantic translation above gives an old-fashioned impression compared to the communicative, and this may please older readers, or those interested in how the ST reads without knowing enough French to read the original. Similarly, the first translation by Scott-Moncrieff of *A la recherche du temps perdu* may be felt by some readers to be 'closer' to what Proust wrote, because composed at about the same time. This perceived closeness may derive in part from adherence to some of the lexical and syntactic features of the original; we have seen repeatedly that on these levels, French tends to retain elements that give an old-fashioned feel when translated literally into English. Proust is of course a rather extreme case, since his syntax is notoriously convoluted, and it is arguable that a good translation should reflect this (the retention of old-fashioned lexis is arguably a different matter). The difficulty is that sooner or later, a translation that reads in a rather old-fashioned way will come to be considered as outmoded to the point of being difficult to read. To take another extreme example, a translation into French of Shakespeare that attempts to reproduce his archaisms is likely to read very oddly, so that one is tempted to say that the French reader who wishes to appreciate these should read him in the original. The essential point here is that a translation is almost always regarded as a secondary text which is not read primarily for its literary interest as expressed in phonoaesthetic terms. In other words, those who read major French authors in translation do so in spite of the translation rather than because of it. The literary qualities of interest in translated work are therefore non-linguistic: subtlety of plot and characterisation, for instance. This suggests that Newmark's category of 'semantic' translation is of more theoretical than practical interest, for everyday text types at least – as opposed to poetry, for instance.

We can perhaps generalise by saying that a French text that is authoritative in the sense discussed above might be a candidate for a translation towards the literal end of the spectrum. However, 'literal' here refers to syntax rather than other linguistic levels. Hervey and Higgins (1992: 61) state categorically that a translation of Proust that disentangles the multiple embedded clauses of the original is a failure. There is however a point beyond which literal translation results in structures that in the TT are ungrammatical: the translator needs therefore to distinguish the threshold between these cases, and those where literal translation gives an unusual stylistic effect that remains grammatical. Much will of course depend on the style of the SL writer; although French tends to tolerate longer sentences than English, Proust's convoluted syntax is a special case.

Linguistic Transposition

Linguistic transposition concerns the grammar, and involves replacing the ST word or structure with a TL word or structure from a different category. We have discussed transposition on numerous occasions so far without referring to it directly as such, apart from a brief mention in the previous chapter. An example of transposition is the replacement of a French noun by another part of speech in English, as in one of Vinay and Darbelnet's examples, the first one cited below. The second concerns transposition from relative pronoun to conjunction. The third shows the common use of a phrasal verb in English:

(6) *Dès son lever*   'After / as soon as s/he gets up'

    ... *aux Etats-Unis, dont le mode de vie lui paraît plus passionnant*

    '... in the United States, where he feels the way of life is more exciting'

    il a traversé le ruisseau en sautant   'he jumped across the stream'

Transposition is very common, and is often obligatory if an idiomatic rendering in the TT is sought. In the first example, the French noun has to be replaced by a verb phrase for a stylistically neutral translation, while a rendering like 'on his / her rising' is possible, but conveys an old-fashioned feel.

In the second example, the relative *dont* reads rather awkwardly if translated literally by 'of which'; furthermore, there is a prescriptive rule against using 'whose' to refer to a non-animate subject, although it is often ignored (and has been in this book). The relative pronoun *dont* is therefore often more idiomatically replaced by the conjunction 'where'. When we consider transposition and the other procedures listed below, we are looking at decisions available after a non-literal translation has been ruled out.

The third example above shows the common case where French has verb + *en* + present participle while French has a 'phrasal verb' – verb + preposition. No choice is available here if an idiomatic rendering into English is aimed at.

It makes sense to think in terms of transposition where we are translating at the level of phrases and longer units that are not set phrases or idioms. To look again at the example in (3) above and reproduced below in (7) with an acceptable translation, we can analyse some of the operations that have taken place using concepts introduced earlier: 'he looked' expands to *il avait l'air,* and clearly French has a noun in this instance where English does not. But when we analyse the phrase further we see that the English phrase is idiomatic: 'to look the picture ...' defies literal translation, as does 'the picture of health'. So we seem to regard a sequence like 'He looked the picture of health' as a single unit and therefore we translate it at this level, rather than on a phrase-by-phrase basis:

(7) 'He looked the picture of health'   *Il avait l'air en pleine forme*

The translation in (7) falls under 'equivalence' discussed below. We look at some further examples of transposition in a subsequent section.

Modulation

This procedure is also common, and concerns principally the semantic level, although syntax is also affected. It involves a change in the viewpoint from SL to TL, as in the following examples:

(8) *objets trouvés*   'lost property'

  chien méchant   'beware of the dog'

  il n'y a pas de quoi   'don't mention it'

  le taux d'abstentions   'the turnout' (in elections)

In these examples, French regards property as found rather than lost, simply describes the dog as dangerous rather than warning against it, states that there is nothing to thank for rather than deprecating thanks, emphasises absence rather than presence. Modulation often concerns set phrases such as those shown above, and is often obligatory, as follows:

(9) *Le moment où ...*   'The time when ...'

Here French selects a conjunction of place, where English has time. Modulation can be optional; Vinay and Darbelnet have the following example:

(10) *Il est facile de démontrer...*   'It is not difficult to show ...'

or *Il est facile de démontrer...*   'It is easy to show ...'

As so often, the translator's intuition needs to be fully tuned in to avoid literal translation. In this category we can also place metaphors, to the extent that the use of a metaphor implies a certain viewpoint. We discuss this issue more fully in the following chapter.

Equivalence, or Pragmatic Translation

This procedure, also common, is a type of modulation that concerns idioms and set phrases, and more generally the 'pragmatic' use of language. The linguistic sub-discipline of pragmatics is concerned with the use of language in context; we explain what this means in the following paragraph. Most of the examples discussed in the preceding sections are independent of context; so for example, we will translate certain syntactic constructions from French by using a phrasal verb, irrespective of what precedes and follows. These examples concern the grammar pure and simple. Purely grammatical also are the cases where the *linguistic* context in which a word is used can affect its meaning: for example, where the sense of *accuser* varies according to the following noun: *accuser reception* 'to acknowledge receipt' against *accuser son âge* 'to show one's age', and so forth.

There are various ways in which language varies according to *social* context. In the preceding chapter we looked at some constructions in French that vary as a function of the social characteristics of the speakers concerned, or the formality of the text: for example, *quand venez-vous?* as against *quand vous venez?*. In examples like these, the stretch of language is linked, by its very structure, to the social and stylistic characteristics of the speech situation. By contrast, the pragmatic level is generally concerned with language that is tied to social context in a different way. Pragmatics is the study of language used in a specific social context to 'do things' rather than 'say things'. Language used in this way will often have a force that goes against what seems to be its literal meaning. In these cases, literal translation may or may not be possible. For example, a speaker may use a 'pragmatic directive' to get someone to do something. The sentence 'Would you mind closing the door?' looks on the surface like a question, and the basic function of a question is a request for information. Despite this, the sentence just quoted is operating as an indirect request or order to close a door. Anyone who ignores the pragmatic force of the question, for example by saying 'No, I don't mind' without closing the door, will be regarded as uncooperative or otherwise inadequate.

Pragmatics is too large a subject to be treated at much length here; Hickey (1998) is a recent and thorough account of the subject considered in connection with translation. We can suggest, very broadly, that stretches of language that have the function of 'doing things' rather than 'saying things' need looking at with care, and are perhaps less likely candidates for literal translation. The linguistic sub-discipline of pragmatics received its first impetus from a book (Austin, 1962) called *How to do Things with Words* (French translation: *Quand dire, c'est faire*). Austin pointed out, as the title of his book implies, that quite often we are doing things, rather than making statements about the world, when we speak or write. Examples are: 'I apologise'; 'I name this ship *The Queen Elizabeth*'; 'I arrest you in the name of the law'. The category of language used to do things is very large. Vinay and Darbelnet have a long chapter entitled 'The Message', much of which is concerned with language use on the pragmatic level. Although we have considered pragmatics under the heading of the 'equivalence' translation strategy, literal translation, modulation, transposition and adaptation are also possible procedures that can deal with problems of the pragmatic use of language. Examples of literal and equivalent translations of a pragmatic use of language are the following:

(11)   *T'as quelle heure?*   'What time have you got?'   (literal)

or   'What does your watch say?'   (equivalence)

This is a translation issue on the pragmatic level because language is being used without literal force, to do something – make a request. Clearly, one does not 'have' the time, and one's watch 'says' nothing. Here English has available two pragmatic ways of requesting the time, although the first is perhaps less current. It is worth noting that one way of requesting the time, perhaps the most direct one, is word-for-word literally identical across the two languages: *Quelle heure est-il*? 'What time is it?'.

As was mentioned above in connection with literal translation, the matching of equivalence can be violated if exoticism or humour are being sought, e.g. 'I say!' *Je dis!*. Stretches of languages used pragmatically can resist ready translation for the reason mentioned in the previous chapter in connection with some syntactic constructions: that is, because they are the object of comment scattered through books of reference, and because they are often composed of frequent words. This is especially true of 'discourse particles' to use the term in linguistics, such as *enfin*. One researcher, Beeching (2001: 104) has listed nine functions fulfilled by *enfin*; clearly, each function is capable of a different translation, as in the following examples:

(12)   1. en dernier lieu (dans un développement ou après une énumération): *Je montrerai enfin que ces deux systèmes sont compatibles*. Translation: 'finally'

       2. marquant le soulagement: *Enfin seuls !* Translation: 'at last!'

       3. bref, pour résumer, en d'autres termes, en effet: *Il est intelligent, travailleur, enfin il a tout pour réussir*. Translation: 'in short', 'in a word'

4. marquant la résignation: *C'est triste mais enfin on n'y peut rien.* Translation: 'after all'

5. marquant une objection à autrui: *Enfin, vous pouvez essayer…* Translation: 'But I mean'

6. marquant l'impatience: *Vas-tu te taire, enfin !* Translation: 'for God's sake!'

7. introduisant un correctif (restriction): *Il pleut tous les jours, enfin presque.* (ou précision): *C'est une robe à peine évasée, enfin presque droite.* Translation: 'well'

8. tout bien considéré, après tout, en somme: *Cet élève qui, enfin, n'est pas sot, ne réussit pas dans son travail.* Translation: 'after all'

9. marquant la perplexité: *Mais enfin, c'est incroyable, une aventure pareille.* Translation: 'I mean'

The examples in (12) show that *enfin* is usually, but not always, translated differently according to its pragmatic force. Other discourse particles capable of different translations according to context are *donc, voilà* and *quoi*. Astington calls this translation issue 'multiple equivalence', and we devote a section to it in the following chapter.

It can be seen from the examples under (11) and (12) that when we talk about the 'pragmatic function' or 'pragmatic force' of a word or phrase, we can mean several different things. Example (11) shows a request for information expressed in an indirect way. The examples under (12) show a discourse particle used in a non-literal way (apart from examples 1. and 2.) to alert the hearer to the speaker's attitude to what is being said. Yet another pragmatic function of language is its use in a 'manipulative' way, alerting the listener or reader to what is following, or demanding attention:

(13)   *remarque, c'est pas toujours facile*   'mind you, it's not always easy'

       écoute, je préfère pas   'look, I'd rather not'

Here the issues are again that literal translation is ruled out, and that the pragmatic force of the uses of *remarque* and *écoute* may not be listed in works of reference. The translation problems in the two examples above are of course quite different: the translation of *remarque* by 'mind you' offers no choice, while a translation of *écoute* is a trap to be avoided, since a rendering by 'listen' rather than 'look' will add forcefulness not intended in the French. The two examples are similar in that in both cases the writer or speaker is doing something (rather than saying something)

with the fragment of language that may rule out litera
can argue that the use of *remarque* in French is a literal
regards what it is doing, which is effectively saying 'pay
I am about to say'. But the English equivalent, 'mind you',
idiomatic. The second example is more complex bec.
distinction between two alternatives must be made.

We look at some further examples of the pragmatic use o. ____ ın
the following section.

Adaptation, or Cultural Transposition

Adaptation is the least literal, or most free, type of translation. Here the focus is on phenomena or practices that are absent in the target culture, rather than operations on linguistic units, although these are of course inevitably concerned. Vinay and Darbelnet (1995: 338) define adaptation as 'The translation method of creating an equivalence of the same value applicable to a different situation than that of the source language'. As an example, the authors suggest that in a country where the fig tree is considered harmful, another tree can be substituted for the fig in the biblical parable. Similarly, a reference to *le cyclisme* in a TT may be suitably conveyed as 'cricket' or 'football' if an allusion to the national sport of each country is intended. The examples taken from 'Adrian Mole' in Chapter 2 show an adroit adaptation, where 'Chinese take-away' is adapted to *petit resto chinois*, reflecting the different eating habits in the two countries. Yet another example is the translation of *il embrassa son père* by 'he greeted his father'. There is a tradition for operas such as *Die Fledermaus*, when staged in translation in a contemporary setting, to contain topical allusions, and this also can be thought as adaptation.

The discussion of *banlieue* earlier in this book can be looked at from the viewpoint of adaptation, since a non-literal translation like 'inner city', 'housing estate', etc., must generally be selected to convey the equivalent in socio-cultural terms. Clearly, judgement needs to be exercised; it would not be sensible, for example, to translate *ETA* as 'IRA' or *Corse* as 'Northern Ireland', even though there are parallels where the France and the UK are concerned. The translator can however consider employing a *specific* adaptation along the lines: 'Corsica, France's Northern Ireland'.

Regarding cultural practices (rather than phenomena) reflected in language, Vinay and Darbelnet have the example of *bon appétit* translated as 'Hi!' In this example, we can imagine a situation in which speaker A sees B sitting at lunch or obviously on the way to lunch, and where a French speaker will tend to say *bon appétit*, an English speaker, while just as likely to express a greeting or good wishes on a given occasion, has not

..e range of fixed 'votive' expressions. By votives we mean expres-
..ns that convey a wish; these are copious in French, have a set structure
and often lack a direct English equivalent, as in the following examples:

(14)   *bonne continuation!*   'take care!'; 'all the best!'

      bonne route!   'safe journey!'

      bon film!   'hope you enjoy the film!'

      bon examen!   'best of luck in the exam!'

Literal force is of course inevitably lost in these cases. The best that can be achieved is faithfulness to the pragmatic function of the TL cultural reference or practice.

Deciding whether a translation requires a search for equivalence or adaptation seems to depend on the linguistic or conceptual distance between the SL and TL sequences. For example, Vinay and Darbelnet give (15) below as equivalence, but (16) as adaptation:

(15)   *Comme un chien dans un jeu de quilles*   'Like a bull in a china-shop'

(16)   *En un clin d'il*   'Before you can [could] say Jack Robinson'

The difference between (15) and (16) is that the image used in (15) in the two languages is essentially the same, but is expressed as it were using different properties. The translation in (15) is therefore a sort of modulation, expressing the concept from a different viewpoint. In (16) the concept is similar but finds very different expression in the two languages; indeed, the English expression is an idiom while the French is fairly transparent. We can perhaps think of equivalence and adaptation as being placed on a continuum rather than sharply demarcated; they share the property of exploiting non-literal translation and focus on socio-cultural phenomena rather than linguistic transformations like noun > verb. But it is apparent that equivalence and adaptation shade into each other, since concepts that are identical across two cultures will have very different modes of expression, as in the examples shown in (13) and (16).

We now consider some other translation procedures beyond the 'seven types'.

Exegetic Translation

The term 'exegesis' is traditionally applied to biblical scholarship, where a text is translated and obscurities explained and commented upon. Exegetic translation is therefore a rather specialised type, not occurring in everyday contexts, and used where practices or phenomena across the two

- Mon Lieutenant, le Général Cambronne vous
demande pour vous dicter cinq lettres !

cultures are different enough to require detailed comment. We have been performing exegetic translation throughout this book, from the point of view of a theory of translation. One can imagine other purposes, to do with language learning: for example, the cartoon above exploits a French idiom and puts it in its historical context using a piece of 'parallel history'. One possible 'exegesis' could begin as follows: the joke in the cartoon depends on the French idiom *'le mot de Cambronne'*, a euphemism for *merde*. The idiom derives from Cambronne, one of Napoleon's generals, who when called upon to surrender at Waterloo is reputed to have replied: *merde!* The euphemism is incidentally of interest to the translator, because (apart from being recalcitrant to translation except through equivalence) it is elusive in reference books: it is listed under *merde* in the *Petit Robert*, but of course one can only find it there if one already knows its meaning; it is however listed under *mot*. The *Petit Larousse* is similarly discreet: it says of Cambronne: *'il aurait répondu à la sommation de se rendre par le mot célèbre auquel reste attaché son nom'*. Which *mot* is not mentioned.

Gist Translation

Gist translation is probably most often practised informally, in other words outside of a professional translation context, when a bilingual is asked to summarise a written document *viva voce*. As in all summary, details and subsidiary arguments are suppressed. It is however possible to envisage other circumstances where translation-cum-summary is carried out: below is the full text dealing with the impact of Human Rights legislation on the right of appeal in the French higher courts, and we can imagine this issue as providing a short article of interest, if only fleetingly and superficially, in an English newspaper. We have already discussed a fragment of this text. The translation below is therefore designed to provide gist, at least to the extent that superfluous material in the ST is left out.

(17)

AU DEBUT DE 2001, LES COURS D'ASSISES CONNAITRONT UNE DEUXIEME VIE

Au 1er janvier 2001, le procès d'assises tel que l'ont connu, <u>depuis deux siècles, des générations d'accusés, d'avocats et de magistrats</u> aura vécu. Au couperet des verdicts succédera, pour celui que la justice reconnaît criminel, un temps inédit: la possibilité, si le jugement ou la peine ne lui conviennent pas, de faire appel et d'être rejugé.

Instaurée conformément aux dispositions de la Convention européenne des droits de l'homme par la loi du 15 juin renforçant la protection de la présomption d'innocence, cette possibilité d'interjeter appel d'une condamnation criminelle (comme c'est le cas pour les délits jugés par les tribunaux correctionnels) constitue une révolution juridique.

Jusqu'à présent, il ne restait au condamné qu'à espérer une faute de procédure – plutôt rare dans les faits – pour voir son procès cassé. En pratique, elle n'en constituera pas moins, pour le monde judiciaire, une révolution culturelle, aux contours imprévisibles.

Concrètement, si les premiers condamnés de l'année bénéficieront automatiquement de la nouvelle loi, tout condamné par arrêt prononcé postérieurement au 15 juin 2000 – <u>c'est-à-dire à partir du vendredi 16 juin 2000</u> – sait d'ores et déjà qu'il pourra lui aussi faire appel de sa condamnation, pour peu que son avocat ait régulièrement formé un pourvoi devant la Cour de cassation.

En effet, le législateur a souhaité que tout recours en instance devant la haute juridiction au 1er janvier 2001 soit susceptible d'être converti en appel à cette date. Or, souhaitant respecter l'esprit de la loi, les hauts magistrats de la chambre criminelle ont décidé ces derniers mois de ne plus examiner les pourvois en attente pour que chacun puisse bénéficier des nouvelles dispositions. Les avocats auront donc <u>dix jours, et dix jours seulement</u>, à partir du 1er janvier, pour confirmer la volonté de leur client d'être effectivement rejugé.

FRENCH CRIMINAL COURTS REBORN FOR THE MILLENIUM

1 January 2001 sees the end of trials in the French Criminal Courts as conducted for two centuries. A new era will follow the irreversible verdicts pronounced in these courts: the possibility of appeal and retrial if those convicted don't accept the judgment.

Introduced to conform to the recent European Human Rights Convention endorsing the presumption of innocence, this new possibility of lodging an appeal against a sentence passed in the Criminal Court, as can already be done in the lower courts, will mean a revolution in the French legal world. Until now, those convicted had to rely on a technicality in their trial to see verdict overturned, which in practice was rather rare. This new procedure will therefore be a cultural upheaval in French law, with unforeseeable outcomes.

In concrete terms, those sentenced early in 2001 will automatically benefit from the new law, while all those pronounced guilty after 15 June 2000 can also appeal against their verdict, so long as they have lodged a valid request in the court of appeal. The French Parliament wanted all cases still pending in the appeal courts on 1 January 2001 to be capable of being converted into an appeal from that date. So, wishing to respect the spirit of the law, appeal judges have decided over the last few months not to examine new appeals, so that all concerned can benefit from the new arrangements. Lawyers will therefore have only ten days, from 1 January, to confirm that their clients want to be retried.

The translation is not much shorter than the original, because of the expansions necessary to adapt the ST for an English readership. Concision has been achieved by eliminating some repetition and redundancy; the most notable examples are underlined in the ST. This is partly a gist translation, and partly a translation adapted to approximate to the snappier style characteristic of English journalism. Note also the tendency for shorter paragraphs in French.

Non-Translation, or Compression

Clearly, there will be occasions where the sensible decision is to leave untranslated a segment of the ST. This procedure differs from non-translation in the form of borrowing as direct importation, discussed above, in that non-translation in the form of compression involves leaving out of the TT elements present in the ST. This will generally occur when the segment contains needless detail that will weary the reader, or information that is difficult to translate concisely because culture-specific, or both – as in the following example. The decision regarding what constitutes 'needless' detail must of course always be taken bearing in mind the skopos or author–reader–text nexus discussed in Chapter 2.

(18) Etudes secondaires de la 6e au baccalauréat, 2e partie au Lycée Fesch d'Ajaccio, sections classiques A (Latin Grec), et pour la 2e

année du Bac et Philo-lettres. Etudes supérieures à Paris à partir de 1948 Lycée Louis le Grand Lettres Supérieures, Première Supérieure. Simultanément études à la Sorbonne Propédeutique, puis Licence de Lettres Classiques.

He went to secondary school at the Lycée Fesch in Ajaccio, specialising in classics and then philosophy and literature. In 1948 he started his higher education in Paris, studying literature at the prestigious Lycée Louis le Grand and doing his first year of university at the Sorbonne at the same time. He subsequently took a degree in classics.

The ST, taken from a brief biographical sketch of the dedicatee of a festschrift, contains details that would need a more or less lengthy circumlocution for full understanding by most English-speaking readers, most notably: *sections classiques A (Latin Grec), et pour la 2e année du Bac et Philo-lettres* and *études à la Sorbonne Propédeutique*. This detail therefore is compressed into a form deemed to be sufficient for the readership of the translation, English-speaking academics.

We can call this procedure either non-translation or compression; we have of course devoted in this book a good deal of space to its opposite, expansion. An expansion worth pointing out in the text above is the addition of 'prestigious' to 'Lycée Louis le Grand'. The motivation is the frequent one of making explicit an attribute that is inherent in the TL term. Note also the sentence-level expansions necessary for translation into English, where French is content with verbless note form; and the use of the historic present in the French, ruled out in English in all but the most poetic literary written texts.

We now examine in more detail transposition and modulation, probably the most frequent translation procedures.

Some Examples of Transposition and Modulation: Astington's Categories

We expressed at the beginning of this chapter the intention to examine translation procedures under broader and less disparate headings. It is true that transposition and modulation are broad categories that can very usefully be borne in mind when translating, but these categories themselves embrace a large and diverse set of linguistic categories and translation procedures that resist systematisation. In the French–English section of his book, Astington has 57 categories, divided between translation procedures and category changes, ranging from 'Abstract → Concrete' through 'De + noun → Adjective', to 'Shift of viewpoint'.

Examples (19) to (75) below illustrate the 57 types. Astington's last category, 'Shift of viewpoint', comes out of order, after the penultimate 'Verb + adverb or adverbial phrase → Verb or verb + preposition'. From this it will be apparent that the categorisation used by Astington is linguistically arbitrary, although frequent in our culture: it is alphabetical. We do not imply criticism by labelling Astington's classification as arbitrary, since he did not set out to classify translation procedures from the linguistic viewpoint. A linguistics-based procedural approach could perhaps have classified procedures in ascending order of linguistic unit, as we have attempted to do in this book using a problem-based approach.

We can perhaps assume that Astington's full list is quite comprehensive, as it is based on 'more than thirty years' experience and on a scrutiny of over 900 passages, 460 French and 450 English' (Astington, Preface). One or more examples are given alongside each category. A classification of this kind illustrates the point that we made in the first chapter of this book, when we suggested that a useful description of the translator's art might result from a 'debriefing' of the kind sometimes carried out with skilled professionals at the end of their career.

When we look at the headings in the French–English section in Astington's book, and consider an example under each, we see that most of the operations discussed are transpositions or modulations. Some are optional, others not. We distinguished between transposition and modulation above by saying that the former is a procedure that operates on word categories, while the latter operates on the point of view. There is however overlap between the two, as a change of viewpoint will often imply a difference in syntax or word category. We shall see further that there is overlap between many of the other categories used by Astington.

(19)   Abstract → Concrete:

   les prix à la consommation   'the price to the consumer'

This is a modulation, since the two languages see the same phenomenon in different ways. It also involves transposition to the extent that we choose to distinguish between concrete and abstract nouns.

(20)   Active → Passive:

   il paraît rarement à New-York   'he is rarely seen in New York'

This is also modulation, and the same remarks apply as to (19), since clearly passive and active sentences have a different syntactic structure. This type of modulation is often optional, although Astington, who devotes nearly two pages to the topic, points out that: 'since the passive is widely used in English, it seems to be the natural translation in many main clauses'.

(21)   Adjective → Noun or noun phrase:

>   *la fraude fiscale*   'tax evasion'

This is a straightforward, non-optional transposition, and is common since the very frequent English adjectival noun + noun sequence is largely absent from French.

(22)   Adjective used as a noun → Noun phrase:

>   *c'est un inconditionnel du pouvoir fort*

>   'he is an unquestioning supporter of firm government'

As above, this is a non-optional transposition. The French use of adjective as noun in this way is allied to the tendency to use past participle as noun, as mentioned in Chapter 3. Astington has as an example of this latter tendency the following: *un déraciné* 'anyone who has been uprooted'. English sometimes has a literal match for the French mode of expression, as in *les blessés* 'the injured'; but a longer English phrase seems usually to be required.

(23)   Adjective → Adverb:

>   *les autres se regardèrent, indécis*   'the others looked at one another, doubtfully'

Once again, this is a non-optional transposition, and quite a common procedure. As stated in the previous chapter, French quite often has recourse to adverbials like *avec joie*, or adjectives with adverbial force. As in the above example, this is necessary quite simply because the adverb associated with the adjective is lacking in French.

(24a) Adjective → Subordinate clause:

>   *cyclique, l'industrie papetière est coutumière de crises*

>   'since it suffers regular fluctuations, the paper industry is accustomed to crises'

As discussed at some length in the previous chapter, this transposition is an example of French ellipsis that most often needs expansion in English. The procedure will almost always be obligatory, though an elliptical construction of the type shown in (24a) will occasionally be found in English, as in the following example, from E.M. Forster's novel, *The Longest Journey* (1984: 182):

(24b) 'Honest, he knew that here were powers he could not cope with, nor, as yet, understand.'

As so often, what is highly literary in English has a wider distribution in French.

(25) Adjective → Adjectival phrase:

le secteur étatisé de l'industrie 'the state-controlled sector of industry'

This obligatory transposition is simply an example of the existence in French of a compact mode of expression that requires expansion in English. Note that Astington's terminology is accurate here: 'state-controlled' is an adjectival phrase contained within the NP 'the state-controlled sector'.

(26) Adjectival phrase → Adjective:

une évocation historique à grand spectacle 'a spectacular historical reconstruction'

Discussed in the previous chapter, this obligatory transposition is a further example of a French PP with adjectival force that translates as an English adjective.

(27) Adverb or adverbial phrase → Adjective:

une ville n'est pas impunément posée sur la plus grosse artère de l'Europe

'a city cannot remain unscathed if it is astride the biggest main road in Europe'

Again as discussed in the previous chapter, this type of transposition is less frequent than the reverse, shown in (29) below, where an English adverb translates a French adverbial. It is worth noting that the Adverb → Adjective transposition in (27) is accompanied by other, more radical adjustments: use of the modal verb 'cannot' plus 'remain' where French simply has the weaker form of expression *être*; and a clause introduced by 'if' in English. We can note that the structure of the French rules out literal translation in this example: 'A city is not situated with impunity on the biggest main road in Europe' reads oddly, because 'with impunity' usually collocates with persons in English. We discuss in the next section more radical, text-level re-orderings of this kind.

(28) Adverb → Phrase (usually adverbial):

très schématiquement, l'historique de la crise est cette fois la suivante

'in brief outline, the history of the latest crisis is as follows'

This type of transposition is essentially the same as in (27). The rendering in (28) is optional, since 'schematically' exists in English. The translation 'very schematically' belongs however to a higher register than 'in brief outline'.

(29)   Adverbial phrase → Adverb:

> *le centre fonctionne sans interruption* 'the centre operates continuously'

We discussed the operation illustrated in (29) in some detail in the previous chapter. Recall that from a functional point of view, the 'Adverbial phrase → Adverb' label is more accurately expressed as 'Adverbial → Adverb'. Transpositions of this type are frequent, and though not always obligatory in the sense that a literal translation is often possible ('without interruption'), the greater frequency of adverbial forms of adjectives in English means that the Adverbial → Adverb operation will often give an idiomatic rendering.

(30)   Affirmative → Negative:

> *le mythe se défend encore assez bien*   'the myth is still not dead'

This is optional modulation, akin to Vinay and Darbelnet's example of *il est facile de démontrer*… translated either by 'it is not difficult to show …' or 'it is easy to show …'. Example (30) is optional because it is possible to formulate an Affirmative → Affirmative rendering, perhaps 'the myth still has some currency'. The translator has no systematic procedure to employ here, only the exercise of native-speaker intuition with a view to determining whether an affirmative or negative rendering is more idiomatic.

(31)   Animate qualities applied to inanimate objects:

> *une angoisse sourde*   'a gnawing anxiety'

Another way of categorising this procedure is by referring to collocation. Astington's comment is that 'cases arise where the two languages do not ascribe the same animate quality'. As in the previous example, no systematic 'procedure' seems available here, beyond the development and exercise of an intuition that alerts the translator to the idiomatic TL collocation.

(32)   'Avoir':

> *elle eut de nouveau ce sourire* …   'once again her face was lit by that smile …'

There is overlap here with 'multiple equivalence', discussed in (44) below and in the next chapter, since the verb *avoir* needs to be translated variously according to the associated noun. The two key elements here are that: (a) a more specific verb is often called for in English when (b) *avoir* has an abstract noun as its object.

(33)   Concrete → Abstract:

   la crise marque un palier   'the crisis is levelling out'

This is another case of overlap between categories in Astington's classification. If we accept that the French mode of expression is more concrete than the English, this may be because the French metaphor strikes the non-native reader more forcibly. We discuss metaphors more fully in the next chapter, but we can point out here that the 'Concrete → Abstract' operation shown above is not absolute, since one can imagine an English rendering that is more abstract still. As we pointed out in Chapter 2, imagery is very common in most types of prose, so much so that it usually passes unnoticed. If we look closely at 'the crisis is levelling out', however, we see that concrete 'level' is being used in an abstract way just as *palier* is in French. One difference is no doubt that English 'level' is more commonly used in the abstract than *palier* is in French. The essential issue here is rather that the French register needs to be matched in English; alternative solutions like 'the crisis is lessening / becoming less acute', etc. are more abstract than 'the crisis is levelling out', and hence perhaps too formal.

(34)   Contraction:

   l'aide aux chômeurs privés de ressources

   'unemployment benefits for those without resources'

The area of contraction is fairly disparate. The example above shows an issue we have already discussed, the reinforcement of French prepositions. Contraction can be used for various reasons; as we saw in a previous section, a common reason is the excision of TT material that would need a long circumlocution for it to be made clear to the ST reader. The contraction (or compression, or non-translation) in (34) has a structural cause, the fact, already noted, that French prepositions often need reinforcement where they can stand alone in English.

(35a)   'Dont':

   la presse, dont je vous rappelle qu'elle est censurée ...

   'the press, and I remind you that it is censored ...'

The issue here is again 'multiple equivalence', the fact that a TL word or phrase can have more than one translation depending on context. We saw above in the section on transposition that *dont* can translate as a conjunction, as in:

(35b) ... *aux Etats-Unis, dont le mode de vie lui paraît plus passionnant*

'... in the United States, where he feels the way of life is more exciting'.

The fact that Astington devotes a page to the translation of *dont* suggests that the problem is not uncommon. The example shown in (35a) shows a relative transposed to a coordinating clause. The other basic operation listed by Astington is the transposition of *dont* to 'with' + present or past participle, as in:

(35c)   *c'est un coteau tranquille dont le flanc escarpé déclive vers l'ouest*

'it is a quiet hill with its steep side sloping west'.

(36)   Emphasis:

c'est que le problème des vacances scolaires est une querelle gigogne ...

'in reality, the school holidays problem is a quarrel with multiple ramifications ...'

We have already discussed emphasis at some length in Chapter 5. Example (36) shows the quite common use of *c'est que* to deviate from the basic SVO sentence structure. Astington's translation is quite a free one; the rendering of *c'est que* by 'the fact is that' is a more obvious and literal solution.

(37a) Expansion:

La querelle de la laïcité 'the vexed question of undenominational schooling'

Example (37a) shows a straightforward case of codability: a compactly encoded French term, *laïcité*, needing expansion in English. This is simply because this issue of the involvement of religion in schooling has been, and to some extent continues to be, a controversial one in France. The other expansion in this phrase from *querelle* to 'vexed question', does not lend itself to such a straightforward explanation: we are simply reduced to saying that the force of French *querelle* cannot be matched by any single word in English, so that it needs expansion to a phrase like 'vexed question' or 'controversial question', or perhaps 'ongoing controversy'.

The 'Expansion' category is one of Astington's longest, and covers nouns, as in (37a); the other major categories are adjectives:

(37b) *ces routes sont maintenant sablées et praticables*

'these roads have now been sanded and are open to traffic'

past participles:

(37c) *ce mort aimé* 'the dead man we had loved'

verbs:

(37d) *pour matraquer l'opinion publique* 'to club public opinion into conformity'

Again, we can say at the simplest level that these examples are structural, and show examples of a more compact mode of expression in French. This is certainly true of (37b) and (37d), which are straightforward cases of French words showing compactness of encoding that is not explicable by cultural factors. The example in (37c) has more to do with syntax, and recalls the cases of ellipsis discussed in the previous chapter.

(38) 'Faire' + infinitive:

cette lettre fait rebondir l'affaire 'this letter gives a new impetus to the affair'

The *faire* + infinitive construction, a 'causative' in the linguistic terminology, can have various translations. A common rendering in English is 'have' + past participle, as in *nous avons fait bâtir une maison* 'we've had a house built'; or in a more old-fashioned register, sometimes used jocularly, 'we've caused a house to be built'. Although Astington has only eight examples of *faire* + infinitive, the translation in every case is non-literal. The conclusion is that the translator will need often to consider a basic recast when confronted with this construction.

(39a) General → Specific:

lequel est le plus important : du pain ou des jeux ?

'which is the more important: bread or circuses?'

The translation procedure of 'particularisation' gives in the TT information that is more narrowly focused than in the ST; or in the linguistic terminology, gives a TT hyponym where the ST has a superordinate. The example shown above concerns an idiom, but productive examples have already been discussed in Chapter 4, where we saw that French *bruit* may require particularisation in English, depending on context. Some other examples given by Astington are:

(39b) *un bruit de verre brisé*   'the tinkling of broken glass'

    les cris des bêtes   'the squeals of the animals'.

These examples concern nouns, but verbs may also call for particularisation:

(39c) *le soir venait rapidement*   'the evening was quickly closing in'

and adjectives:

(39d) *les loups voyageurs*   'the roaming wolves'

The 'General → Specific' operation is the counterpart of Specific → General in (67) below, where the TL lacks a more narrowly focused term.

(40)   Impersonal → Personal

        il me semble être estimé de tout un chacun

        'I dare say I am well thought of by all and sundry'

The constructions *il me semble* + infinitive, as well as *je crois* + infinitive, are not uncommon, and need obviously a non-literal translation: *oui, je crois en avoir quelques-uns* 'yes, I think I have some'.

(41)   Impersonal use of verbs:

        Du brick il ne restait plus rien   'of the brig nothing now remained'

This is an optional transposition, since 'there now remained nothing of the brig' is also possible. However, the literal translation conveys more formality.

(42a) 'Learned' vocabulary → 'Everyday' vocabulary:

        l'ordinateur raisonne toujours juste sur n'importe quelles données et cette intolérance contraint l'intelligence humaine à une ascèse nouvelle

        'the computer makes unerring deductions from any given data and such intolerance subjects human intelligence to a new and harsh training'

Astington's example of *ascèse* translated as 'harsh training' is one of the more interesting (because difficult) cases of the greater currency of Latinate vocabulary in French compared to English. We have touched on this subject in previous chapters, pointing out for example that *exégèse* is usually better translated as 'hypothesis' or 'theory' than the more learned 'exegesis'. Astington makes the distinction between cases where on the one hand, the translator has a choice between an English learned and everyday word or phrase, as in French *pyromane* translated as learned 'pyromaniac' or everyday 'fire-raiser', 'fire-bug' or 'arsonist'; and on the other hand, those cases where no choice is possible. Astington considered the second, non-optional category at some length. This category includes not only nouns, as in (43a), but also verbs, as in:

(42b) *pulvériser*   'to reduce to rubble'

past participles, as in:

(42c) *retraite anticipée*   'early retirement'

adjectives, as in:

(42d) *hippique*   '(horse) racing'

and phrases, as in

(42e) *stimulateur cardiaque*   'pace-maker'

As ever, the trap is literal translation, as in the *exposition canine* example discussed in Chapter 3.

(43) Metaphors :

> *La Corse est une île, pas besoin de faire un dessin*
>
> 'Corsica is an island, there's no need to spell it out / labour the point'

This is a very straightforward example of the replacement of an idiomatic metaphor in the SL by another in the TL. Astington devotes over three pages to the subject, and includes metonymy under metaphor. We discuss both devices more fully in the next chapter.

(44) Multiple equivalence in some commonly occurring words and expressions:

> *on ne pouvait pas ne pas la trouver belle, émouvante, jusqu'au drame*
>
> 'you could not but find her beautiful, touching, dramatically so'

Again, we discuss the category of multiple equivalence more fully in the following chapter, because it is very large and disparate. The problem in (44) is the translation of *jusqu'à*, which requires a non-literal rendering in this context. The crucial phrase here is 'in context'; the essence of multiple equivalence is that the translation of some commonly occurring words and phrases will differ greatly depending on the surrounding context.

(45)   Negative → Affirmative:

    il n'en a pas été de même dans   'things were different in the
    la rue   street'

This is the counterpart of category (30) above, the 'Affirmative →
Negative' modulation. Again, the essential issue turns on what the translator feels is the idiomatic value of the translation, since 'things were not
the same in the street' is obviously a possible rendering.

    Categories (46), (47), (49) and (50) below all concern French–English
denominalisation, discussed in Chapter 3. The four examples show the
various ways in which the French noun can be rendered. The extent of the
phenomenon is reflected in the space devoted to it by Astington: over four
pages, out of the 70 in the French–English section of his book.

(46)   Noun → Adjective:

    un flot de cheveux bruns   'flowing brown hair'

(47)   'De' + noun → Adjective :

    Des mesures de rétorsion   'retaliatory measures'

(48)   Noun + 'de' + noun → Noun + noun :

    une période de décalage   'a time lag'

This is the very common procedure whereby the French post-modifying
construction translates as English adjectival noun + noun. The preposition
de is of course not the only one used: *à* and *pour*, among others, are also
found.

(49)   'De' + abstract noun + adjective → Adverb + adjective:

    les policiers sont d'un mutisme complet sur cette affaire

    'the police are completely silent about this affair'

(50)   Noun → Verb :

    il y a un constat de frustration des jeunes

    'it is acknowledged that young people are frustrated'

(51)   Order of elements within the sentence:

    il ne quitte pas son dictionnaire 'his dictionary never leaves his side'

The example in (51) shows modulation or change of viewpoint, and is
fairly straightforward since it involves only one element in the SL

sequence. We discuss this issue more fully in a separate section below, where we consider more radical re-ordering concerning the whole sentence.

(52)   Passive → Active:

> *les kiosques à journaux ont été dévalisés*   'the newspaper kiosks have sold out'

As Astington states, and as we pointed out in the previous chapter, this change of category is less common than Active → Passive when doing French–English translation. Note that the English rendering is in fact a middle rather than active construction. The transposition is optional in this case, with something like 'the newspaper kiosks have been cleaned out' as a possible solution.

(53)   Past historic:

> *Il monta de la terre un soufflé brûlant. Puis il plut*
>
> 'There arose from the earth a burning breath. Then down came the rain'

We looked in Chapter 3 at some cases of the unusual use of the past historic. Astington remarks that 'a more roundabout expression is sometimes required to render the value of the past historic in English'. The function of the past historic is generally to present a new state of affairs, and when this new state arrives abruptly, as in (53), the translator may feel that expansion is necessary.

(54a)   Past participle with a noun or pronoun → Clause or present participle:

> *il distinguait les mouvements confus des légionnaires accourus au tumulte sur la plage*
>
> 'he could make out the disordered movements of the legionaries who had rushed down to the beach in a tumult'

In (54a) the issue is the expansion in English of an elliptical phrase, discussed in the previous chapter. Astington also includes absolutes in this category, as in:

(54b)   *son déjeuner expédié, le frère aîné sortit*

> 'having polished off his lunch, the elder brother went out'

The translation in (54b) is optional, since in a higher register 'his lunch polished off, the elder brother went out' is also possible.

(55)   Past participle reinforcing a preposition or prepositional phrase →
        not translated into English:

   des fenêtres munies de rideaux verts   'windows with green curtains'

This is the well-known issue, discussed in the previous chapter, of the
French tendency to reinforce a preposition, typically with a past or
present participle. Note that we have already looked at this issue under
'Contraction', in (34) above. As in (34), the contraction required is linguistically structural.

(56)   Past participle used as a noun → Phrase or clause:

   des disparus   'missing persons'

As pointed out in (22) above, French can use a past participle as a noun
more frequently than English, and expansion is usually needed when
translating.

(57)   Personal → Impersonal:

   nous sommes évincés de tous les moyens d'information

   'access to all the media is denied to us'

This is the counterpart of the 'Impersonal use of verbs' category, discussed
in (41) above. As with other abstract categories, like Active → Passive and
Affirmative → Negative, there is often choice, and the translator needs to
consult intuition. So a more literal use of the ST in (57) like 'we are being
excluded from access to all the media' is also worth considering.

(58a)   Phrase → Clause:

   faute de comprendre les causes, on s'efforce alors d'agir sur les symptômes

   'because the causes cannot be understood, efforts are then directed
   towards acting on the symptoms'

We can regard the procedure in (58a) as a fairly complex case of denominalisation, since the NP *faute de comprendre les causes* is transposed to a
subordinate clause organised around a verb. A more literal rendering is
possible, along the lines of 'for want of understanding the causes ...',
although as so often the more literal solution is the more formal. The
'Phrase → Clause' heading illustrates Astington's tendency to group
disparate grammatical categories together. He refers to the type of phrase
shown in (58a) as an 'infinitive phrase', and the other two sub-categories
grouped under the 'Phrase → Clause' heading are quite different syntactically. The second and third sub-types show ellipsis again:

(58b) *touriste en Italie, bien sûr, vous irez au restaurant*

'when you are holidaying in Italy, you will of course eat out'

(58c) *nous sommes têtus, parce que Bretons*

'we are obstinate, because we are Bretons'

Astington calls constructions of the type shown in (58b) 'noun phrases in apposition', but it seems preferable to think of them as examples of ellipsis as they need expansion in English. The example in (58c) is also elliptical; Astington groups sequences of this type under the heading 'phrases with prepositions and conjunctions'. This illustrates again the point made in Chapter 5, namely that we can look at syntax from several points of view. Astington's viewpoint is structural (an SL phrase becomes a TL clause), while very often in Chapter 5 we adopted what could be called a procedural or process-based viewpoint: apposition and ellipsis are procedures that writers perform on the structures of the language.

(59a) Plural (of abstract nouns) → Singular

   des rires fusèrent de toutes parts   'laughter broke out on all sides'

In this example the translator is in danger of too close an adherence to the SL form, since 'laughs broke out on all sides' is acceptable in English, but 'laughter' is more idiomatic. Again, intuition is the best guide. Other cases may require more thought, as in:

(59b) *il avait des audaces*   'he was full of audacity'

(60)   Prepositional phrase → Preposition

   on a organisé un vin d'honneur à l'intention des délégués

   'a reception was given for the delegates'

Here we have the same issue as in (34) and (55). This time the SL preposition is reinforced with a noun.

(61a) Prepositions, difference in usage in the two languages:

   une retraite à taux plein   'retirement on full pay'

There are many examples of the difference in usage of prepositions across English and French, although not many should cause problems of French–English decoding or encoding. The problem usually occurs in the opposite direction, where for example, an English speaker is in danger of saying or writing *je suis venu sur l'avion*. The essential problem is that the use of a preposition in a given context is quite often arbitrary: so French has *la clef est sur la porte* and English 'the key is in the door'. Astington does provide one example in this category that has the potential to cause mistranslation through misunderstanding of the SL:

(61b) *les attaques de femmes sur la voie publique*

'the attacks on women in public thoroughfares'.

(62) Present participle → Clause:

aucun établissement scolaire n'étant à l'abri, il importe qu'on réfléchisse sur le trafic de la drogue avant que le drame ne se produise

'because no educational establishment is immune, it is imperative that people should give serious thought to drug trading before a tragedy occurs'

On the level of syntax, the procedure shown in (62) could also be labelled 'Clause → Clause'. Recall that in our discussion of the difference between a sentence and a clause in Chapter 5, we said that a sentence must contain a finite verb, one that is not an infinitive or a present participle. The sequence *aucun établissement scolaire n'étant à l'abri* is therefore a clause, and the issue here is the translation of a French clause containing a present participle with an English one presented by a conjunction, in this case 'because'.

(63) Present participle → Preposition:

descendant la Tamise, traversant la Manche, remontant la Seine

'down the Thames, across the Channel, and up the Seine'

un navire qui appareille et va filer, traversant la mer transparente

'a ship which is casting off, about to speed off over the translucent sea'

Astington has only three examples under this heading, but they all illustrate, albeit in a less direct way, the same principle shown in (34) and (55): the greater tendency in English to use prepositions without any reinforcement by a noun or part of a verb. The issue in (63) is that French does without prepositions entirely, while the English translator intuitively has recourse to them.

(64a) Pronominal verbs:

des économies s'imposent   'economies are absolutely necessary'

Pronominal verbs are those that occur with a preceding pronoun that is sometimes loosely called 'reflexive'. It is worth being aware of the difference: a reflexive verb is properly so called in a sentence where the action turns back or 'reflects' upon the subject – where subject and object are the same, as in *elle s'est coupée*. Astington states that 'these verbs are rarely reflexive or reciprocal'. An example of reciprocal use is: *les loups s'entredévorait* 'the wolves were devouring each other'. Astington devotes three pages to this category and has six sub-categories. Four of these express passive meaning, which suggests it is the most common translation of the pronominal construction. We looked at a straightforward instance of this in the chapter on syntax. A further example is as follows:

(64b) *les pêches se dégustent à tout moment de la journée*

'peaches can be enjoyed at any time of day'

More complex examples are *se faire* + infinitive:

(64c) *son absence s'est fait cruellement sentir* 'his absence was keenly felt'

and the use of *se voir* + infinitive, and more rarely, *s'entendre* and *se laisser* + infinitive, all with passive force:

(64d) *ce gouvernement se voit confier une double mission*

'this government has been entrusted with a two-fold mission'

nous ne voulons pas nous entendre dire ...   'we do not want to be told ...'

je me suis laissé dire que c'était aussi l'opinion de la plupart des membres ...

'I have been told that such was also the opinion of the majority of the members ...'

The final use of pronominal verbs is to express what Astington calls 'progressive meaning', that is the idea of an ongoing process. It is however worth pointing out that progressive meaning is inherent in many of the verbs in Astington's examples under this sub-heading:

(64e) *les chutes de neige vont s'espacer*   'snowfalls will become rarer'

le pétrole se fait rare   'oil is becoming scarce'

(65a) Relative clauses:

Le spectacle pittoresque qu'offre le célèbre marché flottant

'The picturesque spectacle provided by the floating market'

This is one of Astington's longer headings: it extends over two pages. He has five major sub-headings and the first, exemplified in (65a), is largely concerned with inverted relative clauses, i.e. those where the verb precedes the subject. As we have suggested elsewhere, this construction is much more common in French than English, so that a quite radical transposition will generally be needed, whether the inversion is in a relative clause or not. The second sub-heading covers the *que + être* construction (or an equivalent verb like *constituer* or *représenter*), usually translated using apposition:

(65b) il *pratique ce sport typiquement écossais qu'est le curling*

      'he goes in for that typically Scottish sport, curling'

The third sub-heading is the 'Relative → Adjective' transposition; the example below also shows inversion, and the procedure is contraction:

(65c) *dans la situation de crise où se trouve*   'in the present world
      le monde   crisis'

The fourth, 'Relative → Preposition', is yet another manifestation of the English tendency to use a preposition where French has a different element:

(65d) *le mouvment qui anime les Canadiens français*

      'the upsurge of feeling among French Canadians'

The final sub-heading, 'Relative → Possessive', comprises transpositions that result in contractions, where English has the possibility of greater compactness:

(65e) *la conception que s'en fait la France*   'France's conception of it'

      le sentiment d'insécurité qui atteint les Français

      'The French people's feeling of insecurity'

(66) Singular → Plural:

      nous avons amélioré la desserte dans les banlieues

      'we have improved services in the suburbs'

The 'Singular → Plural' category should not usually give trouble, as the translator's native-speaker intuition will supply the suitable form. This transposition seems less common than its counterpart, 'Plural → Singular' (59), judging by the amount of space devoted by Astington to each: a page and a half for 'Plural → Singular', only half a page to the reverse.

(67)   Specific → General:

on reconnaît qu'il s'est révélé orfèvre en la matière

'it is generally admitted that he has shown himself to be an expert in the matter'

The rendering of the particular or specific by the general is often discussed in the translation literature. It occurs, obviously, where there is a gap in the TL; in this case we are dealing with a metaphorical use of *orfèvre*, literally 'goldsmith', as 'expert'. The problem is that the French metaphor has no stylistically neutral English equivalent: a term like 'boffin' is too narrowly focused on science, while 'whizz' is too colloquial. This procedure is the opposite of particularisation, shown in (39) above as 'General → Specific'.

(68a) Subjunctive:

qu'il puisse y avoir en Angleterre un impôt sur l'hypocrisie

'if there could only be a tax on hypocrisy in England'

There is overlap here with the 'multiple equivalence' category above, since the translator's problem is to render the subjunctive in a way that is idiomatic in context. This example shows the advantage of familiarity with the various functions of the subjunctive expressed through *que +* subjunctive verb form: here the function, in the jargon, is 'optative', or the expression of a wish. A contrasting function expressed by the same form is 'jussive', or the issuing of a command, as in:

(68b) *qu'il entre* 'tell him to come in'

qu'on me lise á ce propos

'people should read my books / what I've written on the subject'

Byrne and Churchill have a very thorough list of the forms and functions of the subjunctive (1993: 358–87).

(69)   'Sentence tags':

où se cachent donc tous ces gens-là ? 'where can all those folks have been hiding?'

This is an area that largely concerns the translation of dialogue. We discussed earlier in this chapter the pragmatic use of words like *enfin* as so-called 'discourse particles': words that are used, as Astington puts it, "to emphasise the point, to involve the listener or reader, or merely to cover hesitation'. Other words looked at by Astington are *voilà* and *voici*. These words and phrases rarely translate literally when they are functioning as discourse particles – as opposed to their 'core' use, where a literal translation will be possible.

(70)   Verb → Adjective:

l'esprit répugne d'instinct à comprendre une telle brutalité

'instinctively the mind is reluctant to take in such brutality'

il ne dédaigne pas à mettre la main à l'ouvrage

'he is not too proud to give a helping hand'

This is a category of procedures that is hard to systematise, since, as the examples show, the French verbs have a compactness that cannot be matched in English. We can also think of these examples as coming under the 'Expansion' heading.

(71)   Verb → Adverb:

il ne tardera pas à neiger   'it will soon be snowing'

The same remark applies here as was made immediately above.

(72)   Verb → Noun:

je respirai profondément   'I took a deep breath'

rien n'était prévu pour s'asseoir   'there was no provision for seating'

These are examples against the prevailing tendency to denominalise when translating from French into English. If there is a principle here, it is, as Hervey and Higgins remark (1992: 215): 'the transposition between nouns and other parts of speech [from French into English] is not one-way. Exceptions to the statistical norm are easy to find'. The examples in (72) are exceptions of this type. Note that these transpositions are optional, so that for instance *je respirai profondément* could also translate literally (and less idiomatically), as: 'I breathed in deeply'.

(73)   Verb → verb + preposition / adverb / adjective:

c'est une piste a suivre   'it's a clue to be followed up'

ne jetons pas cette chance   'let us not throw away this chance'

l'explosion l'avait a peu   'the explosion had left it more or less
près respecté*   intact'

The procedure here, very obviously, is expansion, caused simply by a more compact expression in French. The first two examples are straightforward, and should cause no encoding problems, as they illustrate the common case of the French verb that stands alone but is expanded in English in a way that is obvious to any native-speaker. The third example is trickier, and needs thought to articulate the idea behind the word.

(74)   Verb + adverb or adverbial phrase → Verb or verb + preposition:

> *il leur a dit tout bas de se taire*   'he whispered to them to be quiet'
>
> *il lavait le pont à jet de lance*   'he was hosing down the deck'

The first example shows compression from French into English. The second shows the frequent operation that uses an English phrasal verb – verb + preposition – to translate the French noun-based adverbial: not 'adverbial phrase', as Astington states.

(75)   Shift of viewpoint:

> *c'est vraiment tourner le dos à la réalité*   'they are refusing to face up to reality'

This example is a modulation, usually defined as a shift of viewpoint; or as the use of different metaphors in the two languages. This example seems optional, since the literal translation 'they are really turning their backs on reality' is an acceptable, if less idiomatic rendering than Astington's.

General Comments on Astington's Categories

We can make several remarks about this classification. Firstly, a good number of the operations listed above have already been discussed in this book. Secondly, there is overlap between the categories: for example, 'shift of viewpoint' (i.e. modulation) is given its own heading, but is also considered under several others: 'Order of elements within the sentence', 'Negative → Affirmative' and 'Verb → Adverb' are all modulations as well as transpositions. Thirdly, all of the operations listed can be classified as transposition or modulation or both. Fourthly, as Astington remarks in his Preface, some operations are more frequent than others, a fact not reflected in the list above, because we have given one or two examples only of each. Some of Astington's headings cover several pages of examples: notably 'Expansion', 'Learned vocabulary', 'Metaphor', 'Multiple equivalence' and 'Pronominal verbs'. This is because these headings are abstract ones that subsume operations on several different word categories, while most of the other headings directly concern operations on word categories. A further, related point is that the 57 categories are mixed: some are directly concerned with operations like expansion and contraction, while others, although they are looked at in terms of the word categories or syntactic categories concerned, can equally be thought about from the viewpoint of expansion, contraction or other operations. Finally, it is worth repeating what we have stated several times above, that where a procedure is optional, the more literal translation is generally the more formal or less idiomatic one. Thus the term 'optional' is used here in a weak sense: sometimes the translator is not obliged by the structures of the SL and TL to choose a certain rendering, but native-speaker intuition needs to be exercised to choose the more idiomatic of the optional renderings available.

Ordering of Elements Within the Sentence

We have already looked at this issue in the previous section, as one of the operations distinguished by Astington. As pointed out above, many of the examples cited by Astington can also be analysed as modulations, as in:

(76)   *il n'y songeait déjà plus*   'it had gone completely out of his mind'

Modulations of this type are also transpositions, although they involve a change in grammatical function rather than category. The example in (76) is an object > subject transposition: the French indirect object pronoun *y* translates as English subject pronoun 'it'. Astington also has subject > object, as in:

(77)   *parce que leur tête ne revient pas à tel ou tel contrôleur*

       'because some tax inspector or other doesn't like their face'

The other transpositions listed by Astington are subject > complement and complement > subject, as in the two following respective examples:

(78)   *les sondages sont sources de controverses*

       'there is much controversy about opinion polls'

       le temps est à l'orage   'thunder is in the air'

The operations in (76)–(78) are working on a single element, whether word or phrase, in the linguistic sequence in question. The other operation of this type listed by Astington is 'Repositioning of adjectival or adverbial phrase', as follows:

(79)   *nous allions chaque après-midi nous reposer sur la terrasse*

       'each afternoon we would go and rest on the terrace'

All of the examples in (76)–(79) show operations that are quite straight-forward because, as stated above, they concern one element only in the sequence. More complex operations need sometimes to be performed; in Astington's words (1983: 47):

> Occasionally, because structures of equivalent meaning are so different in the two languages or because equivalent verbs have different 'constraints' (for example some verbs can have only an animate subject or an animate object), the elements in the sentence have to be re-arranged.

Astington calls this 'complete reconstruction'. The difference between this and what is shown in (77)–(79) is plainly that complete reconstruction involves the re-ordering of more than one element, while the operations in (77)–(79) concern one only. Astington has the following example of complete reconstruction, shown in (80) below. Some of the operations in (80) are of more interest than others, but the general point is that the translator is obliged in this sequence by the structures of the two languages to re-order and recategorise elements in a thoroughgoing way. The most radical recast concerns the verb *se voulait*, which is transposed to the adjective 'forced'. Other transpositions and re-orderings are more routine and in any case obligatory, like *faire un geste* > 'wave' and the displacement of *de sa main libre* to the left in the TL sequence.

```
         1        2              3      4      5
(80)  elle leur fit un geste qui se voulait joyeux de sa main libre

         2        5        1      3      4
      she waved her free hand to them with forced gaiety
```

We can question whether re-orderings of this kind are 'occasional', as Astington states; intuition and experience suggests, on the contrary, that they not unusual. Recall the translation of the Human Rights passage from *Le Monde*:

(81)   Au couperet des verdicts succèdera, pour celui que la justice reconnaît criminel, un temps inédit: la possibilité, si le jugement ou la peine ne lui conviennent pas, de faire appel et d'être rejugé.

'For those found guilty, an unprecedented era will follow these brutal and irreversible decisions: the possibility of appeal and retrial if they do not accept the judgment or sentence.'

Although no radical transpositions of the *se voulait* > 'forced' type have been performed here, the ST sequence of phrases has been altered quite considerably. Certainly the translator needs to be ready to do a radical re-ordering if it is felt that an idiomatic TT requires it.

Types of Procedure: Cultural or Linguistic?

A perusal of Astington's book leaves the reader with the impression that transpositions and modulations are the most common types of translation procedure, but this simply reflects the bias of the book. After reading *Faux Amis and Key Words* by Thody and Evans, a different impression is gained. The seven types of Vinay and Darbelnet discussed above can be categorised as cultural-linguistic or linguistic, following the distinction made throughout this book. It seems likely that of the two broad types, the purely linguistic operation is more frequent, although the frequency will depend on the text type in question. But on the whole, one might risk the generalisation that the grammar – concerning mostly transpositions – will most often present translation difficulties. We cannot really rationalise this, beyond making the descriptive statement that transposition is very often called for simply because French and English will often express a given meaning using words and phrases from different grammatical categories.

The problem is to synthesise a very detailed classification like Astington's together with a broad one that includes transposition (and sometimes modulation) as superordinate categories grouping every operation that is purely linguistic. A possible answer is for the translator to develop the habit of having constantly in mind, on the one hand transposition and modulation, and on the other hand the habit of applying these to the appropriate word or phrase category as each difficulty is encountered.

high-flown phrases like 'innumerable centuries'. A similar effect is achieved by the use of 'ingredients' in a scientific application. A further device is the repetition of 'interesting'. Successful translation seems possible in principle here, although a very high level of craftsmanship, largely depending on the manipulation of collocational patterns, would be required of the translator for a successful rendering. This is of course true irrespective of the direction in which the translation is performed; at least where humour of this type is in question.

The Text Level

Although translation problems at the text level, that is the level beyond the sentence, are by no means trivial, they are difficult to discuss in the item-based way that we have used so far. This is because they concern larger units that are harder to define, classify and analyse. The following example is taken from *La Fabrique sociale de l'économie* by Pierre Bourdieu, a leading French Marxist sociologist not noted for his ease of readability. This example is therefore rather extreme. While it is true in general that French tolerates longer sentences than English, the extract quoted below is outstanding in having a sentence, coinciding with a paragraph, of 141 words. We have to wait until line nine, or word 75, for the main verb, *favorisé*:

(3) La mise en place, au mois de septembre 1966, du marché hypothé-caire qui ouvrait aux banques la faculté d'offrir des crédits à long terme et de réduire l'apport initial et qui venait s'ajouter aux nouvelles modalités d'intervention offertes aux institutions finan-cières, bancaires ou non bancaires (création du compte d'épargne-logement, prêts spéciaux différés du Crédit foncier, remplacés en 1972 par les prêts immobiliers conventionnés, allongement des crédits bancaires-CCF à moyen terme, crédits promoteurs, etc.) a favorisé un financement bancaire massif de la construction qui a profité surtout aux constructeurs les plus importants: alors qu'en 1962, les banques ne distribuaient que 21,7% des crédits au logement, leur part s'élevait en 1972 à 65,1%, tandis qu'à 1'inverse la part du secteur public tombait de 59,7% à 29,7% et celle des préteurs de caractère non financier de 18,5% en 1962 à 5,2% en 1972.

The instinct of the translator into English will be to bring up the main verb closer to the phrase with which it is associated, *la mise en place [...] du marché hypothécaire*. This involves quite a radical recast of the original, involving the shifting downwards of the list of the various *modalités d'in-tervention* and the insertion of a sentence break after *constructeurs les plus importants*, as follows:

(4)   The setting up in September 1966 of the home-loan market, enabling
      banks to offer long-term credit as well as to reduce the deposit
      required from borrowers, and increasing the number of new services
      capable of being offered by financial institutions, whether banking or
      non-banking, favoured a massive financing by banks of house-
      building which mainly benefited the biggest building firms. These
      new services included the home-savings account, special deferred-
      repayment loans issued by the Crédit Foncier, replaced in 1972 by
      state-approved home-loans, the extension of medium-term loans
      issued by the CCF, loans issued by house builders, etc. Thus, while in
      1962 banks issued only 21.7% of home loans, their share rose to 65.1%
      in 1972, while in contrast the public-sector market share fell from
      59.7% to 29.7%, and the share of non-profit-making lenders fell from
      18.5% in 1962 to 5.2% in 1972.

Our second example concerns journalistic French, which tolerates interrogatives in headlines to a greater extent than English – indeed, French
newspaper headlines are in general wordier and less playful than English,
if one compares like with like (*The Guardian* and *Le Monde*, for instance).
This example is best discussed on the text level because it illustrates the
need to examine the relation between two juxtaposed sentences, and
consider the possibility of coalescing the sense of the two into one. Some
additional text has been retained to give an idea of the overall sense of the
piece.

(5)   **Le nouvel impôt sur le revenu est-il économiquement efficace ?**
      C'est évidemment la thèse que fait valoir le gouvernement. Celui-ci
      fait observer qu'en procédant dès 1997 à 25 milliards de francs d'al-
      lègement d'impôt – ce à quoi il faut ajouter diverses mesures, dont le
      déblocage anticipé des primes liées aux plans d'épargne populaire
      (PEP), pour un montant de 15 milliards de francs –, il contribue à
      soutenir la consommation des ménages et, ce faisant, la croissance.
      De plus, dans une logique libérale, il souligne que la baisse des taux
      d'imposition, notamment les plus élevés, contribue à stimuler l'ini-
      tiative et à encourager l'effort.

      [...]

      La réforme est-elle socialement juste ?
      Le gouvernement plaide en ce sens. D'abord, il rejette la critique
      selon laquelle la reforme serait en réalité un cadeau fait aux «riches»,
      les Français les plus défavorisés, ceux qui ne paient pas l'impôt sur
      le revenu, ne bénéficiant pas de cette baisse fiscale.

(6) **French Government claims new income tax rates more effective**
The French government has claimed that by cutting income tax by 25 billion francs in 1997, along with various measures like the early introduction of incentives linked to popular savings plans, worth 15 billion francs, it is boosting household consumption and therefore growth. Using free-market logic, the government also claims that lowering income-tax rates, especially the highest, will stimulate initiative and encourage individual effort.

[...]

Government argues tax reform is fairer
The government rejects the criticism that the reform is really just a present for the rich, while those worst off, who pay no income tax, will not benefit from the tax cuts.

Source: Le Monde Fiscalité 13.2.97

In these examples, the ST uses the device, rather unusual in English, of using the headlines as an integral part of the text. The first sentence of the body text in each paragraph effectively constitutes the second element of the argument. By contrast, the TT conforms to the frequent practice of using the headline as a summary of the following paragraph, allowing the reader to decide whether what follows is of sufficient interest to scan further. It can be noted that the ST headlines also have this summarising function, while at the same time the headline in both paragraphs is also the first element of substantive information. We discuss the text level in more detail below, in the section on coherence and cohesion.

Improving the Source Text

The previous section raises the question of how far the translator should be seeking to improve the ST. Among other things, the extract from Bourdieu discussed above illustrates that writers who are perhaps working under multiple pressures, no doubt including tight deadlines, are capable of producing prose that is less than ideal, as in the initial passage:

(7) La mise en place, au mois de septembre 1966, du marché hypothé-caire <u>qui ouvrait aux banques la faculté</u> d'offrir des crédits à long terme

The translation offered previously compressed the phrased underlined above into: 'enabling banks'. We can speculate that Bourdieu's formulation illustrates the principle enshrined in Pascal's famous apology in a letter to a correspondent:

> Je n'ai fait [cette lettre] plus longue que parce que je n'ai pas eu le loisir de la faire plus courte.

It is a matter of common observation that a hasty formulation is generally less compressed than one having benefited from careful drafting over a longer period. This is of course a constraint that can also weigh upon the translator.

Aside from wordiness, a further problem is repetition. It is sometimes said that 'avoidance of repetition is the first rudiment of style', and certainly unintentional repetition must be scrupulously avoided by careful drafting, redrafting and editing. Judicious repetition, as in the Salinger passage above, is of course an entirely different issue. The following sentence shows careless repetition:

(8)   Un trou noir imprime sur l'espace environnant une très forte empreinte gravitationnelle qui se traduit par l'accrétion de toute parcelle de matière.

The two closely related words, *imprime* and *empreinte*, give an unfortunate effect. The translator certainly needs to improve the ST here:

(9)   A black hole imposes on the space surrounding it a very strong gravitational imprint, resulting in the accretion of all particles of matter.

Metaphor

Aside from verbosity and clichés, another sign of rapid drafting (or careless writing) is the mixing of metaphor, as in the following example taken from the French popular science journal *Sciences et Avenir*, concerned with the cloning of animals:

(10)   Si on ne peut remédier à cet écueil, le clonage perd une part de son intérêt puisque incapable de produire autre chose que des animaux « nés vieux ».

This issue is of some theoretical interest. The italicised phrase *remédier à cet écueil* may seem odd to a non-native reader, since the literal meanings of *remédier* and *écueil* could well be the first ones that come to mind. Seeming mixed metaphors like this will (or should) force themselves on the translator's attention, as a result of intense concentration on the ST. Consultation of a dictionary will of course show that both words, beyond their literal meaning, are commonly used in a figurative sense; literally 'to cure', *remédier* is perhaps most suitably rendered here as 'solve'. The

French verb has therefore a wider polysemic range than the literal English equivalent. Similarly, *écueil*, literally of course 'reef' but figuratively 'pitfall' or 'stumbling block', can have for a non-francophone reader an odd collocational effect. Canvassing of native speakers in fact shows that the phrase is not very readily apparent as a mixed metaphor. A neutral translation such as 'solve this problem' seems adequate here; or if a metaphor is sought, something like 'avoid this pitfall'. Mixed metaphors in the TT can therefore produce, because of their relative unfamiliarity, a kind of 'static' that may not impinge on the francophone reader. In practical terms, there should be little risk of the translator's rendering literally a mixed metaphor such as that shown above.

As stated previously, a metaphor is an implicit comparison, most often using imagery. An explicit comparison (a simile) will obviously use a word such as 'like' or 'as': 'My love is like a red, red, rose'. Metaphor either suppresses the comparison: 'My love is a red rose'; or simply substitutes the image for what it is being compared to: *écueil* for *problème*. On the subject of the translation of metaphors generally, one or two points may be made. Firstly, there are cases where no choice is possible: *une puce* (in the computing sense) is 'a chip' in English. A case like this poses no practical problem, but is of interest to the student of translation because 'chip' and *puce*, although both metaphors, are not perceived as such; in the jargon they are 'dead metaphors'. Only the non-native student of French will perhaps be struck, at first encounter, by the fact that French compares an integrated circuit to a flea.

Where there is choice, the non-native may be in danger of performing a literal translation on a metaphor that the composer of the ST did not in fact see as a metaphor. This is an example of 'over-translation' in Vinay and Darbelnet's definition of the term: seeing two linguistic units where in fact there is only one. The classic example of this is translating *aller chercher* by 'go and find' rather than 'fetch', and the basic issue, as so often, is the need to shake oneself free of the influence of the TT. We can view the needless translation of TL metaphors as over-translation in the sense of seeing two linguistic units where in fact there is only one, since there is the basic propositional message conveyed by the metaphor as well as the image, which it may or may not be profitable to translate. The following example shows an apparent metaphor which is probably best left untranslated. The headline in (11) below is taken from the French magazine *La Recherche*, directed towards an educated but non-specialist readership and so more or less equivalent to *New Scientist*. The article is about black holes; we discuss a longer extract more fully in a subsequent section on lexical cohesion:

(11)   Comment s'alimente un trou noir?

This example shows quite clearly the possibility that an English-speaking translator may see a metaphor where none is intended. As we argue more fully below, a neutral translation like 'How is a black hole sustained?' seems preferable to an attempt to match the metaphor. This is in contrast to the following headline:

(12)   Téléverbier va atteindre de nouveaux sommets

In this example, since Téléverbier is a ski-equipment company, is seems reasonable to assume that the metaphor is intended, and since an equivalent is readily available in English, the SL metaphor can be matched: 'Téléverbier to scale new heights'.

   The fact that metaphors are often not perceived as such by those who use them is one reason for the prevalence of clichés. A speaker who utters the following sequence is presumably unconscious of the hackneyed nature of the imagery contained in it, and of the incongruous mixture of the three metaphor-clichés:

(13)   'We were in at the deep end, but we got out by the skin of our teeth, flying by the seat of our pants'

This is not an invented example, although admittedly it is drawn from speech not writing. The mitigating circumstance in speech is obviously that the speaker is performing 'on-line', composing and talking at the same time. Writing of any pretension needs to be swept clean of barbarisms like this. Neither can the translator be insensitive in this way; the essential task is to determine whether what looks like a metaphor in the ST is genuine, or only looks like one because of the translator's relative unfamiliarity with the SL. In the former case, the translator needs to consider selecting an equivalent metaphor if one is available; in the latter case, a neutral translation must be found. We discuss metaphor further in relation to coherence and cohesion below.

Metonymy

   Metonymy, a common device, substitutes the whole for the part, or the part for the whole. So, 'the hall' can be used to stand for the audience contained in it (as can *la salle* in French); a further example is *verre* representing the drink it contains: *si on prenait un verre?* Substituting the part for the whole, the second sub-type of metonymy, seems commoner than the whole for the part. An English example is 'the Crown', which frequently represents its wearer or the institution itself. A less stuffy example is the US English use of 'ass' to refer to its possessor: 'your ass is mine'. Very obviously, part-for-whole references like 'Ten Downing Street' and *Matignon*, which substitute the locality of the UK and French governments for the governments themselves, cannot transfer literally because they are culture-specific. A translation of *Matignon*, the French Prime Minister's residence, will generally have to be 'the French government', 'the French Prime Minister' or something suitable to the context. Apart from this, the translation of metonymy can raise problems of recognition: *l'homme du 18 juin* is General de Gaulle, an important date in his career representing the man himself. The problem with metonymic devices of this kind is that they tend not to be listed in works of reference. The remaining issue, as ever, is finding a good equivalent. The French refer to their nation's children as *nos chères têtes blondes*, but no very current metaphoric or metonymic reference appears to exist in English: perhaps 'the nation's future'? But French and English metonymy often differ in quite obvious ways: *toujours les mêmes têtes* 'the same old faces'. Here, while both French and English have part-for-whole metonymy, a different part is exploited in each case but straightforward equivalence is easily found.

The example of the *verre* above illustrates that metonymy in the SL sometimes needs to be neutralised in the TL. One obvious translation of *si on prenait un verre?* is 'shall we go for a drink?', where the English mode of expression is not metonymic and therefore neutral. Another example in the opposite direction is the following, taken from a publicity leaflet for the AGORA range of Renault buses:

(14)   AGORA accorde naturellement une place essentielle à la recherche de la rentabilité et de la productivité : il est possible d'effectuer la plupart des opérations de maintenance *à hauteur d'homme*, et l'accès à tous les organes mécaniques est aisé.

'The AGORA range naturally gives high priority to low operating costs and high productivity: easy-access mechanical systems mean that most maintenance procedures can be carried out *at eye level*.'

Coherence and Cohesion

The difference between coherence and cohesion is discussed in several textbooks of linguistics and translation. Occurring on the more abstract level, coherence implies an intelligible progression of ideas through a text. For a text to make sense, the progression needs to be logical, and must also be sufficiently explicit and rational, in the sense of referring overtly to concepts shared by writer and reader. Discussions in the literature tend to imply that cohesion, or the explicit, concrete marking of the more abstract flow of an argument, is the more superficial level, as in the following definition from Gardes-Tamine (1992: 148):

> la cohérence et la cohésion se distinguent en ce que la première s'appuie sur des relations sémantiques et logiques, alors que la seconde n'implique que des relations morpho-syntaxiques et lexicales

Coherence and cohesion are however interdependent, rather than arranged hierarchically, as is implied by Gardes-Tamine's use of 'only' to qualify 'lexical and morpho-syntactic relations'. A text often quoted in the literature to illustrate the coherence–cohesion distinction is that devised by Yule (1985: 105–6). We discuss it in adapted form below.

(15)   My father once *bought* a really *expensive* <u>Lincoln convertible</u>. He managed it by *saving every penny* he could. It was dark blue with masses of <u>chrome</u> and a <u>fawn leather top</u> and it used to <u>guzzle gas</u> like there was no tomorrow. That <u>car</u> would be *worth a fortune* nowadays. However, he sold it *for peanuts* to a collector of <u>old automobiles</u> to help *pay for* my college education. Despite everything, sometimes I think I'd rather still have that <u>rag-top</u>, *or the money*.

Text (15) is *coherent*, as it presents a series of ideas that we recognise as progressing in a rational way. It is also *cohesive*, in possessing lexical and grammatical elements that provide signposts forward through the text, making the progression easier to perceive. Following the distinction established in Chapter 3 between lexical and grammatical words, we can point out threads of lexical cohesion in text (15), in the different car vocabulary (underlined), and vocabulary relating to money (italicised); and expressions of time: 'once', 'nowadays', sometimes'.

Grammatical cohesion is evident in noun + pronoun sequences: 'my father' … 'he managed it'; 'Lincoln convertible'… 'it was dark blue'; logical connectors: 'however', 'despite everything'; tenses: 'bought', 'did it', 'was dark blue', 'used to', 'would be', 'sold it', 'I think', 'still have'.

Consider now the following text, adapted also from Yule and designed to illustrate lack of coherence:

(16)   My father bought a Lincoln convertible. The car driven by the police was red. That colour doesn't suit her. 'She' consists of three letters. However, a letter isn't as fast as a telephone call. Call me stupid if you like. People who like cars are stupid.

Text (16) is incoherent, as there is no logical progression between its elements. It is a series of statements each of which is independent of the preceding one. However, it is furthermore only superficially cohesive. For instance, the noun phrase 'the car' in the second sentence does not convey *anaphoric* reference (does not refer back) to the Lincoln; it refers forward (has *cataphoric* reference) to 'driven by the police'. So, there is no connection between 'Lincoln convertible' and 'the car' except at the surface level.

Contrast the following progression, from text (15):

(17)   My father once bought <u>a really expensive Lincoln convertible</u>. <u>That car</u> would be worth a fortune nowadays.

Here, 'that car' refers to Lincoln convertible and recapitulates the concept as 'given' information. Something new is then said about the given. The given > new alternating structure is quite common at the text level. So:

(18)   My father once bought a really expensive Lincoln convertible [NEW]. That car [GIVEN] would be worth a fortune nowadays [NEW]. However, he sold it [GIVEN] for peanuts to a collector of old automobiles [NEW] to help pay for my college education.

In text (16) the structure is:

(19)   My father bought a Lincoln convertible [NEW]. The car [NEW] driven by the police was red [NEW].

Text (16) is therefore incoherent on the surface, as well as lacking cohesion at a deeper level.

Anaphora, Cataphora

As mentioned above, anaphora is reference back:

(20)   My father once bought <u>a really expensive Lincoln convertible</u>. < <u>That car</u> would be worth a fortune nowadays.

Cataphora, a less common cohesive device, is reference forward, often to introduce a list. The second example below shows a celebrated piece of cataphora, from the opening of the American Declaration of Independence.

(21)   Mes objections sont les suivantes: > en premier lieu ...

'We hold these truths to be self-evident, that all men are created equal, that they are endowed by their Creator with certain unalienable Rights, that among these are Life, Liberty and the pursuit of Happiness.'

The following piece of journalism has a complex structure of text-level cataphora, with anaphora at sentence-level:

(22) **Mauvais oeil**
      Ce sont de petites bêtes silencieuses au long bec emmanché d'un long cou. Elles perchent haut pour se faire oublier. Dans leur nid d'acier, elles dominent la ville. On les trouve partout : sur les routes, aux carrefours, au-dessus des caisses de supermarchés, dans les garages et le métro, aux abords des squares, aux portes des immeubles… Depuis peu, elles se glissent jusque dans nos chambres, furtives et obstinées. Comme une irrépressible pandémie, elles prolifèrent sans qu'on y prenne garde. Ce sont les caméras de télé surveillance.

In (22), we are obliged to wait until the very last sentence to learn the lexical item referred to (*les caméras de télé surveillance*) by the long series of cataphoric elements in what precedes. A structure such as this is presumably designed to induce the reader to persist to the end of the paragraph, but carries the risk of causing irritation. As mentioned above, anaphora is much more frequent; we seem to prefer to have the informative, lexical element in a text conveyed to us first, since we find it more comfortable to keep it in mind and refer back to it when prompted by anaphoric elements. Newspaper articles typically have an anaphoric structure that enables readers to scan the main elements in the text, as indicated by the headline, sub-headlines and lead paragraph, so they can pursue the item in greater detail if they wish.

Translating Coherence and Cohesion

As Hervey and Higgins point out (1992: 51) 'while coherence is clearly culture-specific in some respects, it may also vary significantly according to subject matter or textual genre'. We can relate this to what was pointed out in Chapter 2 in connection with the more frequent use of metaphor in informative texts. As stated previously, the extract under (23) below is taken from the French magazine *La Recherche*. We can see a thread of lexical coherence running through this first paragraph that depends on a sustained metaphor.

(23) **Comment s'alimente un trou noir?**
      Un trou noir imprime sur l'espace environnant une très forte empreinte gravitationnelle qui se traduit par l'accrétion de toute parcelle de matière. Les espaces intersidéraux sont toutefois tellement vides de matière que les millions de trous noirs d'origine stellaire qui peupleraient la Voie lactée sont astreints à de très longues périodes de sevrage.

The title seems to initiate a 'sustenance' theme through the use of the verb *s'alimenter*. This verb has, of course, as well as its literal reference to feeding, the more abstract sense translatable by 'supply': *l'appartement s'alimente en gaz* 'the flat uses gas'. The title would therefore appear to be better translated using an abstract verb like 'sustain': 'How is a black hole sustained?' rather than 'How is a black hole nourished?', which reads rather oddly. As with the mixed metaphor discussed above, we cannot be sure whether the choice of verb reflects a deliberate decision to set up a chain of lexical coherence. However this may be, the correspondence lower down is quite striking, at least to a non-native translator: that which links *Voie lactée* and *sevrage*. Here, the reference to a black hole as if it were an animate being is quite clear: the pristine sense of *sevrage* is 'weaning', and the extended sense is also perhaps translatable as 'weaning', as in the sequence *le sevrage d'un toxicomane* 'weaning an addict off drugs'.

There *seems* therefore to be a link here between 'Milky Way' and 'weaning': the issue here is essentially similar to the mixed-metaphor problem discussed previously. So we are faced with the 'equivalence' problem discussed in the previous chapter, since the translator may feel that a link of lexical cohesion has been established by the author of the ST. Most of the time, this feeling must remain in the realm of conjecture, although in some circumstances the translator may be so fortunate as to be able to consult the author: translators working for organisations like the EC, the UN and NATO, for example. But most of the time the best recourse available will be to a native-speaker. The problem in this particular instance is caused by the different lexical choices available in the two languages: *Voie lactée* translates most obviously as 'Milky Way' (although something like 'our galaxy' is also possible) and the concrete English term points up the connection between 'milk' and 'weaning'. For the French reader, the more abstract *Voie lactée* is a step removed from the everyday *lait*. In any event, it would be difficult to reproduce the 'milk' – 'weaning' link in English, as the collocation reads oddly:

(24)   *les millions de trous noirs d'origine stellaire qui peupleraient la Voie lactée sont astreints à de très longues périodes de sevrage*

'the millions of black holes of stellar origin which are thought to populate the Milky Way are subjected to long periods of weaning'

The following version reads more idiomatically:

(25)   'the millions of black holes of stellar origin which are thought to populate the Milky Way are deprived of sustenance for long periods'

In other words, a more abstract translation seems suitable here. The essential problems remain the identification of a metaphor in the ST that is live for a native-speaker; and the subsequent attempt to render it idiomatically in the SL.

A more straightforward example is the following, the first paragraph of an article about the Euro from *Ouest-France*:

(26)   Les banquiers-accoucheurs ont de quoi pavoiser. L'euro n'est pas seulement bien né, sans pépin clinique de dernier minute, sans ratage informatique. C'est un beau bébé … qui fait déjà de la politique en bombant le torse face au dollar. Histoire de marquer clairement ses prétentions à être le challenger offensif de l'envahissant cousin d'outre-Atlantique, c'est-à-dire à devenir une monnaie mondiale de réserve. D'emblée il joue dans la cour des grands, même si le dollar, assis sur un leadership politique, économique et militaire a de puissantes ressources.

In this passage, the chains of lexical cohesion are so obvious and persistent that we cannot doubt their intentional character. The 'baby' image is established almost immediately *(accoucheurs – bien né, sans pépin clinique – beau bébé…)* and maintained until a military or bellicose chain starts to interweave with it. The intention here is beyond doubt: the translator's problem is how to deal with the metaphors: reproduce them in the same form, find a different set or select neutral renderings. As with the *trou noir* passage, the selection of neutral translations will weaken the cohesive chains in the ST, but explicit cohesion seems characteristic of French more than English.

Apart from the use of metaphor to bring about text cohesion, a difference between French and English which is often pointed out is that which concerns the use of grammatical words (metaphor concerns lexical words, obviously). As Fuller points out (1973: 10), a phrase like *ainsi que* is sometimes in danger of being over-translated, in a sequence like:

(27)   les architectes et les médecins font défaut, ainsi que les hommes de science

Fuller remarks that 'if the *ainsi que* is translated by "as well as", it may suggest a difference of emphasis not intended in the French, where its purpose is merely stylistic. Hence it may be better to translate it merely as "and"'. A translation like the following may therefore suffice:

(28)   there is a shortage of architects, doctors and scientists

Other conjunctions similar to *ainsi que* are *aussi bien que* and *de même que*. As suggested above, the general tendency seems to be to mark cohesion in French in a more explicit way than in English, using more linguistic material. This may explain the tendency, discussed previously, to reinforce prepositions in French.

Multiple Equivalence

In earlier chapters we have touched repeatedly but briefly on the concept of multiple equivalence. In Chapter 6 we alluded to the concept as one of Astington's categories, giving the example of the preposition *jusqu'à* that differed from the usual literal renderings such as 'until' or 'up to' in sometimes requiring a non-literal rendering in context. As we stated earlier, the crucial phrase here is 'in context'; the essence of multiple equivalence is that the translation of some commonly occurring words and phrases will differ greatly depending on the context. Very obviously therefore, the term 'multiple equivalence' refers to the possibility of several renderings by which a single SL element may be translated in the TL. It will be recalled that Astington's full section heading is 'Multiple equivalence in some commonly occurring words and expressions'. At ten pages, this section is by far the longest in the 70-page French–English section of Astington's book. This concept is well known to translators, and the procedure associated with the concept is referred to variously. A common term is 'particularisation', which may seem jargonistic but in fact refers fairly transparently to the use of a particular word or phrase in the TL to translate an SL term that is more general, or of wider scope.

When we look at Astington's section on multiple equivalence, we see that particularisation is the procedure that is applied, and that the problems behind the procedure fall into two main categories. The first is our old friend collocation, as we shall see below. The second is hard to define with equal precision, since it is generally concerned with a longer stretch of language – as opposed to collocation, which usually involves just two words. The second category covers *s'agir, ce* + noun + *si* + adjective, *combien, falloir* and *guère*. The basic issue here, as we have stated repeatedly, is that these items need to be translated suitably in context. The difficulty is that the solution is by no means always so clear-cut as is the case with collocation, where thorough ransacking of works of reference and other resources will usually turn up the suitable translation. So the essential issue is always the idiomatic translation in context, but collocation is easier to think about.

Astington looks at the following 20 items under multiple equivalence: (*large* and *largement* are treated under the same heading):

> *s'agir; beau; bien; bon; ce* + noun + *si* + adjective; *combien; davantage; déjà; falloir; fort; grand; gros; guère; important; jusqu'à; large, largement; mal; mauvais; on; petit*

We now look briefly at these in turn. The translation of the impersonal verb *s'agir* often differs from the usual renderings such as 'it is a matter / question of', which one encounters when first learning French, and which, as Fuller remarks (1973: 10) 'recall the schoolroom'. Fuller suggest various ways of translating *il s'agit de*: 'the point (aim, idea, intention, object, point at issue) is; what is wanted is; the feature to note is; … is involved; … is at stake' where the suspension points indicate a noun with which *il s'agit de* is associated. A further example of Fuller's brings out the point that the construction can sometimes be left untranslated:

(29)   … *un autre fait important. Il s'agit de* …

not   '… another important matter. It relates to …'

but   '… another important matter is …'

Astington (1983, pp. 31–2) lists sixteen examples under *il s'agit de*; two taken at random are as follows:

(30)   *Il s'agit d'une véritable démythification*   'The aim here is to explode a myth'

        Pour les uns, il s'agit d'un manoeuvre de strangulation de la presse

        'Some see in this a manoeuvre to strangle the press'

Ten of Astington's 20 items are adjectives, and the problems they present have already been discussed in Chapter 4. The issue is generally collocation, as Astington's examples concerning *beau* demonstrate:

(31)   *un beau geste*   'a noble gesture'

        une belle réussite   'an outstanding success'

Here the translation of *beau* depends on the noun that it qualifies; there is some scope for choice here, so that 'a fine gesture' also seems acceptable to render *un beau geste*. There is little to add beyond what was said on this topic in the chapter on words in combination; we are looking here at the French side of the phenomenon whereby 'dry' in 'dry voice', 'dry book', etc. will have a different translation into French. We can emphasise again that the translator's intuition needs to be finely tuned to the collocational patterns of the TL, and this is a stringent requirement since by no means every possible rendering of a common SL adjective is to be found in dictionaries or translation textbooks. We suggested above that consultation of 'works of reference and other resources' will generally turn up the solution; other resources will of course be other (perhaps older) native speakers.

Other adjectives and adverbs in this category and discussed by Astington are: *bien; bon; combien; davantage; déjà; fort; grand; gros; guère; important; large, largement; mal; mauvais; petit.* We give examples of each below, as well as of the other 20 items on the list.

(32) *je suis bien obligé de recevoir*   'I just have to entertain'

   gardez-vous-en bien!   'avoid that at all costs!'

(33) *le bon sondage, c'est le résultat des élections*

   'the (only) reliable opinion poll is the election result'

   Gore Vidal nous décrit la Floride de la bonne société

   'Gore Vidal describes for us high-society Florida'

The issue here is again collocation, with the adverb *bien* and the adjective *bon* needing an idiomatic translation in context.

(34) *cet élément si compliqué*   'such a complicated element'

   ces siècles si mal connus que nous appelons le haut moyen âge

   'those curiously little-known centuries which we call the Early Middle Ages'

Judging by Astington's examples, the *ce* + noun + *si* + adjective construction is most often translated by 'such' + adjective. Of his seven examples, five are translated in this way. The second example above shows that a non-literal rendering is sometimes called for.

(35) *on voit combien les accords de Helsinki sont bafoués*

   'it can be seen to what extent the Helsinki agreements are flouted'

Here the problem is simply that, as Astington points out, 'a literal translation of *combien* is not always acceptable in English'. The problem is hard to systematise, and we are reduced to saying that *combien* is more mobile, or has a broader scope, than English 'how much', since *combien* is sometimes substitutable, as here, for *dans quelle mesure* or *à quel degré*.

(36) *nous comprenons davantage la partie colossale qui est en jeu*

   'we realise more clearly the colossal stakes that are to be played for'

The adverb *davantage* is of course usually an elegant synonym of *plus*. Now and then, as the example above shows, expansion is needed to give a suitable translation that collocates with the verb selected.

(37)   *sur la terre ferme, elle ne doit déjà pas être gauche, mais sur la glace, c'est*
       le comble de la prestesse légère

       'she cannot be ungainly even off the ice ...'

As with *davantage*, close attention to context is needed to ensure that *déjà*
is not unsuitably translated in its usual sense.

(38)   *il faut s'attendre à une évolution*   'stormy weather is to be
       orageuse   expected'

The case of *falloir* is similar to that of *s'agir* in that both are frequent and
that the rendering that first comes to mind is often to be avoided.

(39)   *l'argument est fort*   'that is a telling argument'

       il va développer un autre thème fort   'he is going to exploit another
                                                  major theme'

The issue connected with *fort*, as these examples show, is straightforward
collocation.

(40)   *un grand vent*   'a high wind'

       le grand air   'the open air'

       un grand commis de l'Etat   'a senior civil servant'

       il avait grand air   'he looked really imposing'

The first two examples of *grand* show straightforward collocation, while
the second two show its use in idioms.

(41)   *un gros baiser*   'a smacking kiss'

       un gros rire   'a loud laugh'

       il sort ses gros pulls 'he's getting out his thick pullovers'

Again we see straightforward collocation at issue here.

(42)   *les choses ne sont guère arrangées depuis samedi*

       'things haven't become appreciably better since Saturday'

       cette rue est située dans un quartier de Paris que les Parisens ne
       connaissent guère

       'this street is situated in a part of Paris of which Parisians are prac-
       tically unaware'

The examples in (42) show the importance, as ever, of translating in
context in an idiomatic way, in this case the rendering of *guère* beyond the

'hardly' that is the straightforward choice. These examples are slightly more complex than straightforward collocation, since they depend on the TL verb that is selected to translate the SL verb. The decision to translate *s'arranger* by 'not to become better' means that an adverb of idiomatic collocation with this verbal sequence needs to be selected, and 'appreciably' is well chosen. A different verb might clearly need a different adverb, and a perhaps more obvious choice like 'to improve' would in fact collocate satisfactorily with 'hardly': 'things have hardly improved since Saturday'. The same argument applies to the second example.

(43)   *on peut s'attendre à des chutes de neige importantes*

       'heavy snowfalls can be expected'

       une charge explosive a provoqué des dégâts importants

       'an explosive charge caused extensive damage'

These again are straightforward examples of collocation. It needs always of course to be borne in mind that *important* is a false friend that as often as not does not translate as 'important'.

(44a) *j'enviais jusqu'au sort du pâtre que je voyais ...*

       'I envied even the lot of the shepherd whom I could see ...'

Astington has only three examples of multiple equivalence as it concerns *jusqu'à*, and two of these translate as 'even', probably the most frequent non-literal translation. The third was discussed in the previous chapter:

(44b) *on ne pouvait pas ne pas la trouver belle, émouvante, jusqu'au drame*

       'you could not but find her beautiful, touching, dramatically so'

This second example shows that a radical redraft is sometimes required.

(45)   *il a une vision large de la clause de conscience*

       'he has an elastic view of the conscience clause'

       ... geste large et verbe haut   '... with sweeping gestures and loud talk'

       ces musiciens amateurs valent largement les professionnels

       'these amateur musicians are easily as good as professionals'

       la direction du parti communiste russe frise largement les soixante-quinze ans

       'the leaders of the Russian communist party are getting well into the mid-seventies'

The first two examples in (45) concerning *large* show straightforward collocation of noun and adjective. The examples concerning *largement* are more complex; as in the case of *guère*. What *largement* and *guère* have in common, quite obviously, is that they are adverbs, and as we suggested in connection with *guère*, the TL adverb selected needs to collocate with the TL verb + noun sequence that is chosen to translate the SL sequence.

In the first example above, the decision to translate *valent* by 'are as good as' means, as with *guère*, that an idiomatic adverb needs to be found. Again, different sequence will call for a different adverb, so that if we translate *valent* as 'are up to the standard of', then 'well' would be the adverb required.

(46)   *ma mère cachait mal son indignation*

    'my mother found it difficult to conceal her indignation'

    la comtesse réprimait mal ses   'the countess could not entirely
    sanglots   stifle her sobs'

    l'un des jeunes était mal tenu   'one of the youths was unkempt'

The examples in (46) show a striking difference between, on the one hand the relative difficulty of translation of *mal* when it qualifies a verb, as in the first two examples, and on the other the ease of translation when *mal* qualifies a past participle functioning as an adjective. Radical solutions are needed in the first two cases, and sequences of this type account for 15 of the 18 listed by Astington. The translation of *mal* when it qualifies a verb is hard to systematise, but solutions will obviously use a negative expression of some kind: most of Astington's translations involve the following: 'cannot' (in a suitable tense) + verb; expressions with 'difficult' or 'difficulty'; 'little' + verb (*on connaît mal* … 'little is known …'). Literal translation of *mal* qualifying a verb must be very rare.

(47)   *il roulait sur le mauvais côté de*   'he was driving on the wrong
    la route   side of the road'

    …situé sur la mauvaise pente   '… placed on the downward path'

The case of *mauvais*, like the other adjectives discussed here, involves simple collocation.

(48)   *on devinait la profonde lueur rouge du dehors*

    'the deep red glow outside could be made out'

    on assure qu'il est déjà engage…   'it is reliably reported that he has
    been signed up …'

    on parlait d'une lourde erreur   'there was talk of a major blunder'

We discussed in Chapter 3 the social-stylistic alternation between *nous* and *on* translatable as 'we', and pointed out that the sociolinguistic value of *on* is very different from English 'one'. Depending on context, the French pronoun can translate as 'we', 'you', 'they', 'people', but as Astington points out 'various combinations of passive and impersonal constructions, together with nominalisation [...] are also possible'. The three examples above show respectively translation by a passive, an impersonal construction and a nominalisation.

(49) *le gouvernement écrase d'impôts le petit peuple*

  'the government crushes the humble folk with taxes'

  les petits Français n'apprennent plus l'histoire de la France

  'French youngsters are no longer being taught French history'

  un petit architecte qui s'installe dans un chef-lieu de canton ...

  'a second-rate architect who sets up in a small country town ...'

The examples in (49) essentially show collocation at work. There seems to be a connection between the frequency of the adjective *petit* and the difficulty of finding an adjective that collocates well in English, and this is true also of the other common adjectives and adverbs listed here, like *bon*, *grand* and *bien*. Contrast this difficulty with the relative ease of translating less frequent adjectives, as in the case of *lourde erreur* in the third example in (48).

To summarise, the translation issues associated with multiple equivalence are disparate, and we can make a broad distinction between the need to particularise prompted by: (1) the wide collocational distribution with different nouns of frequent adjectives like *bon*, *grand* and *important*; (2) the need to perform more complex operation on adverbs, as in the case of *guère* and *largement*; (3) the wide range of reference of the pronoun *on*; (4) the wide scope of *s'agir* and *falloir*. This last case is the hardest to explain in linguistic terms, and we can only describe the problem by saying that *s'agir* and *falloir* are 'broad-spectrum' verbs that very often need particularisation in English.

Punctuation

As so often the main issue is encoding rather than decoding: there are differences in practice across the two languages, but what is important is the accurate reproduction of the TL practice. For example, as Judge and Healey point out (1990: 389) French does not add a comma after the last item in a list, while English does:

(50) *il possedait des moutons, du bétail, des cochons et de la volaille*

  'the farmer owned sheep, cattle, pigs, and poultry'

We touched on punctuation indirectly in the chapter on syntax when we discussed the greater tendency in French to isolate clauses between full stops. This tendency is connected to what we might call the 'structural' aspect of punctuation. By this we mean differences across the two languages that isolate or emphasise certain structural elements like phrases or clauses. It is only occasionally that punctuation indicates a difference in meaning, as in the well-known difference between 'defining' and 'commenting' relative clauses where the use of a comma distinguishes the two types:

(51)   My brother who's a pilot …

       My brother, who's a pilot …

In the first sequence, the absence of a comma after 'brother' indicates that the speaker has more than one brother, and that one of them is a pilot. The relative clause is distinguishing or defining the brother in question. In the second sequence, the comma indicates that the speaker has only one brother, and is providing further information or commenting on him. This is not a translation issue because the two languages use a comma for the same purpose. It is however a point of grammar that needs to be mastered in the interests of good composition.

The colon is more widely used in French than in English; in the latter language its chief functions are to introduce a list or quotation, while in French, as Chuquet and Paillard point out (1989: 420): '[les deux points] annoncent le discours direct, introduisent une citation, annoncent une énumération, expriment une conséquence, une synthèse, et préparent la chute d'une phrase'.

A further important difference between the two languages is in the use of the semi-colon, which seems more frequent in English. In this connection Chuquet and Paillard remark that (1989: 419) 'on constate une plus grande densité des virgules en français […]', and the passage cited below shows a French writer (Gadet, 2003: 105) using first a colon, then a comma where a translator would use semi-colon:

(52)   Le rapport entre façon de parler et situation n'est alors pas automa-
       tique: les locuteurs peuvent réorienter un discours, par exemple
       vers le familier, rendant ainsi le context plus familier […]. Loin que
       le social, le contexte et l'identité soient des données stables, le
       discours les crée tout autant qu'il en est le produit.

       'The relation between speech style and situational context is not
       therefore a mechanical one; speakers can redirect a speech situation
       in a more colloquial direction, thus creating a less formal situation.
       Far from the social dimension being the stable variable, in this view

it is rather speech context and identity that are stable; speech style creates them as much as being their product.'

As so often, this is a tendency that admits of many exceptions. As we said above, the crucial point is to have mastered the TL use of the semi-colon and other punctuation marks. Less experienced writers of English tend to use a comma where a semi-colon is required. As Judge and Healey (1990: 433) express the matter: '[The semi-colon] indicates the syntactic completeness of the sentence which it terminates, but stresses the semantic ties of that sentence with what follows'. In other words, the semi-colon links two closely related *sentences*, as in the English translation in (52).

Even more than the semi-colon, the apostrophe is the great punctuation shibboleth. The classic test of advanced understanding of the apostrophe is the ability to distinguish between the following:

(53)   They're keeping up with the Joneses

       We've been invited to the Joneses'

We can contrast the structural aspect of punctuation with purely conventional differences across French and English. An example of a conventional difference is the expression of decimal numbers in the two languages; French uses a comma where English has a full stop. In such cases the translator simply needs to be aware of the different conventions, and this is an aspect of the close attention to detail required for conscientious work. A gross difference of quantity can however occasionally result from the failure to substitute full stop for comma: *6,170 millions* '6.17 million'. Conversely, where English has a comma, as in '12,000', French has a full stop or, increasingly, a space: *12.000* or *12 000*.

Judge and Healey (1990: 430–5) have a fairly extensive discussion of the differences between English and French punctuation. Partridge (1999) is a good book-length guide to punctuation in English. Grevisse (1986) has a long section on French punctuation. Demanuelli (1987) is a book-length treatment of punctuation differences between French and English.

The Translation Commentary

The translation commentary is an exercise that is quite often set on advanced courses: at Masters level and for professional examinations set by bodies like the Institute of Linguists, who set out the following rationale (taken from their website at www.iol.org.uk):

Candidates [when doing a translation commentary] are required to raise *significant* issues relevant to an analysis and translation of the text set. They should comment on translation decisions taken or not taken, explaining how choices they have made adequately or inadequately reflect features and aims of the source and target texts. Candidates are encouraged to view commenting as a useful opportunity to reveal to the examiners thought processes and strategies behind the translation submitted (emphasis in original)

The Institute of Linguists exercise is an annotated translation rather than a translation commentary. Conceptually there is little difference between the two exercises, but they differ in form: by the former term is meant a translation accompanied by annotations that comment on points of difficulty in the source text and suggest possible solutions. Adab (1993, 1996) in two books focusing on the annotated translation in both directions (respectively French–English and English–French), provides numerous examples of the exercise. A translation commentary typically comments on the ST as a whole, looking at translation issues of the sort we have discussed throughout this book: the text type; the author's intention or 'audience design'; the register(s) of the text; translation loss or compensation; cultural equivalence; acceptability; any linguistic dissymmetries that may be present across the source and target languages; procedures that may be necessary; and other pertinent issues. The annotated translation tends to be more item based than the translation commentary, but naturally the latter exercise also considers individual translation cruxes.

As is implied in the Institute of Linguists formulation cited above, the aim of the exercise, from the examinee's point of view, is to demonstrate awareness on the translator's part of some of the difficulties that the ST raises. From the examiner's viewpoint, the aim is of course to promote this awareness, as is stated elsewhere in the Institute of Linguists document: 'Good annotations relate to process and strategy; they explain how relatively problematic translation points have been addressed and how choices made adequately or inadequately reflect features and aims of the source and target texts'. This quotation brings out the point that the translator needs frequently to be thinking in terms of *process*: 'what am I doing at this point?'; 'what are the choices available?'; 'what is the underlying meaning?'; 'what is the fundamental problem?'; etc. This is in contrast to an attitude that lays stress merely on the *product*, and risks limiting itself to the question: 'what is the dictionary translation for this word?'.

An adequate annotation or comment needs therefore to show a reasonably sophisticated degree of awareness of, to quote the Institute of Linguists again, 'anything that causes a pause in the normal flow of the translation and makes the candidate ponder how best to put across an idea of something that would constitute an issue for all translators [...]'. The Institute of Linguists give some examples of inadequate annotations: 'I don't understand this expression', 'this is difficult', 'hard to translate' or 'untranslatable because too French', 'an Anglo-Saxon expression', 'not in my dictionary'. These are unacceptable because they offer no analysis and show no linguistic awareness of the nature of the problem.

Example of a Translation Commentary

Below we provide a translation commentary written in a mixed style, showing some features of the commentary as well as some annotations. We distinguish between cultural-linguistic and linguistic translation problems.

A preamble might take the following form: 'The ST is from the French serious weekly magazine *Le Nouvel Observateur,* and is adapted from an article entitled 'Les nouveaux bourgeois'. This term refers to those 'baby-boomers' or 'fifty-somethings' of the post-1945 generation who are prosperous, having benefited from the post-war economic boom, but who are also politically liberal, and anxious not to be associated with the traditional stuffy bourgeois image of previous generations. The term itself needs some thought, as it is not yet a set phrase in French but seems to have been coined fairly recently, perhaps on the analogy of *les nouveaux riches,* to describe a social group that has only recently caught the attention of commentators. Since both 'nouveau' and 'bourgeois' can be found in an English dictionary, the translator can assume that the phrase *les nouveaux bourgeois* will be transparent enough to be left as a borrowing after an initial gloss along the lines suggested above. The pejorative English label 'champagne socialist' is fairly close to the *nouveau bourgeois* concept, but narrower in scope because concentrating on political attitudes. By contrast, the term *nouveau bourgeois* refers to a wider range of attitudes than the political.

'The text is a fairly typical *Nouvel Observateur* piece in being informative but also expressive. It is quite informally written, but the style varies within the text, with some use of formal and even archaic language use for special effect. The article is rather subversive, reflecting the political tendency of the publication, and is of course very allusive because written for a readership fully conversant with French 'culture', both popular and high. Some allusive terms transcend the two cultures in question, while others do not.'

Some elements of interest for the commentary are underlined in the text. The list below is of course not exhaustive. We have stressed cultural elements because these are more prominent, and comment on some of the more purely linguistic issues has already been made elsewhere.

Pour les nouveaux bourgeois, le chapitre des contradictions existentielles n'est pas moins fourni. Les années passant, il devient moins
commode de vivre en bourgeois tout en se pensant en rebelle. « Les
riches soixante-huitards ne se racontent plus qu'à eux-mêmes qu'ils
restent en révolte contre le système. Mais l'auto-persuasion à ses
limites, remarque Vincent Grégoire, consultant du bureau de style
Nelly Rodi. Le regard que les 20 ans posent sur leur père agit à cet
égard comme un révélateur. Ils ne croient pas une seconde que cet
homme qui se dit libre puisse vivre comme eux dans l'instant et dans
la fantaisie. » Quant aux 30 ans qui montent, ils déploient un style
plus subtil et surtout plus festif que celui de leurs aînés. Verres
Duralex et cristal dépareillés, Adidas séries limitées, disco-paillettes
et humour 10e degré.

Ce code étranger donne aux cinquantenaires l'impression d'être un
peu coincés. Autre symptôme du temps qui fuit : l'énervement du
nouveau bourgeois contre l'inconsistance et la vulgarité des séries télé
pour ados, du langage banlieue, de la techno et du rap qui déferlent
dans son logis. Son rejet de la nouvelle culture hip-hop qui séduit tant
les jeunes le prend en écharpe. Passe-t-il sans le savoir à côté d'une
vraie tendance ? A-t-il raison de mépriser ce brouet à la sauce
marketing ? Est-il en train de renoncer à ses convictions antiracistes ?
Il ne peut décider. Pour contrebalancer cette perte de contact avec les
générations montantes, son hédonisme est du genre généreux. « Il a
tendance à gâter ses proches. Il n'hésite pas à donner 6 000 balles par
mois à ses enfants étudiants plutôt que de leur dire : 'Tu mangeras des
croûtons en attendant l'héritage', affirme Régine Lemoine Darthois,
PDG d'Euromap. Il espère que son argent, son expérience, sa culture
leur serviront quand même un peu. Mais il ne peut se départir d'un
sentiment d'incertitude et de précarité quant à la perpétuation du
confort intellectuel et matériel qu'il a atteint. » (© *Le Nouvel
Observateur*)

Comments on Underlined Items

Le chapitre des contradictions existentielles

Concentrating firstly on *chapitre*, this can be looked at as a false-friend
problem, or from the point of view of polysemy; or indeed both, since as
we pointed out in a previous chapter, some false friends pose problems
because of their polysemic value. Although in the present context 'the
chapter of existential contradictions' is not totally unacceptable so long as
a suitable translation for *fourni* is found, the translator needs to be aware
that French *chapitre* has several related meanings, and is capable of a non-

literal translation according to context. Probably 'question' is a better rendering here, and 'existential contradictions' would need to be loosened up too as it reads very pompously in English. A sentence like 'The question of the contradictions in their lives is no less pressing' is perhaps suitable in avoiding much of the Latinate vocabulary of the ST. At the same time there are perhaps 'existentialist' resonances in the original that would be lost if this solution were adopted.

Les années passant

A purely linguistic issue: this is an absolute construction that needs expansion in English, as French tolerates absolutes more readily than English. While 'the years passing' is possible, the feel is too archaic for the text type. Suitable translations could be 'as the years pass'; 'with the passing years', etc.

Soixante-huitards

The most obvious issue here is the prominence in the French collective memory of the May 1968 protests, which are of specialist interest in the UK. The phrase needs expansion along the lines: 'those old enough to have taken part in the French student protests of 1968', with explanation of what these were depending on the intended readership. There is translation loss involved here because an unwieldy expansion would be needed for most UK readers; and of course the linguistic issue is once again codability, the fact that languages encode culturally important concepts in a compact way that often needs expansion in translation. Clearly therefore, an attempt to match the compactness of the original by coining 'sixty-eighter', on the analogy of 'forty-niner', is pointless because the allusion would only be understood by an English reader capable of reading the French original.

A further problem is that the suffix *–ard* often carries a pejorative suggestion, as in *chauffard* 'bad driver', *motard* 'motorcycle cop' or 'dangerous motorcyclist'. Consultation of native speakers suggests that the suffix does carry a derogatory overtone in *soixante-huitard*, but this would be hard to convey compactly. Analogous overtones are conveyed in UK English by various suffixes: compare 'Trotskyist' as opposed to 'Trotskyite', or even more sharply, 'Leftist' versus 'Leftie'.

L'auto-persuasion

The issue here is the familiar one of learned vocabulary in French. A well-known example is l'*Autodidacte* in Sartre's *La Nausée*, translated in some editions as 'The Self-Taught Man', in others as 'The Autodidact'. In the present case there seems little choice in the translation of *auto–*, as the prefix has a narrower distribution in English than French, at least in everyday language. The obvious translation is 'self–', which by association seems to call up 'delusion': is 'self-delusion' too strong a translation here? Expansion to 'the ability to fool yourself' has less compactness, but arguably more accuracy.

Humour 10e degré

This phrase depends on the common idiom *prendre quelque chose au deuxième / second degré* 'to look below the surface of something' (Collins-Robert), in other words to refuse to take something literally or at face value. A related expression is *l'humour second degree* 'tongue-in-cheek-humour' (Collins-Robert) which is essentially conveying the same idea, as tongue-in-cheek humour can be hard to detect. The phrase *humour 10e degré* simply extends this series. No equivalent exists in colloquial English, although one does talk about 'levels of meaning'. A neutral translation like 'super-subtle humour' may be the best that can be hoped for.

Langage banlieue

The term *langage* is of some theoretical interest, since French explicitly distinguishes between *langage* and *langue*. The former is the language of a sub-group, or language considered in its physical realisation, the latter the more general and abstract term. In other words, we have a difference of hyponymic organisation between the two languages. This distinction does not cause a problem of practice, as both terms translate as English 'language'.

The term *banlieue* is often translated as 'suburbs', and as we have pointed out previously, to the extent that the *banlieues* are typically large, recent (post-war) and low-quality housing developments located at some distance from the city centre, the term 'suburb' is denotationally accurate. But the term 'inner-city', although not accurate in denotation, captures more closely the English connotation of *banlieue* in the measure that the term evokes inadequate housing, high rates of crime and unemployment, and a large immigrant population. But 'inner-city language' sounds odd, because in contrast to France, few very striking linguistic innovations are associated with the English inner cities; the meaning could perhaps be rendered as 'the sloppy / incomprehensible / street language of young people'.

Qui déferlent dans son logis

The jocular use here of *logis* seems designed to establish a contrast between the 'superficiality and vulgarity of the TV series for teenagers […]' and the relative staidness of the 'nouveau bourgeois'; this is achieved by the selection of the slightly archaic *logis*. It is worth pointing out in passing that *inconsistance* is a false friend, and does not mean 'inconsistency'. This latter term translates into French as *incohérence*.

A translation of *logis* by 'abode' may convey the effect aimed for in the ST, although expansion to something like 'peaceful abode' or adaptation to 'civilised home' is perhaps preferable in conveying the conflict between the generations that is the focus of the sentence. The translator needs of course to be aware of the stylistic value of the French term *logis*. A translation of the sentence beginning with '*l'énervement* ...' might read: 'The irritation of the nouveau bourgeois at the superficiality and vulgarity of TV series for teenagers, at young people's incomprehensible language, at the techno and rap that flood into his peaceful abode / civilised home ...'.

6000 balles

Here the problem is the stylistic value of colloquial vocabulary in French, as discussed in a previous chapter. A further complication is that since the phrase occurs here in speech imported into the text, the translator can consider rendering *balles* by the equivalent colloquial word in English. The translator is fortunate in having an equivalent word available in this instance. But given the copiousness of these colloquial words in French, and the fact that almost everyone seems to use them, the translator needs to consult his / her intuition to determine whether 'quid' would give the same stylistic effect in English.

PDG

Concise expression in French means loss in English, as 'chairman and managing director' is rather unwieldy. Reduction to 'managing director' or the acronym 'MD' gives a shorter and more familiar solution, but is less accurate. 'CEO' is worth considering if it is felt that the US acronym would be familiar to UK English readers. The use of acronyms and abbreviations is quite common in fairly informal French, and is often quite hard to match: *système D, BCBG*, etc.

Concluding Remarks

At the end of an MA translation class recently, a specialist of translation who had been observing the present author teaching the class remarked: 'Your approach is very bottom-up'. Out of the blue, the jargon was rather disconcerting, but the remark referred to the relatively item-based linguistic approach characteristic of this book. It hardly needs to be said that this is by no means the whole story when considering translation problems. We emphasised at the outset the limitations of a purely linguistics-based approach to translation: like many interdisciplinary enterprises, translation studies is an 'uncomfortable' discipline that is still struggling to assert its autonomy. Venuti (1998: 1) is perhaps the sharpest critic of a linguistic view of translation, deploring 'linguistics-oriented approaches that offer a truncated view of the empirical data they collect'. We do not deny that our view in this book of the task of translation is truncated. Other important aspects of that task, like the aesthetic and the socio-cultural, have been less fully treated here, or barely mentioned. This is not because they are unimportant, but because, as we pointed out in Chapter 1, these aspects lie outside the scope of the branch of linguistics we have adopted here, in practice if not in principle. The approach to translation sketched in this book should therefore be seen as complementary rather than exclusive. Similarly, the Anglo-American, culturally hegemonic view of translation criticised by Venuti (1998) and referred to in Chapter 2, while undoubtedly valid in a broader perspective, is only of marginal interest here, since our subject is translation between two *langues de culture*.

Returning to the limitations of the bottom-up approach referred to above, recent pragmatic and cognitive approaches to language and translation take the view that the reading, understanding and production of language are not bottom-up processes that start from the smallest units (morphemes, words, sentences) and end with the largest (larger text units, the text itself), but rather top-down processes that take these latter elements into consideration first. To the extent that we have looked at this top-down approach, our analysis has been conducted, in Chapter 2, from the viewpoint of text type and skopos. The limited measure in which we have examined the top-down approach certainly does not imply that we wish to decry it, and we acknowledge that the translator needs constantly to bear skopos in mind – both initially and throughout the rendering of any text. We can call this a pragmatic view of translation in the sense that pragmatics is concerned with language beyond the smaller unit, and can concern the whole text. As we pointed out in Chapter 6, pragmatics is a wide-ranging discipline that can be of relevance in many levels in translation.

The cognitive aspect of language and translation has been sporadically and indirectly referred to here, but it is very important. It is concerned with issues of cognition – knowledge and understanding – within and beyond the text. The translator needs an adequate 'cognitive baggage', the real-world or 'encyclopedic' knowledge necessary for full understanding of a translation text, as well as sensitivity to the 'cognitive context'. This latter term refers to points in a text where ambiguity is present owing to a difficulty in determing the author's *vouloir dire* or intended meaning in the immediate context. To the extent that we considered this, it has been in connection with word-meaning dependent on the lexical relations in the two languages: polysemy, synonymy and hyponymy. Meaning in context is the watchword in this regard. Nor can cognitive baggage be separated from cognitive context; the last translation problem we discussed above, example (52) concerning speech style studied from the sociolinguistic viewpoint, shows the need to translate a phrase like *façon de parler* in the context as 'speech style'. Elsewhere in the same book a different rendering might be suitable: the technical 'idiolect', the literal 'way of speaking', etc. At the same time, 'encyclopedic' knowledge of linguistics is needed to enhance sensitivity to the wider context in which the book is set, in this case the relevant academic sub-discipline.

The broadest generalisation regarding translation that we can risk is a truism, namely that the translator needs to be guided by broad principles, since only these can be of wide application. There is a parallel here with language learning, where the learner must internalise a grammar, in the sense of a set of rules, and a lexicon, in order to be able to generate the grammatical sentences of the target language – once again, because all of the possible sentences cannot be learned by rote, since their number is indefinite. Therefore we propose finally one or two general remarks designed to summarise the mass of detail and numerous examples in the preceding pages.

Firstly, we repeat that it can be useful to have constantly in mind the transposition and modulation procedures until these become second nature. Secondly, it is not enough to say simply that translation is a double process of SL decoding and TL encoding; expanding on this we can perhaps say that the central challenge of translation is to reconcile what is idiomatic with what is accurate. This means avoiding the influence of SL words and structures *where suitable* – a crucial qualification. To take a very simple example, an inexperienced translator who sees the phrase *compagnie aérienne* may find it hard to struggle free from the SL sequence to find the phrase that will come unbidden when no SL influence is at work: 'airline'. Instead, the structure of the SL sequence may prompt 'air company', 'aircraft company', 'aerospace company', etc., etc. This is a case of 'over-translation' of the type that needs constantly to be guarded against.

To use a mixed metaphor, over the last seven chapters we have done little more than scratch the surface of the tip of the iceberg of the French–English translation enterprise. This book, in conjunction with many others, is a starting-point; a *point d'appui*, scarcely a *tête de pont*.

References

As is conventional, these references list all and only the works referred to in the text. In the following section we list some of the key texts in the translation literature.

Adab, B.J. (1993) *Annotated Texts for Translation: French–English*. Clevedon: Multilingual Matters.

Adab, B.J. (1996) *Annotated Texts for Translation: English–French*. Clevedon: Multilingual Matters.

Amis, K. (1986) *The Old Devils*. Harmondsworth: Penguin.

Amis, K. (1991) *The Amis Collection. Selected Non-fiction 1954–1990*. Harmondsworth: Penguin.

Armstrong, N. (2001) *Social and Stylistic Variation in Spoken French. A Comparative Approach*. Amsterdam and Philadelphia: Benjamins.

Astington, E. (1983) *Equivalences. Translation Difficulties and Devices, French–English, English–French*. Cambridge: Cambridge University Press.

Atkins, B.T., Duval, A. and Milne, R.C. (eds) (1998) *The Collins-Robert French Dictionary* (5th edn). Glasgow / Paris: Collins / Dictionnaires Le Robert.

Atkins, B.T.S. and Zampolli, A. (eds) (1994) *Computational Approaches to the Lexicon*. Oxford: Oxford University Press.

Austin, J.L. (1962) *How to do Things with Words*. Oxford: Clarendon Press.

Baker, M. (1992) *In Other Words. A Coursebook on Translation*. London: Routledge.

Bassnett, S. (1991) *Translation Studies* (revised edn). London: Routledge.

Batchelor, R.E. and Offord, M.H. (2000) *Using French: a Guide to Contemporary Usage* (3rd edn). Cambridge: Cambridge University Press.

Battye, A., Hintze, M-A. and Rowlett, P. (2000) *The French Language Today. A Linguistic Introduction* (2nd edn). London: Routledge.

Beeching, K. (2001) La Fonction de la particule pragmatique *enfin* dans le discours des hommes et des femmes. In N. Armstrong, K. Beeching and C. Bauvois (eds) *La Langue française au féminin. Le sexe et le genre affectent-ils la variation linguistique?* (pp. 101–22). Paris: Editions l'Harmattan.

Bell, A. (1984) Language style as audience design. *Language in Society* 13 (2), 145–204.

Byrne, L.S.R. and Churchill, E.L. (1993) *A Comprehensive French Grammar* (4th edn, rewritten by Glanville Price). Oxford: Blackwell.

Catford, J.C. (1965) *A Linguistic Theory of Translation. An Essay in Applied Linguistics*. London: Oxford University Press.

Chuquet, H. and Paillard, M. (1989) *Approches Linguistiques des problèmes de traduction*. Paris: Ophrys.

Corréard, M.-H. and Grundy, V. (eds) (2001) *The Oxford-Hachette French Dictionary* (3rd edn). Oxford / Paris: Oxford University Press / Hachette.

Coveney, A.B. (2000) Vestiges of NOUS and 1st person plural verbs in informal spoken French. *Language Sciences* 22 (3), 447–81.

Crystal, D. (1991) *A Dictionary of Linguistics and Phonetics* (3rd edition). Oxford: Blackwell.

Culler, J. (1976) *Saussure*. Glasgow: Fontana.

Demanuelli, C. (1987) *Points de Repère: Approche interlinguistique de la ponctuation français-anglais*. St-Etienne: CIEREC, Travaux LVIII.

Duneton, C. (1978) *La Puce à l'oreille: Anthologie des expressions populaires avec leur origine*. Paris: Stock.

Ellis, N.C. (1996) Sequencing in SLA: phonological memory, chunking and points of order. *Studies in Second Language Acquisition* 18, 91–126.

Forster, E.M. (1984) *The Longest Journey*. London: Arnold.

Fowler, H.W. (1983) *A Dictionary of Modern English Usage* (2nd edn, revised by E. Gowers). Oxford: Oxford University Press.

Fuller, F. (1973) *A Handbook for Translators*. Gerrards Cross: Colin Smythe.

Gadet, F. (1997) *Le Français ordinaire* (2nd edn). Paris: Armand Colin.

Gadet, F. (2003) *La Variation sociale en français*. Paris: Ophrys.

Garat, A.-M. (1992) *Aden: Roman*. Paris: Seuil.

Gardes-Tamine, J. (1992) *La Stylistique*. Paris: Armand Colin.

Germain, C. (1981) *La Sémantique fonctionnelle*. Paris: Presses Universitaires de France.

Grevisse, M. (1986). *Le bon usage* (12th edn, revised by André Goosse). Gembloux: Duculot.

Hemingway, E. (1954) *The Sun Also Rises*. New York: Charles Scribner's Sons.

Hervey, S and Higgins, I. (1992) *Thinking Translation. A Course in Translation Method: French to English*. London: Routledge.

Hickey, L. (ed.) (1998) *The Pragmatics of Translation*. Clevedon: Multilingual Matters.

Hudson, R. (1996) *Sociolinguistics* (2nd edn). Cambridge: Cambridge University Press.

Hymes, D. (1972) Models of the interaction of language and social life. In J. Gumperz and D. Hymes (eds), *Directions in Sociolinguistics: The Ethnography of Communication*, (pp. 35–71). New York; London: Holt, Rinehart and Winston.

Jones, M.A. (1996) *Foundations of French Syntax*. Cambridge: Cambridge University Press.

Judge, A. and Healey, F.G. (1990) *A Reference Grammar of Modern French*. London: Arnold.

Ketteridge, J.O. (1956) *French Idioms and Figurative Phrases*. London: Routledge & Kegan Paul.

Kirk-Greene, C.W.E. (1981) *French False Friends*. London: Routledge & Kegan Paul.

Koessler. M. and Derocquiny, J. (1928) *Les Faux amis: ou, les trahisons du vocabulaire anglais*. Paris: Vuibert.

Labsade, F. Tétu de (1990) *Le Québec – un pays, une culture*. Montréal: Boréal.

Leech, G. (1981) *Semantics. The Study of Meaning* (2nd edn). Harmondsworth: Penguin.

Lodge, D. (1997) *The Practice of Writing*. Harmondsworth: Penguin.

Lodge, R.A. (1989) Speakers' perceptions of non-standard vocabulary in French. *Zeitschrift für Romanische Philologie* 105 (6), 427–44.

Lodge, R.A., Armstrong, N., Ellis, Y. and Shelton, J. (1997) *Exploring the French Language*. London: Arnold.

Lyons, J. (1968) *Introduction to Theoretical Linguistics.* Cambridge: Cambridge University Press.

McCarthy, P.J. (1986) *Introduction to Arithmetical Functions.* New York: Springer-Verlag.

Mandelbaum, D.G. (ed.) (1958) *Selected Writings of Edward Sapir in Language, Culture and Personality.* Berkeley and Los Angeles: University of California Press.

Matthews, P. (1981) *Syntax.* Cambridge: Cambridge University Press.

Milroy, J. (1992) *Linguistic Variation and Change. On the Historical Sociolinguistics of English.* Oxford: Blackwell.

na Gopaleen, Myles (Flann O'Brien) (1968) *The Best of Myles. A Selection from Cruiskeen Lawn.* London: MacGibbon & Kee.

na Gopaleen, Myles (Flann O'Brien) (1973) *The Poor Mouth (An Béal Bocht),* trans. P.C. Power. London: Hart-Davis MacGibbon.

Newmark, P. (1988) *A Textbook of Translation.* Hemel Hempstead: Prentice-Hall Europe.

Partridge, E. (1999) *You Have a Point There. A Guide to Punctuation and its Allies.* London: Routledge.

Pinker, S. (1994) *The Language Instinct.* New York: William Morrow.

Queneau, R. (1959) *Zazie dans le Métro.* Paris: Gallimard.

Queneau, R. (2000) *Zazie in the Metro,* trans. B. Wright. Harmondsworth: Penguin.

Rat, M. (1957) *Dictionnaire des Locutions françaises.* Paris: Larousse.

Rey, A. and Rey-Debove, J. (eds) (1986) *Le Petit Robert: Dictionnaire Alphabétique et analogique de la langue française.* Paris: Les Dictionnaires Robert.

Salinger, J.D. (1958) *The Catcher in the Rye.* Harmondsworth: Penguin.

Saussure, F. (1973) *Cours de Linguistique générale,* C. Bally, A. Sechehaye, A. Riedlinger and T. de Mauro (eds). Paris: Payot.

Slobin, D. (1979) *Psycholinguistics* (2nd edn). Glenview, IL: Scott, Foresman.

Thody, P. (1997) *Don't do it! A Dictionary of the Forbidden.* London: Athlone Press.

Thody, P. and Evans, H. (1985) *Mistakable French. Faux Amis and Key Words.* New York: Hippocrene Press.

Van Roey J., Granger, S. and Swallow, H. (1998) *Dictionnaire des / Dictionary of Faux Amis, français-anglais, English-French* (3rd edn). Paris: Duculot.

Venuti, L. (1995) *The Translator's Invisibility. A History of Translation.* London: Routledge.

Venuti, L. (1998) *The Scandals of Translation. Towards an Ethic of Difference.* London: Routledge.

Vermeer, H.J. (1989) 'Skopos and commission in translational action', trans. Chesterman, A. In A. Chesterman (ed.) *Readings in Translation Theory* (pp. 173–87). Helsinki: Oy Finna Lectura Ab.

Vinay, J.-P. and Darbelnet, J. (1995) *Comparative Stylistics of French and English. A Methodology for Translation.* Amsterdam and Philadelphia: Benjamins.

Wray, A. (2002) *Formulaic Language and the Lexicon.* Cambridge: Cambridge University Press.

Yule, G. (1985) *The Study of Language.* Cambridge: Cambridge University Press.

Other Texts on Translation

Like the translation industry, the translation literature is substantial. Below is a selection of the texts that are frequently referred to, as well as some reference books (Baker; Picken; Shuttleworth and Cowie). Readers interested in investigating further will of course wish to consult references in the books listed.

Baker, M. (ed.), with Malmkj'r, K. (1997) *Routledge Encyclopedia of Translation Studies*. London: Routledge.

Bassnett, S. and Lefevere, A. (1998) *Constructing Cultures: Essays on Literary Translation*. Clevedon: Multilingual Matters.

Chesterman, A. (ed.) (1989) *Readings in Translation Theory*. Helsinki: Oy Finna Lectura Ab.

Chesterman, A. and Wagner, E. (2002) *Can Theory Help Translators? A Dialogue Between the Ivory Tower and the Wordface*. Manchester: St. Jerome.

Durieux, C. (1988) *Fondement Didactique de la traduction technique*. Paris: Didier Erudition.

Fawcett, P. (1997) *Translation and Language: Linguistic Theories Explained*. Manchester: St. Jerome.

Gentzler, E. (1993) *Contemporary Translation Theories*. London: Routledge.

Lefevere, A. (1977) *Translating Literature: The German Tradition From Luther to Rosenzweig*. Assen and Amsterdarn: Van Gorcum.

Lefevere, A. (ed.) (1992) *Translation / History / Culture*. London: Routledge.

Maillot, J. (1981) *La Traduction scientifique et technique*. Paris: Technique et Documentation.

Munday, J. (2001) *Introducing Translation Studies: Theories and Applications*. London: Routledge.

Newmark, P. (1981) *Approaches to Translation*. Oxford: Pergamon Press.

Newmark, P. (1993) *Paragraphs on Translation*. Clevedon: Multilingual Matters.

Newmark, P. (1998) *More Paragraphs on Translation*. Clevedon: Multilingual Matters.

Nida, E. (1964) *Towards a Science of Translating*. Leiden: E.J. Brill.

Nord, C. (1997) *Translating as a Purposeful Activity: Functionalist Approaches Explained*. Manchester: St. Jerome.

Picken, C. (1989) *The Translator's Handbook* (2nd edn). London: Aslib.

Schäffner, C. and Kelly-Holmes, H. (eds) (1995) *Cultural Functions of Translation*. Clevedon: Multilingual Matters.

Shuttleworth, M and Cowie, M. (1997) *Dictionary of Translation Studies*. Manchester: St. Jerome.

Trosborg, A. (ed.) (1997) *Text Typology and Translation*. Amsterdam and Philadelphia: Benjamins.

Wagner, E., Bech, S. and Martinez, J.M. (2001) *Translating for the European Union Institutions*. Manchester: St. Jerome.

Wilss, W. (1996) *Knowledge and Skills in Translator Behavior*. Amsterdam and Philadelphia: Benjamins.

Reference books

The translator needs to call upon as many reference tools as will help in the accurate rendering of a text: general and specialist dictionaries, encyclopedias, thesauruses, style guides, all in either paper or electronic form. It hardly needs to be said that on-line tools are increasingly copious and flexible, but the computer-literate translator is perhaps in danger of overlooking more traditional aids. We have already referred to Fowler as the most compendious guide to acceptable usage in standard written English; at the same time, journalists' style guides often provide good guidance to accurate and concise expression. A style guide often preferred is that of *The Economist*, and indeed the writing in that journal is admired by many professional translators.